WAR AND MEMORY AT THE
TIME OF THE FIFTH CRUSADE

War and Memory at the Time of the Fifth Crusade

MEGAN CASSIDY-WELCH

The Pennsylvania State University Press
University Park, Pennsylvania

Library of Congress Cataloging-in-Publication Data

Names: Cassidy-Welch, Megan, author.
Title: War and memory at the time of the Fifth Crusade / Megan
Cassidy-Welch.
Description: University Park, Pennsylvania : The Pennsylvania State
University Press, [2019] | Includes bibliographical references and index.
Summary: "Explores how the Fifth Crusade was remembered and
commemorated during its triumphs and immediately after its disastrous
conclusion. Provides a study of medieval war memory, showing that in the
early decades of the thirteenth century, remembering war was an important
means of creating and expressing collective and individual belonging"—
Provided by publisher.
Identifiers: LCCN 2019007016 | ISBN 9780271083520 (cloth : alk. paper)
Subjects: LCSH: Crusades—Fifth, 1218–1221. | War and society—
History—To 1500. | Memorialization—History—To 1500. | Collective
memory—History—To 1500.
Classification: LCC D165 .C37 2019 | DDC 956/.014—dc23
LC record available at https://lccn.loc.gov/2019007016

Copyright © 2019 Megan Cassidy-Welch
All rights reserved
Printed in the United States of America
Published by The Pennsylvania State University Press,
University Park, PA 16802-1003

The Pennsylvania State University Press is a member of the Association of
University Presses.

It is the policy of The Pennsylvania State University Press to use acid-free
paper. Publications on uncoated stock satisfy the minimum requirements
of American National Standard for Information Sciences—Permanence of
Paper for Printed Library Material, ANSI Z39.48-1992.

CONTENTS

Acknowledgments (vii)

Introduction *(1)*

1   Preparatory Memory: Managing Remembrance *(18)*

2   Eyewitnessing and Remembrance Work *(42)*

3   Remembering Crusaders *(62)*

4   Remembering Loss *(85)*

5   Places of Remembrance *(106)*

6   Coming Home: The Materials of Memory *(125)*

Conclusion *(148)*

Notes (155)

Bibliography (181)

Index (199)

ACKNOWLEDGMENTS

This book emerged from a research project funded by the Australian Research Council (ARC) through its Future Fellowship scheme from 2011 to 2015, with additional support from the Australian Research Council Centre of Excellence for the History of Emotions. I am very grateful to the ARC for its assistance over a number of years. Work for the book was completed at Monash University. I thank Monash for its generous support from 2011 to 2017.

Many people read drafts of various chapters, heard some of my thoughts at conferences and symposia, and inspired my thinking on the topics of memory, the Crusades, and war. I thank members of my research group at Monash, participants at the biennial conferences of the Australian and New Zealand Association for Medieval and Early Modern Studies, the American Historical Association, the International Medieval Congress at Leeds, the MARCO Symposium at the University of Tennessee at Knoxville, the Medieval Academy of America, the University of Amsterdam, the University of Adelaide, the University of Sydney, the University of Queensland, the Australian Catholic University, the University of Western Australia, and the University of Melbourne.

I thank many Crusades scholars for their wonderful work in this rich field and for their inspiring conversations, especially those who worked with me on other publications related to this volume. In the latter category, I particularly acknowledge Anne E. Lester, M. Cecilia Gaposchkin, Jessalynn Bird, Elizabeth Lapina, Jan Vandeburie, Thomas Smith, Nicholas Paul, William Purkis, Lee Manion, Rebecca Rist, James Naus, Vincent Ryan, Jochen Schenk, Sarah Lambert, Ana Rodriguez, Carsten Selch Jensen, Darius von Güttner Sporsynksi, Guy Perry, Christopher MacEvitt, Jonathan Harris, Alex Mallett, and Katherine Allen Smith, all of whom in various ways contributed to (and in the case of Anne Lester, coedited) publications and the ideas that underpin this book. The Crusades scholar to whom I owe an enormous debt of gratitude is the late James M. Powell, whose groundbreaking *Anatomy of a Crusade, 1213–1221* remains the go-to book for the Fifth Crusade and on whose scholarship I have relied so much.

I thank the Société archéologique de Namur for permission to use the images in this book, the Bibliothèque nationale de France, the British Library, the library at Gray's Inn, the Vatican Library, the Koninklijke Bibliotheek van België, Leiden University Library, Douai's Bibliothèque municipale, Monash University Library, the National Library of Australia, and the Fisher Library at the University of Sydney. Particular and heartfelt thanks go to Julianna Grigg for her RA and editorial work throughout the life of this project. Without her careful assistance, this book would not have been completed—at least, not on time. I particularly thank Julianna for her work on the maps included in the book. I also thank Kimberley-Joy Knight, whose careful editing and bibliographic assistance greatly improved this book.

The Centre for Medieval and Renaissance Studies (CMRS) at Monash University provided a home for me to write this book and mull over medieval things with a group of wonderful colleagues. The postgraduates of the CMRS created a warm and stimulating intellectual environment while I was at Monash, and the staff of the center—especially Peter Howard (director), Constant Mews, Carolyn James, and Kathleen Neal, and Clare Monagle—were the best of colleagues. Thank you to all of them.

And my final debt of gratitude is reserved for my family. This is the third book that my beloved husband has seen me write. Without his support and the love of my two sons, it could not have been completed, so it is to them—Steve, Robert, and Timothy—that this book is dedicated.

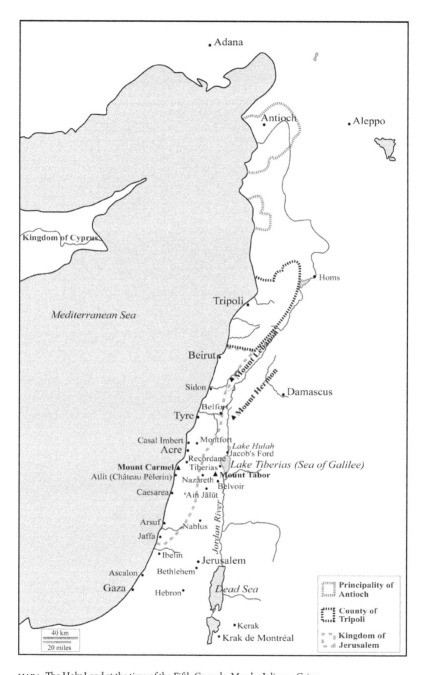

MAP 1 The Holy Land at the time of the Fifth Crusade. Map by Julianna Grigg.

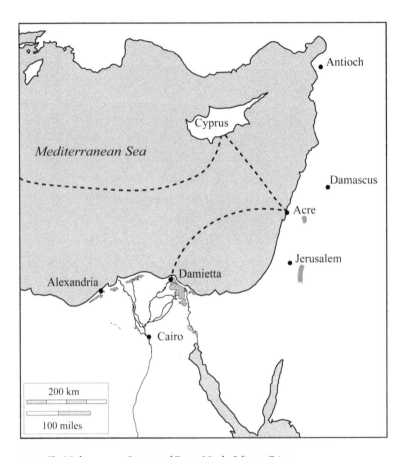

MAP 2 The Mediterranean, Cyprus, and Egypt. Map by Julianna Grigg.

MAP 3 The Fifth Crusade mobilization. Map by Julianna Grigg.

Introduction

> We, however, are confident that the Lord will soon bring to a happy conclusion the enterprise he has started so well. So that men shall praise the Lord for his works, and for his wonderful works to the children of men, glorify him, give him thanks for the things which he has done with you.
>
> Pray for our dead companions, Master Walter of Tournai . . . Master Constant of Douai . . . John of Cambrai . . . lord Reinier. . . . Our servant H. and others. . . . Pray for those dead companions.
>
> As for me, I was ill for two months before Damietta, and almost died, but the Lord has kept me alive till now, possibly to pay for my sins with pain and tribulation.
>
> —JACQUES DE VITRY

Jacques de Vitry, preacher of the Crusades, bishop of Acre, and eventually cardinal bishop of Tusculum, wrote several letters while accompanying the armies of the Fifth Crusade to Egypt. An eyewitness to the progress, brief triumph, and eventual failure of the Crusade, Jacques was one of the campaign's most important reporters. With Oliver of Paderborn (schoolmaster and ultimately bishop of Cologne), Jacques communicated news from the battlefront in Egypt, wrote of victory, and explained defeat. He wrote six letters while on Crusade, four of which were composed and sent from Egypt during and after the siege of Damietta. These letters reported the military progress of the Crusade and simultaneously reassured the recipients that the Egyptian campaign was God's work in action. In so doing, Jacques's letters sought to locate the action of war in a longer story of biblical history and divine will. This was a story that was very familiar to his readers and to Crusade participants. At the same time, Jacques's letters commemorated fallen crusaders, naming them as pious instruments of God and sometimes martyrs, men who had "departed from us in this exile and joined the Lord in happiness." The letters also provided Jacques with an opportunity to communicate something of his own experience at war, although as a cleric and not a soldier. He inserted tantalizing glimpses of his subjective emotional state at various points throughout the letters, rarely discursively but still clearly enshrining his own presence in the history of this most promising but ultimately disappointing Crusade.

Jacques de Vitry's Crusade letters are some of the many sources for the Fifth Crusade in which remembering is prominent. As the above quotes from Jacques's letters indicate, remembering took a number of shapes for medieval people—eschatological, collective, and individual. Crusading itself was steeped in the language of memory by the time of the Fifth Crusade: indeed, from the capture of Jerusalem by the armies of the First Crusade in 1099, participants in the subsequent crusading movements increasingly thought of their actions in ways that recalled events of past Crusades and the events of biblical history. They understood holy war as vengeance for the loss of Christ's inheritance, and they saw themselves more and more as engaging in a tradition undertaken previously by their families, communities, and regions. Crusading in the early thirteenth century was not only an act of love, as Jonathan Riley-Smith famously asserted, but an act of remembrance.[1] Remembrance was articulated in Christian terms and in familial terms, as a collective endeavor and as an individual activity. Remembrance was intrinsic to motivating, justifying, and defining crusading. By the time Jacques was writing his letters home from the Fifth Crusade, memorial and commemorative ideas had come to be central to all forms of communicating the events and the ideas of the Crusade.

This book asks two main questions: Why was remembering war so important in the early thirteenth century, and what purposes did remembrance serve? As will become clear in what follows, remembering became integrated into the war experience in different and new ways at this time, both during and after the conflict. This was due to the particular and recent history of the Crusades, which stimulated a renewed interest in the articulation and communication of remembrance. The overall argument of the book is that crusading possessed a unique temporal and spatial logic in which remembering was central. Crusading asked its participants (whether combatants or otherwise) to look both forward and backward in time for the justification and meaning of their spiritual and military actions in the present. Remembering the past both stimulated action and shaped future understandings of the triumphs and bitter defeats of the Crusade. In the case of the Fifth Crusade, which took place after a series of challenging losses in a number of theaters of crusading warfare and ultimately involved loss itself, remembrance was a significant means of explaining and expressing the sometimes devastating nature of military activity while communicating ongoing optimism about the eschatological efficacy of crusading itself.

WAR MEMORY

That remembering war should be so entwined with cultural and social practices and collective and individual identifications will be unsurprising to modern readers. In Western culture, especially, what Jay Winter called the "memory boom" of the twentieth century is not just an academic interest but a practice performed by countless others as part of societal life.[2] Collective rituals such as national memorial days, the perpetuation of national stories about war and battle as transformative historical moments, the construction of monuments memorializing war, and the existence of veterans' associations with sometimes powerful political reach are all examples of how war is not just integrated into but integral to the performance of Western cultural identities. There are historical reasons for this interest in war memory, as a vast historiography on memory in modern Western culture attests. Kerwin Klein neatly summarizes:

> We have, then, several alternative narratives of the origins of our new memory discourse. The first, following Pierre Nora, holds that we are obsessed with memory because we have destroyed it with historical consciousness. A second holds that memory is a new category of experience that grew out of the modernist crisis of the self in the nineteenth century. . . . A third sketches a tale in which Hegelian historicism took up premodern forms of memory that we have since modified through structural vocabularies. A fourth implies

that memory is a mode of discourse natural to people without history, and so its emergence is a salutary feature of decolonization. And a fifth claims that memory talk is a belated response to the wounds of modernity.[3]

Klein alerts us to modern historical conditions as precipitating a sort of epistemic shift in memory. Pierre Nora thought similarly. In a still influential but problematic exploration of history and memory, Nora posits that by the final decades of the twentieth century, spontaneous memory had been suffocated by the rise of history and its claims to the past. Memory as an active and dynamic lived practice was lost, and we now have only "ersatz memory"; memory "crystallized" around *lieux* (sites), as *milieux* (environments) of memory are no more. For Nora, the "quintessential repository" of unadulterated collective memory was rural peasant culture: precolonial, premodern, medieval.[4] For others, modernity itself has produced a "crisis of the self," a dissociative break from the past that was experienced subjectively and as a collective sensibility, particularly as a result of the First World War. Paul Fussell thought that the war created ironic skepticism and bitter disillusionment. He found its literature (especially), eschewing romanticized tales of valor and chivalry, was sharply different from pre-twentieth-century writing—this was "goodbye to Galahad," in the words of Siegfried Sassoon.[5] Others have seen the wars of modernity as precipitating the disenchantment of war: martyrdom and the Western Christian interpretation of death that had framed the rhetoric of sacrifice in centuries prior are now abandoned. These old symbols of sacrifice and redemption can be co-opted into the modern structural vocabulary of memory, but they have been historicized in the context of the contemporary rather than the past. As Stefan Goebel has recently shown, the medieval past was a significant semiotic source for the commemorative and memorial efforts of the First World War.[6] But whereas Goebel understands this medievalism as asserting a creative continuity with the longer past, it could also be seen as restating once again the rupture between the premodern and the modern in the form of nostalgia. Recourse to medieval images in war memorials, for instance, is more of a nod to an imagined and vanished past (itself the product of Victorian dreaming) than an uncomplicated and reassuring narrative of continuity.[7]

The political context for much of this historiography is the nation-state, "imagined communities" with "invented traditions" that assert political meaning for war and for memory.[8] Historians like Geoffrey Cubitt and Jay Winter have suggested that the twentieth-century memory boom may be in part attributed to disengagement with progressivist narratives of nationhood after the Second World War. Cubitt suggests that as the idea of the nation as a moral project—enshrined in foundational texts like laws and constitutions—broke down in the second half of the twentieth century, remembering war came to be performed in ways that are not "official" nationalist assertions of direction and purpose. So although nations continue to ask citizens to die in their defense, "the nation" itself is now merely one agent of remembrance, and its claims to nationalist certainty have been fundamentally diminished by, inter alia, the political and critical work of decolonization and postcolonialism, the "dissolving tendencies of mass culture," and globalization.[9]

A critical moment of this shift was the Holocaust, which, as Alon Confino asserts, added moral force to the quest to remember, brought to the fore the terminology of witnessing and trauma, and asked for repentance from the culpable.[10] Remembering the Holocaust acknowledged its uniqueness as a "convulsion" in historical time while challenging the claims of the nation regarding identity formation and cultural dominance.[11] The practice of history itself changed after the Holocaust, according to Confino, not because memory was suddenly invented as a topic for historical inquiry, but because memory was now an epistemological and hermeneutic category that could be deployed to understand the upheavals of the recent past. This, in Peter Carrier's words, was a new genre of historical writing: Holocaust "memoriography" attends to the historical work of understanding how the Holocaust has been remembered or forgotten and to the history of the Holocaust itself.[12] The memory boom, therefore, has long been connected to the disruption of political and social narratives of progress located within nationalist parameters—the end of the "master narrative," as Klein puts it.[13]

Such explanations for the general rise of modern memory recognize unique historical conditions. But they also create a temporality premised on abrupt historical transformations, including the institutionalization of "history," new sensibilities born of trauma, and—most especially— the shattering impact of war. These are epistemic and paradigm shifts, the shock of which is signified by the words used to describe them—*wounds, crisis, dislocation, convulsion.* Yet if we widen our perspective on the issue of war memory, it is almost immediately clear that remembering war is not simply a product of modernity. War memory has a much longer set of histories, many of which have nothing to do with a dramatic split between modernity and premodernity (both of which are problematic categories in themselves) or with the paradigm of the nation-state and its testing. In light of that, as I have outlined above, modern memory is frequently conceived as emerging from a particular time and premised on a historical temporality that emphasizes rupture, difference, and a departure from the premodern, interior, and collective crisis. It seems important to question the place of war memory in a more distant past. Moreover, the organizing context of the nation-state as the driver of memorial culture and a monolithic formation against which remembering pushes does not help us when we think about the longer history of war memory.[14] This book suggests that understanding how Crusade memory functioned requires quite precise historical contextualization and sensitivity to the many social and cultural forces that influenced its practice. At the same time, frameworks for understanding modern memory can offer medievalists hermeneutic and epistemological tools—which must be carefully deployed—for considering premodern forms of remembering war.

It is the broad task of this book to trace what remembering war meant to medieval people in order to offer a contribution to both medieval history and the history of war memory. First, I want to show that remembering war is not a specifically modern concern. It is perfectly clear that some features of war memory are specific to our own era, and I do not challenge that these are connected with the specific conditions of contemporary history. The programmatic construction of war memorials and monuments, the rise and influence of veterans' associations, new media through which war stories are told and reported are examples. But other features of remembering war are much older. Medieval people also privileged the eyewitness and oral testimony as primary conduits through which memory flowed. They gave transcendent meaning to war through commemorative practices such as liturgical procession and collective prayer. War memory communicated and perpetuated bigger collective truths about duty and belonging in the context of Christendom. Families used remembrance of war to tell stories about their ancestors and to create traditions. These were communicated in specifically medieval ways, but as in our own time, such ideas were always culturally meaningful. At the same time, the looseness of historical periodization is exposed by looking at war memory before the nation-state.

MEMORY, TEMPORALITY, AND THE CRUSADES

I am also interested in understanding the temporality of medieval war memory. How did medieval conceptions of the link between the past and present inform remembrance of conflict? A growing literature on medieval memory continues to show that memory was thought to operate in specific cognitive and epistemological ways in medieval culture. As Mary Carruthers showed a number of years ago, theologians like Hugh of Saint Victor thought that the memory occupied a space in the body or soul. To him, remembering meant both the capacity to bring to mind things learned, seen, or experienced and an instrument of order and composition. The interior ability of an individual to store, collate, and retrieve information from the memory enabled the production of understanding and knowledge.[15] This "art of memory" was also predicated on the idea that past and present were fluid, that the things of the past could be brought to the present for practical and psychological benefit. Monastic novices, for example, used memory as a way of creating monastic time. A thirteenth-century English *Speculum novitii* told a novice to use liturgical time to bring to mind biblical history and scenes from the life of Christ:

> At Lauds, think of the apprehended Christ. At Prime, think of Christ standing before Pilate.... During Terce, think of Christ raised on the cross.... At Sext, think of the darkness which fell upon the earth up to the ninth hour.... At None, think of Christ dying.... At Vespers, run back to the Lord's cross ... [at] Compline, think how you are ... watching the Lord's tomb so that when he arises you can run and ... hold his feet.... Think of the resurrection when you wake up; arrange the breadcrumbs on your dinner plate in the shape of the cross to remind yourself of the crucifixion; as you process into church, think of your life as a pilgrimage journey to heaven; as you climb into bed, think of the entombment of Christ.[16]

Such memory work was deeply experiential and even emotional. However, this did not mean that one must have *actually* experienced something in the past to be able to remember it. In the case of the monastic novice, remembering Christian history was a way of ridding himself of distracting personal memories from the time he had spent as a member of secular society and replacing those "real" memories with new ones that were shared by other members of his community.[17]

These examples illustrate some features of medieval memory that may resonate with historians of contemporary memory. Memories are something that communities are thought to share. In the monastic world, remembering is clearly an important tool of socialization. And remembering is a way of identifying with something collective—a community, a form of spirituality, a tradition or culture. At the same time, remembering in Latin Christianity is a way to bring together the earthly and heavenly realms. In other words, medieval memory was a distinctive combination of the individual's interior capacity to capture, store, retrieve, and use the past and the collective, the terrestrial, and the eschatological.[18]

Perhaps no other group in Western medieval society was so acutely aware of the importance of memory as crusaders. As individuals under oath, they were part of a collective endeavor, the rhetorical justification of which stressed action—performed in memory of Christ's sacrifice—to defend and liberate Christ's patrimony. Preachers encouraged men to take up the cross using the memory of biblical exhortation—"If any man would come after me, let him deny himself and take up his cross and follow me" (Matthew 16:24) was a typical refrain.[19] The rhetoric of unity was not necessarily matched by the reality of crusading, which, as Michael Lower and others have argued, was not the uniform mass movement we imagine it to be until careful efforts by the thirteenth-century papacy widened opportunities to participate.[20] Yet Crusade preachers and chroniclers communicated crusading as a communal effort from the very beginning and continued to do so throughout. They asserted that Western Christians were a distinctive group with distinctive religious obligations. Even Crusade failures could be a collective responsibility, as the *peccatis exigentibus* (because of our sins) explanation for continued failure indicates.

Those who preached and wrote about the Crusades of the twelfth century also crafted a vision of time in which the biblical past and the crusading present were brought together in a new and urgent way. Crusaders had always been equated with figures from biblical history, understanding themselves to be the new Israelites—specifically the Maccabees—or new apostles, and this continued into the thirteenth century.[21] Guibert of Nogent thought that the armies of the First Crusade were like the Maccabees in that they fought for "the sacred rituals and for the Temple"; *Quantum praedecessores*, Pope Eugenius III's call for the Second Crusade in 1147, used the example of Mattathias to inspire crusaders to triumph;

and in Pope Gregory VIII's great crusading letter of 1187 that preceded the Third Crusade, *Audita tremendi*, he told future crusaders to heed the example of the Maccabees, who thought that "it is better for us to die in battle than to witness the desecration of our nation and our saints."[22] There was more to these inspirational figures than mere similitude. The tasks of biblical heroes and contemporary crusaders were each part of a trajectory of sacred history that followed sacred time. Current events were part of this eternal, transcendent story. As Jay Rubenstein has shown, there was an apocalyptic dimension to this temporality from the start, and this was integrated into the historical accounts of the Crusade.[23] After the loss of Jerusalem in 1187, this was even more pronounced, as the loss of vast tracts of the Holy Land and the city of Jerusalem itself occasioned profound anxiety about the meaning of Saladin's victory. Thus, from the twelfth century, crusading temporality was eschatological in many ways. By taking up the cross, crusaders were placing themselves in a time frame that ran parallel to the terrestrial lapse of time in days and years. They were actors in an eternal history; Peter the Venerable called them the "army of the living God."[24] Their work was part of God's plan. "It is not for us to know why He would do this," wrote Pope Gregory VIII about the loss of Jerusalem, but it was certainly the *negotium Christi*, the business of Christ, for all crusaders to participate in its recovery.[25]

Crusading was also an individual activity. Each crusader made an individual vow of commitment to take up the cross—the *votum crucis*—and each participated in a later ritual of departure that eventually included individual blessing and the bestowing of a cross, staff, and pilgrim's scrip.[26] The reward for crusading—the remission of sins—was offered to individuals, and it was the individual who would be solely accountable for his actions on the Day of Judgment. The relationship between pilgrimage and the Crusade helps contextualize the very subjective character of this form of holy war, as has been recounted by historians since the publication of Carl Erdmann's *Die Entstehung des Kreuzzugsgedankens* in 1935.[27] As with other pilgrimages to holy places, crusading was a religious journey conducted for devout purposes. Its character was also penitential, and at least for the twelfth century, crusading could be designated a *peregrinatio* like many others. Pilgrimage contained its own temporality too, which was simultaneously retrospective and forward-looking—pilgrims looked "backward in gratitude" and "forward in hope."[28] Looking at Crusade memory allows us to understand the differentiated temporalities of the medieval period without the linear and progressivist narrative of the modern as its frame. Remembering made sense of this temporality.

The third aim of this book is to look closely at the world of early thirteenth-century crusading to understand why and how war memory was important at this particular historical moment. Part of the answer lies in the diversification of crusading in the first two decades of the thirteenth century. After 1187, the Latin Kingdom of Jerusalem was reduced to a string of cities that ran from Tyre to Jaffa along the Syrian coastline and the island of Cyprus. The vast swathes of territory captured during the course of the First Crusade had been lost incrementally over the course of the twelfth century, and although Jerusalem continued to be the focus of crusading calls in the early thirteenth century, the Holy Land was not the principal theater of war during the first decade of that century.[29] The Fourth Crusade was conducted in the Byzantine Empire; the Albigensian Crusade was conducted in southern France; the Crusades against the pagan Livonians took place on the Baltic coast. The so-called reconquest in the Iberian Peninsula also absorbed the rhetoric of the Crusade during this time. At the same time, the targets of crusading were increasingly diversified too. There had been military activity against the Wends of northeastern Germany and Poland in the mid-twelfth century as part of the Second Crusade (fought on three fronts in the Holy Land, Portugal, and eastern Europe), but it was in the early thirteenth century that the Crusade became institutionalized as an appropriate instrument of defense against a range of groups within and outside western Europe—even those who, like the Byzantine Greeks or the "Cathars" of Languedoc, thought of themselves as Christian. During the same period, opportunities for participating in crusading activities were opened up, and the conceptualization of crusading was increasingly sharpened.[30] Recruitment, financing of crusading, and redemption of vows were all transformed under the pontificate of Innocent III as a part of his agenda of moral reform, and crusading itself was reinvigorated.

Most importantly for this book, the early thirteenth century was a time of "intense reflection" on the crusading past.[31] This has been most thoroughly analyzed by Nicholas Paul, whose study of family memory and crusading has paved the way for a number of recent studies in this field.[32] Paul found that across the Latin West during the "long" twelfth century, narratives of the crusading past, particularly those communicated in family or genealogical histories, created and transmitted family traditions around crusading and its value. The genre of aristocratic family history writing had its heyday during the twelfth and early thirteenth centuries, and these texts are important sources for both understanding what we might call aristocratic self-fashioning and the creation and importance of ancestral traditions. Noble families found in the Crusades—especially the First Crusade—inspiration, instruction, and venerability, all of which were reflected in the commemorative texts they commissioned. But by the early thirteenth century, things were changing. Paul notes that although crusading ancestors remained a source of pride for noble families throughout the thirteenth century and beyond, once "the living memory of twelfth-century crusading slipped away and was replaced by literary imagination and chivalric pageantry, a new crusading era, born in the aftermath of the Third Crusade, began, populated by new heroes who fought in new landscapes."[33] The foundational First Crusade narratives were being transformed by vernacular histories and by the advent of crusading romance. This is a period of significant transformation in the history of crusading in relation to the conduct and conceptualization of the Crusades and in the relationship between the crusading past and the crusading present. How this affected or stimulated remembrance is a central question of this book.

THE FIFTH CRUSADE

The particular focus of this book is the Fifth Crusade, which was the product of a renewed push to recapture Jerusalem (lost to the armies of Saladin in 1187) by Pope Innocent III and his successor, Pope Honorius III. First enunciated in the 1213 bull *Quia maior*, the formal call was issued as part of the Fourth Lateran Council in 1215, and the Crusade was subsequently preached across northern Europe and beyond by a number of high-profile and experienced preachers, Jacques de Vitry, Robert of Courçon, and Oliver of Paderborn among them. In 1217, the Crusade was under way in the Holy Land (with some northern crusaders having engaged in military activity in Portugal along the way), but it changed direction in 1218 when it decided to attack Egypt.[34] The port city of Damietta was besieged and eventually captured that year, but it was lost in 1221 after the costly decision to advance up the Nile toward Cairo resulted in negotiation and truce with the Ayyubid sultan Al-Kamil. The Crusade ended with the evacuation of all crusaders (after some of high rank served a period as hostages) by the end of 1221. The Fifth Crusade had a number of distinctive features, in both its planning and its execution: it was well organized, well financed, and under the control of the pope—at least at the outset. Papal control of Crusade planning was in part a response to the disastrous Fourth Crusade—its diversion to Constantinople had been explained away by the time of *Quia maior* but remained a controversial episode, especially in the East.[35]

However, papal control of the Crusade did not translate to clear leadership of the Crusade; indeed, the "leadership question" has long been identified as one key reason the Crusade ultimately failed. No single leader was put in place to coordinate the Crusade before it began, although there were many contenders—the king of Jerusalem, John of Brienne; the emperor, Frederick II; the papal legate Pelagius, bishop of S. Albano (who arrived in September 1218); King Andrew II of Hungary; Leopold, Duke of Austria; King Hugh of Cyprus; and Bohemond IV of Antioch. Guy Perry's new biography of John of Brienne notes that although the king of Jerusalem emerged as the Crusade's de facto leader, this had not been planned by Pope Innocent III or his successor, Honorius III (who preferred Andrew of Hungary).[36] Perry notes that the leadership question was the symptom and result of the way that Crusade participation worked. Contingents large and small formed, arrived, and departed with their own leaders: in James Powell's words, "The crusaders were not a standing army in the field awaiting a commander . . . they were a force."[37] So although the blame for the failure of the Fifth Crusade has often been attributed to individuals—the procrastination of Frederick II, whose promise of manpower never materialized, or the conflict between Pelagius and John of Brienne at Damietta—there was also a structural weakness in the leadership of the Crusade in general.

Interest in the leadership of the Crusade stems from its earliest historiography, which was undertaken by Reinhard Röhricht in the nineteenth century. Röhricht was an antiquarian and schoolteacher and was one of the first to consider the Fifth Crusade as a focused area of study. His 1891 *Studien zur Geschichte des fünften Kreuzzuges* was supplemented by a number of works on German pilgrimage to the Holy Land during the crusading period; articles on key figures of the Crusade including Oliver of Paderborn, Jacques de Vitry, and Frederick II as sources; and his collection of the charters and documents of the chancery of the Latin Kingdom of Jerusalem.[38] Röhricht was part of a constellation of nineteenth-century scholars who gathered around Comte Paul de Riant's *Société de l'orient latin*, the academic society for the study of the Crusades and the group that essentially founded modern Crusades scholarship. The scholars of this period were typical of their time: they were interested in the documentation of the events they sought to describe (hence the many editions that emanated from this group), and they wrote mostly top-down and narrative history, with an emphasis on leadership, papal directives, and aristocratic participation.[39]

The transformative historiographical moment for this Crusade came in the later twentieth century with James Powell's 1986 monograph *Anatomy of a Crusade, 1213–1221*. Powell was the first to offer a social history of the Fifth Crusade that synthesized the turn in Crusade studies to analyzing the preparations and background of crusading with questions of motivation.[40] His approach was innovative in a number of ways. He was concerned with moving away from the question of conflict between Crusade leaders as the dominant interpretive framework of the Crusade and was clear that the Crusade ought to be seen as part of a more general effort of renewal and reform for Christendom. He also argued that this was an especially important Crusade, as it "was being forged into an instrument for the moral transformation of society."[41] Powell's careful evaluation of the planning, recruitment, financing, and conduct of the Fifth Crusade has stimulated further studies on the culture and papal direction of the Crusade. Historians have recently begun to recognize the active and distinctive role of Pope Honorius III in the Crusade, and a new edition of some key papal documents has now brought some of the letters and bulls to a wider audience.[42] Thomas Smith, in particular, has shown how Honorius should be viewed not as a passive inheritor of the views of Innocent III but as a "shrewd and calculating politician."[43] New studies of key figures such as John of Brienne now pay more attention to the broader context from which participants in the Crusade came.

This turn to context has been the defining feature of the most recent historiography. Historians have increasingly considered the Fifth Crusade as part of a more general discourse of religious renewal in the medieval West, which encompasses monastic and clerical reform, new attention to preaching, and perhaps most distinctively, conversion.[44] In a number of studies, Jessalynn Bird shows that the sermons and preaching of the Crusade reflected long intellectual and spiritual lineages and that from the late twelfth to the mid-thirteenth century, Crusades exhortations were included in sermon collections authored by networks of writers with connections to the Parisian masters.[45] At the same time, Crusade exhortations increasingly reflected a growing interest in conversion as one of the aims and instruments of crusading.[46] Such missionizing efforts are particularly associated with the Franciscans, who were active in Morocco during the time of the Fifth Crusade and whose founder, St. Francis of Assisi, was present in Egypt in 1219 in a delusional attempt to persuade the sultan Al-Kamil to convert to Christianity.[47] But in more general terms, the conversion agenda was part of a much broader program of renewal that was supposed to see Christendom expand farther than ever before. Crusading as an instrument of Christian expansion was linked to simultaneous efforts to deal with heresy within Western Europe, to eradicate the vestiges of paganism in the East and the Baltic, and to encourage all Christians to reform themselves through the sacrament of confession, participation in the Eucharistic ritual, and prayer.

The sources for the Fifth Crusade are diverse. The most well-known narrative accounts are Oliver of Paderborn's *Historia Damiatina* (composed between 1217 and 1222); the sources collected by Röhricht—the *Gesta crucigerorum Rhenanorum*, the *Gesta obsidionis Damiatae*, the *De itinere Frisonum*, and John of Tulbia's *De domino Iohanne rege Ierusalem* and *Liber duellii christiani in obsidione Damiate*—and to a lesser extent, the *Historia orientalis* and *Historia occidentalis* of Jacques de Vitry.[48] Several local and regional chronicles also report the Crusade in varying degrees of detail and emphasis on local participants, including the *Chronicon* of Emo of Wittwerium, which is an important source for the Frisian participation; the highly problematic extensions and versions of William of Tyre's *Historia rerum in partibus transmarinis gestarum*; the *Chronica majora* of Matthew Paris; the *Flores historiarum* of Roger of Wendover; and Ralph of Coggeshall's *Chronicon anglicanum* for the English view.[49] The preliminary expedition to the Iberian Peninsula is reported in a number of texts, including monastic chronicles and poems.[50]

One distinctive feature of the early thirteenth-century Crusade texts is the richness of eyewitness accounts. Oliver of Paderborn and Jacques de Vitry are especially important sources for our understanding of the Crusade because they preached and recruited for it in Europe, they traveled with it to Egypt, they witnessed the progress and eventual demise of the Crusade, and throughout this period, they wrote about it. As I discuss in the second chapter of this book, eyewitnessing was both a significant source of authorial authority in the Middle Ages and a particularly important element in the construction and communication of memory. The letters of Jacques de Vitry are crucial in this regard. His epistolary texts were written before, during, and after the Crusade, and with others (including Oliver of Paderborn's *Historia*, which was originally written as a letter), they form an especially insightful set of texts. Charters and other "administrative" or "official" documents are also important written sources for this book. Although charters for the Fifth Crusade are sometimes scattered and are probably fewer than those that survive from the First and Second Crusades, for instance, they nonetheless provide useful insights into the preparations for crusading; relationships between individuals, families, and their religious associations; and, as I show in chapter 1, the expectation that individual crusaders would be remembered. The testaments and wills included in monastic and other cartularies are especially informative.[51]

Places and objects are also important sources for this Crusade. It seems that as the targets and locations for crusading diversified in the early thirteenth century, there arose considerable local and regional efforts to memorialize the Crusade outside the Holy Land. Although places with tangible links to biblical history remained central to the crusading imaginary, locations such as Lisbon and Damietta also grew to become sites of memory that were particularly meaningful to specific groups of crusaders and their descendants. Acts of remembering (whether material, spiritual, or performative) constructed new holy places on the edges of what the crusading enterprise was traditionally thought to be. The locations encountered by those who actively participated in the Crusade became sites of memory in a number of ways, as I discuss in chapter 5. Lisbon, the port city of Damietta in Egypt, and Mount Tabor in the Holy Land assumed importance during and after this Crusade as commemorative landscapes associated with sacred history (recent or biblical) and previous crusading activity. At the same time, places more conventionally associated with the Crusade, including Jerusalem, retained their value, as the *Descriptio terre sancte*, *Historia de ortu Jerusalem*, and *Historia regum terre sancte* of Oliver of Paderborn reveal.[52] The material fabric of memory is also rich for the Fifth Crusade. For the Holy Land, many of the relevant relics, souvenirs, tombs, coinage, and buildings for this period have been conveniently identified by Jaroslav Folda.[53] Of particular interest for chapter 6 of this book are the objects associated with Jacques de Vitry, now part of the Treasury of Oignies at Namur in Belgium.[54] These objects, which include Jacques de Vitry's miter, portable altar, episcopal rings, reliquary of the Holy Cross, and gemstones, tell unique stories about the connections between places, the custodianship of remembrance, and the links between past and present. These principal sources for the Fifth Crusade are mostly clerical or monastic, although the diversity of genres allows for some broader contextual claims to be made for them, as I discuss throughout.

REMEMBRANCE PROJECTS

The terminology of memory is notoriously loose, and its categorizations are many. In this book, I mostly use *memory* to refer to an interior, individual cognitive capacity. I use the term *remembrance* in a broader sense to suggest the cultural and sometimes collective work of bringing the past to light for a variety of purposes. Thus *remembrance* functions in the way suggested by Emmanuel Sivan and Jay Winter, who describe it as "a strategy to avoid the trivialization of the term 'memory' through inclusion of any and every facet of our contact with the past, personal or collective. To privilege 'remembrance' is to insist on specifying agency, on answering the question who remembers, when, where, and how? And on being aware of the transience of remembrance, so dependent on the frailties and commitments of the men and women who take the time and effort to engage in it."[55] In this book, I am especially concerned with understanding how war has been remembered, memorialized, and commemorated. I focus on a relatively short period of time around the 1220s in the context of what Jan and Aleida Assmann have termed "communicative memory"—that is, the ways in which remembering is formed, articulated, and expressed within a few generations or within living memory of an event.[56] The concept of communicative memory is helpful for considering the historical moment in which remembering is understood to be important. The immediate shaping and transmission of memory can tell us much about decisions to remember and to forget, about the processes of remembering and commemorative forms, and about how past peoples' imagined memory can be useful and meaningful. Moreover, the interplay between individual experienced memory and the articulation of remembrance in a culture is a fruitful way to examine how meaning is created and attributed to historical phenomena more widely.

The Fifth Crusade took place at a significant time for the expression and communication of memory and remembrance of war. The relative longevity of the crusading movement by the second decade of the thirteenth century, its generational and ancestral pull, and its diverse locational presence all affected how war was remembered at that time. Remembrance itself became integrated into the war experience in different ways—through letter writing, the collection of objects, the memorialization of sites, and the fabrication of heroes and villains. It was during this period that the unique temporal and spatial logic of crusading came to incorporate remembrance as a central component. Remembering war was powerful during the time of the Fifth Crusade because it was a useful epistemological tool to explain and provoke actions and events. The many remembrance projects—textual, material, and visual—that were undertaken during this moment of the early thirteenth century tell stories of hope and fear, conflict and loss, and survival and death in the context of violent conflict and its aftermath. This book examines those stories.

CHAPTER 1

Preparatory Memory

Managing Remembrance

Remembering does not suddenly begin when a war ends. Almost as soon as they had taken up the cross and begun making their preparations for departure on a Crusade, medieval soldiers were clearly concerned about how they and their actions would be remembered—individually and collectively. In pragmatic documents usually analyzed to uncover motives for crusading (such as charters or wills and testaments), a sense of the power of remembering is also evident. In Crusade chronicles and eyewitness accounts, the stirring words of prayer and encouragement that were delivered to nervous crusaders on the eve of battle sometimes included the promise of future collective remembrance as a motivation to fight. For crusaders and those who wrote about their battles, remembering was understood to reach beyond the individual to descendants and coming generations, including potential future crusaders. Remembrance, then, was an ongoing set of processes that was iterated, shaped, told, and retold from the first moments of a soldier's identification as a crusader.

The crusaders of the Middle Ages are not the only combatants to project their wishes onto the future by means of text. Battlefront correspondence, wills, and memoirs from modern conflicts proliferate in archives, in libraries, in family histories, and online, while the letters of farewell composed by these soldiers reveal that departure for war provokes both introspection and a desire to take care of family and friends left behind. Some of these contemporary missives even echo concerns that would be familiar to medieval combatants—the fate of the soldier's remains, the disposal of property, and the religious rituals of remembrance. When twenty-one-year-old lieutenant Tommy Kennedy realized that he was near death in January 1945, he wrote to his mother with some quite pragmatic advice about how to remember him: "Hold a nice service for me in Blksfield & put head stone in new cematary [*sic*]," he wrote from a Japanese POW warship in the Pacific.[1] Kennedy's letter, scrawled on the back of a family photo he had taken with him to war, attempted to direct a future that he would not himself see. These letters often express resolve, occasionally regret ("I should have gone to college," wrote one young American soldier from Iraq), and consolation; they make emotional and hopefully enduring connections with loved ones.[2] They are frequently described as poignant, heartbreaking, and sad, and our emotional responses to them are more than slightly influenced by broader cultural and political representations of the conflicts from which they emerge.

Contemporary communiqués from doomed soldiers also remind us that, though remembrance can be managed by those who seek to be remembered, the ways in which this might be accomplished are always historically contingent. Although combatants have long wished to shape how they will be remembered, the contexts, genres of text, and narrative choices they make are very much dependent on time, place, and discourse. How this worked in the crusading period is explored in this chapter. Specifically, I look at what I term "preparatory memory," or the formation of personal and collective remembrance in advance of combat by those who were about to go to war and those who encouraged them. My interest lies in how individuals and groups tried to influence and manage how they would be remembered once they had gone on Crusade and perhaps died. How did individuals want to be remembered? How did they go about determining how they would be remembered? And why was it important to be remembered not just as soldiers or knights but specifically as crusaders—those signed with the cross (*crucesignati*) and part of the army of the Lord (*exercitus Domini*)? In asking these questions, I consider how frameworks of remembering were constructed and used by both individuals and groups with particular and sometimes similar interests in establishing and influencing crusader memory. Overall, I suggest that crusaders and the contemporaries who wrote about them used remembrance as a way of clearly identifying with the Crusade as a spiritual community of which they were a constituent part.

For medieval people, remembrance was always a means of claiming membership in particular groups, which might include families (as Nicholas Paul has so powerfully demonstrated), monasteries, or networks of patronage and other associations.[3] Commemorative practices, liturgical activity, the writing down of the past, and the mnemonic performance of music in monastic settings were all ways of creating and building communities that called for specific types of identification. The Crusade too was a community of remembrance, whose participation required not just a vow and service but also an individually transformative and deeply binding identification with a group. Individuals who offered instruction about the disposal of their property and the treatment of their remains should they die on Crusade used those directions to locate their future remembrance in the context of crusading. The writers of texts focusing on particular events reminded crusaders to remember the need for and meaning of those battles, using these narrative spaces to connect crusading and remembrance.

In the broader historiography of war memory, the relationship between the memories of individuals and the collective memory of groups has mostly been approached in the context of either the appropriation and politicization of memory by the nation or the distinction between "private" and "public" memories.[4] Others have focused on the domination of the "public" over the "private" as time goes on as a part of the evolution of cultural memory, finding that the individual memories of a veteran eventually become influenced and then subsumed by the politics of national commemoration.[5] Medievalists too have mostly been interested in the relational qualities of remembering, especially the ways in which memory was deployed to create "useable pasts" or how communities of memory were formed and operated.[6] For historians like Elisabeth Van Houts, remembering the medieval past requires both oral tradition and written culture in male and female lay and religious spheres, while for others like Patrick Geary, the institutionalization of memory is a product and reflection of the increased monastic use of the written work (and archives).[7] In the context of the Crusades, memory as a "medium of identity formation" has been recently prominent. Paul and Yeager, for instance, have argued that for crusaders, remembering was a social process and that the Crusades themselves provided a "dynamic framework for the development and performance of medieval identities."[8] In a recent issue of the *Journal of Medieval History*, Anne E. Lester and I suggested that memory and the associated practices of remembrance and commemoration were, for crusaders, social acts that "grew out of and were practiced in social groups, drawing together families and kin, confraternities and parishes, monks, nuns and patrons." The unique nature of the Crusade as both religious and military phenomenon opened up myriad possibilities for social and cultural identities to develop and flourish. These identities reflected and required both the individual and the group.[9]

Following this scholarship, this chapter shows that remembering is both a social process and a tool of socialization. In the specific context of the early thirteenth century, it is also important to be reminded that memory work was a part of a more widespread identification with the Crusade, even among those who did not participate in combat. Although crusaders who traveled to the Holy Land and Egypt on the Fifth Crusade managed their future memory by identifying themselves specifically as crusaders, their networks and communities were increasingly drawn into the work of crusading by participating on the "home front." It was at the time of the preaching of the Fifth Crusade that the prayer and liturgical work done by Christians in Europe could be newly described as crusading.[10] Pope Innocent III's statement in *Quia maior* that a Crusade vow "may be commuted, redeemed, or postponed by apostolic command" meant that those who could not fight could now still take up the cross with the promise of the commutation of their crusading vow into a monetary payment or the sending of a proxy to the battlefront. These new crusaders could also benefit from the promise of remission of sins. These practical and spiritual innovations meant that more people than ever before could call themselves crusaders, and it also meant that the community with which crusaders could identify was even larger. Processes of remembering and identification with the Crusade were especially heightened at this time.

INDIVIDUAL REMEMBRANCE

There is clearly much that is conventional in the ways crusaders tried to manage their memories. Ordering their affairs, distributing property, and giving instructions for burial and ongoing rituals of remembrance (such as Masses) were all typical means by which many medieval pilgrims (not just crusaders) linked the present and the future by asserting themselves as pious individuals. Mostly we know about these attempts to organize and perpetuate memory from charters and testamentary documents such as wills, which grew in use during the eleventh century to formalize, document, and enforce the wishes of an individual. These sorts of documents have long been acknowledged by historians of the Crusades as especially insightful in relation to motivations for crusading. Jonathan Riley-Smith, Marcus Bull, Giles Constable, and many others have used charters to argue for the centrality of piety as a motive for crusading and to establish crusading itself as a religious movement that reflected and generated the many sweeping spiritual changes and reforms of the Gregorian period and beyond.[11] By mapping statements of purpose contained in charters, pious benefactions, and donations, historians have shown that seemingly formulaic, indeed prosaic, records of the transfer of rights and property are rich sources for cultural, social, and religious history. As "practical instruments of memory," charters and wills are especially useful for exploring how individuals understood their own places in family, community, and cosmos. Indeed, wills and charters read as intensely personal documents; they establish relationships between an individual and those important to him or her, they communicate not only the proprietary wishes of a person but how he or she wanted to be perceived after death, and they entrust the memory of an individual to significant others. To a large degree, they are texts that project an individual's self-representation forward into the future in perpetuity.

Scholarship on medieval charters in particular has often emphasized the highly mediated nature of these sources. It is clear that Crusade charters composed by monks or clerics, for example, must be contextualized as representing institutional as well as individual wishes. However, some years ago, Giles Constable rejected the outright dismissal of Crusade charters as clerical documents that "did not express the true sentiments of the crusaders themselves."[12] Constable was speaking of the pious statements made in charters and their use as evidence of crusaders' motivation. He suggested that the concomitant evidence of the "demonstrable sacrifice" of property and family may support the claim, now generally accepted among Crusade historians, that concern for eternal welfare was the most significant underlying motivation for participation in the Crusades of the long twelfth century.[13] Crusade charters (and testaments) can be read as remembrance texts, but it is also important to recognize their mediated contexts too. Copies of charters now entered in cartularies, for example, may not necessarily be faithful replicas of the original document. Formulaic *arengae* may be read as textual acts designed (as Brigitte Bedos Redak suggests) to "maintain a process of textualization which would assure these acts' ongoing canonization as discursive practices."[14] And the not infrequent forging of charters must also be acknowledged. The most famous set of these is probably the so-called Collection Courtois, which was discredited long ago but not before leading many noble European families astray with unfounded claims to ancestral involvement in the crusading past (including the Fifth Crusade).[15]

For the Fifth Crusade, both charters of donation before departure and last wills and testaments are scattered. The diverse regional contingents of crusaders who departed for the Crusade during the period of 1217–20 came from various locations and different record-keeping cultures. This means that there are more wills for Italian crusaders and those who supported the Crusade through bequest from places like Genoa, where the notarial culture was strong, as it was in Catalonia.[16] A large number of well-known late medieval testaments survive from towns such as Douai, but locating testaments from before 1250 in Flanders and France is often a matter of trawling through dozens of monastic cartularies or individual archives.[17] For the Levant, the records of the military orders are important repositories for this period, particularly the records of the Hospitallers, whose hospital cared for sick and dying pilgrims and crusaders and whose *ordines* instructed the brothers on compiling last testaments in the Holy Land. The Teutonic Knights too, whose fortunes rose significantly as a result of the Fifth Crusade, kept records of donations through charters and, less frequently, wills. A few testaments that were made at the battlefront in Egypt can also be found. Again, these are scattered. Nonetheless, testamentary texts survive in sufficient number to isolate some common features that may illuminate the practice of preparatory memory.

If the famous mid-thirteenth-century Castilian law code *Las siete partidas* is any indication, will making was generally understood to be extremely important for all soldiers, even those on the very brink of death on a battlefield:

> When a knight desires to make his will and does at home or anywhere else, except in the army, he should make it in the same way as other men do . . . but if he is compelled to make it while in the army, it will then be sufficient if he does do in the presence of two witnesses. . . .

> And if, while he is in action and seeing that he is in danger of death, he wishes to make a will at that time, we decree that he can do so in any way that he is able and desires, either verbally or in writing. He can also write it with his own blood on his shield or on any of his arms, or he can by forming letters in the earth, or in the sand.[18]

This directive indicates that the context of combat could escalate the importance of making a will, although it was clearly ideal for a knight to have one written in a less urgent environment before setting out for war. The formality of will making was also flexible for those on the battlefront, and this extract from *Las siete partidas* shows that both words and writing could be meaningful and presumably binding if a will was made in the thick of battle or its aftermath. Here, the important aspect of will making is its communicative function. For those at war, it did not matter if there was no notary, no parchment, and no scribe. What mattered was the expression of wishes somehow to someone who could then transmit the information from the battlefield or deathbed to home.

Some testaments survive from Damietta for the Fifth Crusade, including the famous will of Barzella Merxadrus, an Italian crusader who made a formal will as he lay dying in a tent outside the city of Damietta in December 1219.[19] Barzella's will tells us that he was a citizen of Bologna, *crucesignatus* (signed with the cross), who had become "gravely ill in the army of the Christians." His clear and immediate identification as *crucesignatus* and a part of the Christian army establishes Barzella's status as a crusader at the very outset of this testament. We know that Barzella was not the only crusader to fall ill at that time—according to Oliver of Paderborn, pestilence had devastated the crusader camp during the winter of 1218–19 and continued to afflict the army for the rest of the Crusade. Barzella himself was accompanied by his wife, whose welfare after his death was clearly a matter of worry for him. He instructed his companions to let his wife remain living in the tent at Damietta "for as long as shall continue to dwell fully and peacefully in the same tent just as she has dwelled in it up to the present, for as long as she shall remain in that same army." Barzella's will draws attention to the presence of women among the crusading army, which by the time of the Fifth Crusade was becoming increasingly uncommon.[20] But his last testament is also a good example of how crusader wills provided for families and spouses as well as institutions and individuals.

Barzella's wife, Guiletta, was his principal heir. She was to receive some of the three bezants designated for his companions "and wife," together with "all other of his goods, movable and immovable, legal rights and actions which she should hold overseas in the army and in the portion that might fall to him from the spoils discovered in the city of Damietta and from the city itself." It seems that Barzella thought not only that he would do well from the outcome of the Crusade but that his wife could remain with the Crusade after his death, at least for some time. For Barzella, his own status as a crusader was in some ways embodied in his wife's continued presence on Crusade after his death; they continued to share a familial or spousal identity through their actions as a part of the Christian army and through the written testament that determined Barzella's wishes on the eve of his death. Spouses and families were the most frequently named groups in crusader wills and testaments and like Barzella's; many crusaders were keen to provide security for their wives. Barzella's own family was from Bologna, and he requested that his mother and brother-in-law still living there were to inherit his other Italian possessions.

Institutions were frequent beneficiaries of both gratitude and bequests in the wills made by crusaders, especially monastic houses and religious orders, which undertook to perform spiritual tasks of commemoration and prayer for the crusader. Masses and prayers in remembrance of individuals were not, of course, reserved for crusaders alone. But both the overt inclusion of a donor's crusader status in the charters recording his or her gift to a medieval religious house and the specific invocation of the memory of a family's generational connection to crusading in charters of confirmation support the suggestion that remembering someone as a crusader was particularly prominent in these documents.[21] To some degree, previous personal connections with religious houses explained why some crusaders favored particular institutions. John of Harcourt, for instance, who drew up his will as he lay dying at Damietta in 1220, continued his family's tradition of supporting the Knights Templar by leaving them some 450 acres of his land in Rothley, Leicestershire. A number of twelfth-century donations to the Templars from the Harcourt family attest to a longer history of association with the order.[22] Gifts to religious houses had long been a common practice in crusading culture, and testaments from twelfth-century Crusades tell a similar story.[23] Gifts of gratitude to the military orders in particular continued to be a feature of testaments in the thirteenth century. Barzella

Merxadrus himself left goods and property to the Teutonic Knights, the Hospitallers, and the Templars in his will, while in 1226 before leaving for war against the Albigensians, Guy of Tremelay gave to the Hospitallers his house at Senon and its rights and dependencies.[24] The Teutonic Knights benefited from the gifts of Lanfranc of Bogossa in August 1218. Gravely ill in the hospital of the Teutonic Knights at Brindisi when he uttered his last wishes on his deathbed (*iacens in lectulo meo gravi infirmitate detentus*), Lanfranc indicated that the Teutonic Knights should receive land, houses, and vineyards for cultivation. Lanfranc's will was not written up by a notary; as a nuncupative will, his wishes were noted and then compiled into a written document later, its veracity attested by a list of witnesses, including the master of the hospital.[25]

Those who were the beneficiaries of the care of the military orders during the course of the Fifth Crusade, like Barzella and Lanfranc, were especially indebted to them. This is very clear in the will of Count Henry I of Rodez, which was first made at Acre in 1221.[26] Henry had a colorful pre-Crusade history of avoiding Count Simon de Montfort during the Albigensian war. De Montfort's armies had invaded and claimed significant portions of land in the south of France, where Henry's own territories lay. To protect his lands and at the instigation of the papal legate Robert of Courçon, Henry finally agreed to de Montfort's overlordship and soon thereafter took up the cross and traveled to Egypt with the Fifth Crusade. His affairs at home clearly concerned Henry as he lay in the hospital of Saint Jean at Acre in 1221, where he drew up his will. In it, Henry declared himself to be afflicted by serious illness (*gravi detentus infirmitate*) but in sound mind. He left numerous properties to the Hospitallers, including the village of Canet; landholdings in Frontignan; all his property, rights, and men at La Bastide-Pradines; various rights of cultivation and grazing; and a number of other properties. These were holdings of significant size and value.

Henry's gratitude to the Hospitallers seems to have grown over the following months as he continued to languish at Acre. In October 1222, Henry added a codicil to his will in which his closeness to the order is even more apparent.[27] In both the initial will and the codicil, he instructed his family to repay the Hospitallers the expenses they had outlaid for him and for the assistance he had received from them in Syria (*multa et magni servicia quamdiu moram in partibus Sirie feci*). But in the codicil, he asked that he be buried "as a brother" (*pro fratre*) of the order rather than simply being buried in their cemetery as he had originally stipulated. He asked his family—"my dearest wife" and "my dearest son"—to protect and defend both the Templars and the Hospitallers. New names were added to the witness list, although Petrus Maurinus, *physicus*, was present both times. Occasionally, specific individuals from the military orders were named as the reason for gift giving in testaments and charters of donation made during the Crusade itself. After the capture of Damietta, Milon de S. Florentin, seigneur of Puits, gave land at Villiers-Vineux to the master of the hospital with an annual rent of one hundred sous "in consideration of the affection" he held for Osbert Gibaut, a knight and brother of the hospital.[28]

Although land and the accompanying rights were the most frequent gifts to military orders and religious houses, individual objects were also bequeathed to them. These items could have pragmatic purposes as well as commemorative functions, and both linked the practice and experience of crusading to individual legacy. Arms and armor were often among the gifts given to the Templars and Hospitallers, as was the case in the will of Barzella, who left "all his weapons and armor and hauberk with one armguard and a coif" to the Teutonic Knights. Barzella was one of many who foresaw that such gifts would have a practical use in equipping future crusaders, and he also specified that his possessions should support someone to remain in the crusader army for a year—to this end, he provided foodstuffs, wine, clothing, and six bezants as well. Gaucher of Le Puiset, Viscount of Chartres, was another who wrote his will during the siege of Damietta in 1219. As he lay dying, he left thirty pieces of silver to commission a knight on horseback to be made for the windows of Chartres Cathedral. Gaucher's wishes were recorded in that institution's cartulary.[29] This charter is short and does not reveal the rather sad detail that Gaucher was with his father, Milo, who died a few days after his son, both having been mortally wounded in a battle fought on August 15 that year.[30] Gaucher's will also charged his wife and mother to make sure that his wishes were carried out.[31]

Wills also shed light on the support for pilgrimages and Crusades from individuals and families who were not themselves participants in a Crusade. Some families offered financial support for a specific Holy Land pilgrimage to be undertaken by a family member, as did William de Bello Campo in 1268, whose will specified that two hundred marks be left to "my son Walter in aid of his pilgrimage to the Holy Land for me and his mother."[32] A sudden flurry of bequests in aid of the Fifth Crusade can be detected in the notarial records of Genoa between August 23 and December 21, 1216, at the time when Jacques de Vitry was preaching vociferously in the city to drum up support. These were mostly general bequests and, as such, could be claimed by papal agents to help fund for any Crusade (not just the Fifth). There are five wills that specifically mention the Crusade—from Betranno de Lavania, who left money "in servicio passagii de Ultramare"; Berta de Gala, "in passagio de Ultramare"; Rustico della Costa, "in passagio Ultramare"; Aidela, wife of Oberti Nigrini, "in servitio passagii de ultramare"; and Montamaria, wife of Martini de Mara, "in servitio passagi ultramarine."[33] The last of these is unusual in that Montamaria seems to have intended to join the Crusade herself.[34] That most of these bequests were made by women supports Powell's contention that the presence of Jacques de Vitry in Genoa during September 1216 had a significant effect on both Crusade recruitment and finances (and Jacques's own observations that women were especially amenable to his preaching).[35]

Crusaders like Barzella were clearly concerned about the fate of their physical remains were they to die during a campaign, and many left instructions in their wills as to where their bodies should be buried. For those like Barzella, whose death was imminent, burial sites were often in the Holy Land itself. Barzella stated that his preferred location of burial was in "the hospital of the Germans in Jerusalem"—that is, the hospital of the Teutonic Knights. For those who were about to depart on Crusade, concern for one's physical body was evident in their last testaments as well. Instructions were often very specific, with some clarifying exactly which body parts ought to be repatriated if it were not possible to bring the entire body home. One example is Hademar of Kuenring, a *crucesignatus* who died in 1217. Hademar asked that at least his heart and right hand be returned for burial at the Cistercian abbey of Zwettl, even if it were not possible to bring back his whole corpse to the monastery that his family had founded.[36] As Nicholas Paul has pointed out, noble families in particular were concerned with gathering together as many of the physical remains of their dead family members as possible, and family tombs were important places where ancestral identities could be communicated by remembering crusader relatives. From the mid-twelfth century, the growing trend to repatriate remains of crusaders coincided with increasing emphasis on the place of burial as a potent site of family memory.[37] This was certainly the case with Saher IV of Quincy, the Earl of Winchester, who succumbed to illness (*gravi infirmitate*) and died at Damietta in 1219. Most of his organs were cremated there and his bones interred at Acre, but his heart and entrails (*cor ejus et vitalia*) were to be brought back whole to the Cistercian abbey of Garendon, a daughter house of Waverley, and buried there. This was one of the abbeys founded by his wife's family in 1133 (the Earls of Leicester) and so had significant family resonance.[38]

When this was not possible, some families acknowledged the care that loved ones had received as patients of the military orders, who also took charge of interment. The Counts of Kybourg, for example, gratefully recognized the care shown by the Hospitallers to their brother Werner, who had died in the hospital of Saint Jean in Acre sometime before 1229. They were grateful that the brothers had buried their brother with appropriate devotion, placing his bones near the holy city of Jerusalem.[39] And Raymond Berengar, Count of Provence, instructed in his will of June 1238 that he wanted to be buried with his father, who lay not in his lands in the south of France but in the cemetery of the Hospitallers in Jerusalem.[40]

The representation of a crusader's last wishes may also be seen in the foundation history of the Cistercian abbey of Zwettl, where Hademar II of Kuenring had intended his heart and hand to be buried. In the monastic text that records Hademar's wishes, an extraordinarily emotional scene of donation and departure is described. Having taken up the cross, Hademar took two of his sons to Zwettl and gave them to the monastery, knowing, as he was reported to have said, that he would never see Zwettl again. Predicting his impending death (*imminente morte*), Hademar spoke to each of his children: "Behold my dear son," he said to his youngest as he commended him to the monastery, "you will always have my name, my bones and my flesh." Turning to the assembled crowd, Hademar spoke of his own certainty that he would die on Crusade and entrusted the weeping community with the care of his soul and his remains. The prayers of the Zwettl monks smoothed Hademar's rough journey across the stormy Mediterranean, but he died on his way home from the Holy Land. His servant collected Hademar's heart and hand and returned them to Zwettl, where, *usque hodie*, the memory of Hademar was celebrated "with vigils and masses and other prayers," just as he had wished.[41] As Hademar's association with Zwettl illuminates, it was often the ritual performance of remembering that a testator or donor was most concerned with ensuring. Prayers and Masses for the safe repose of the crusader's soul are frequent in the charters and testaments, and they were to be performed not only regularly but also forever. As a founder of Zwettl, Hademar could be ensured that the monks of his abbey would continue to sing his name and keep a place for his remains.

Donations and testaments recording the disposal of property, acknowledgment of religious orders, and support for the Crusade and the care of the body are also texts that craft remembrance of individuals and groups through the careful delineation of relationships. They situate the crusader in a series of networks of belonging and affiliation that were hoped to endure beyond the grave. These networks were familial and institutional and reflected preexisting bonds of connection and affection. By naming the various communities to which individual crusaders were attached, soldiers entrusted remembrance of their lives and deaths to those communities. Yet in the end, it is still the testator or donor's voice that echoes loudest in these wills and charters. Although to some degree the notary who recorded and transcribed the wishes also mediated the testator, notaries were always careful to state that they had added nothing to the will aside from the wishes of the testator. Through these formal documents, individual crusaders tried to speak to the future with direct instruction, ordering that their families, kin, and beneficiaries follow their wishes. By so doing, crusaders also staked a claim in how they would be remembered. When Barzella Merxadrus left five bezants for his funeral, burial, and the singing of Masses, he was both guiding his own transition from life to death and, at the same time, positioning himself as a pious crusader, worthy of ongoing remembrance.

These wills and testaments may be seen as very routine bequests in a number of ways. They followed standard testamentary formats and performed the usual functions of disposing of property and looking after loved ones. Where they involved religious institutions, they usually prioritized ones with which the individual or his or her family had a direct and historical connection. In the context of crusading, however, these sorts of documents, which drew on long-standing traditions of bequest, must also be understood in terms of their memorial function. This is not merely commemorative but tied to deliberate and individual identification with the Crusade, either by naming oneself as a crusader, as did Barzella Merxadrus, or by affiliation with the military orders. As with modern soldiers' farewell letters, they are documents of detachment from the present and attachment to the future. They shared much with any other will or bequest, but their crafting in the context of the Crusade adds a subjective identification with crusading to their purpose.

ON THE EVE OF BATTLE: INSPIRATION, CONSOLATION, AND MEMORY

How crusaders were to be remembered can also be read in narrative sources such as exhortations and prayers recited before battle. These "speech acts"—textual utterances that serve particular narrative functions—are included in a number of chronicles throughout the crusading period and take various forms. They are not, as John Bliese pointed out, "verbatim reports" of words uttered before battle. Rather, they reflect and project the rhetorical and spiritual ideas of the chroniclers who composed them.[42] On the First Crusade, for example, Fulcher of Chartres included in his *Historia Hierosolymitana* some rousing words from King Baldwin, who is said to have spurred on his soldiers thusly: "Fear nothing. Conduct yourselves manfully and you will be mighty in this battle. . . . If you survive as victors, you will shine in glory among all Christians."[43] A famous scene from the Seventh Crusade (1248–50) gives a prominent place to the rousing prebattle oration of the French king Louis IX, who is reported as having addressed the nervous crusaders about to disembark their vessel at Damietta:

> My friends and vassals, if we remain undivided in love, we shall be unconquered. It is not contrary to God's will that we have been so unexpectedly conveyed here. Let us disembark on these shores, however strongly they are guarded. I am not the King of France; I am not the Holy Church: it is surely you who are the king, and you who are the Holy Church. I am only one individual whose life, when God wills it, will be snuffed out like any other man's. For us, every outcome means deliverance: if we are defeated, we fly forth as martyrs; if we are victorious, the glory of the Lord will be proclaimed and that of all France—indeed of Christendom—will be enhanced. Surely it is madness to believe that the Lord has roused me to no purpose. He Who provides everything has through this designed a mighty business. Let us fight on Christ's behalf, and He shall triumph in us, giving the glory, the honour and blessing not to us but to His Own Name.[44]

King Louis IX is represented here as reaffirming the basic precepts of crusading—that the impending battle was God's will, that death in battle had a higher purpose and meaning, and that the crusaders were equal in the eyes of God. At the same time, his words project into the future how crusaders themselves would be remembered—either as glorious martyrs or as victorious defenders of God and France. By including these words in his letter about the Seventh Crusade, for example, Gui of Melun drew attention to the importance of the battle that was about to occur and also to the reassuring nature of the king's words. These words were deliberately inspiring as well as calming; they communicated the larger significance of crusading actions while soothing the fears of those about to engage in combat. They also invoked the consolation of future remembrance of the Crusade not as an opportunity for individual posthumous glorification but as a way of contributing to the greater and enduring glory of God.

Although the Fifth Crusade reports no long speeches of the sort declaimed by King Louis IX, there are a number of examples of prebattle words of motivation in some historical accounts.[45] These words are intended to fulfill a number of functions, such as reminding soldiers and future readers of the collective effort of crusading and its transcendent rewards and offering consolation and encouragement to immediate listeners. The *Gesta obsidionis Damiatae* is particularly full of these sorts of motivational inclusions, which are mostly in the form of prayers. In this text, both rousing and consoling words are included in response to descriptions of the army's fear or moments of despair. When the crusaders came to Pelagius in November 1218, crying to him that they would all die in the desert "like dogs and beasts," the legate is said to have held up his hands to heaven, asking Christ to send angels to guide the army and help them overcome nonbelievers. He spoke of Christ's redemptive capacity, reminding the despairing troops that Christ, as the living son of God, was sent to the world for them.[46] When the army feared defeat after a storm later that month, Pelagius offered them words of comfort and once more reminded them of the larger purpose of their travails. He asked them whether it was better to die with the love of God or to live in captivity in a foreign land—"nonne melius est mori in bello amore Domini nostri Ihesu Christi quam in aliena terra sicut captivi vivere?"—and he rallied the army to increase its efforts to cross the river.[47]

These sorts of words are often included in conjunction with reports of other precombat rituals, such as confession and participation in communion. Both were forms of liturgical supplication that Cecilia Gaposchkin has recently identified as becoming systematic during the Fifth Crusade.[48] Other forms of motivational action were performed by both the senior ecclesiasts and other pilgrims who joined the Crusade (and who are often represented as offering spiritual support before battle). Before the critical battle for the chain tower at Damietta, for example, it is recorded that not only did "the clergy, barefoot, walk as suppliants on the shore" but the Patriarch of Jerusalem "lay prostrate in the dust before the wood of the Cross" as the clergy "garbed in liturgical robes cried out to heaven."[49] The crusaders assembled as a group on the eve of February 5, 1219, and although rain and winds "added much peril and difficulty to our men," reported Oliver of Paderborn, still they heard the office of the Mass at early dawn.[50] And the prayers and tears of "pilgrims, nobles and commoners" motivated and strengthened the army before the attack, according to Jacques de Vitry, who also told of these people throwing themselves on the sand and covering their heads with dust in a penitential performance.[51]

But it is words of prayer that are represented as being especially effective before battle, according to the *Gesta obsidionis Damiatae*. The supplications that are recorded in this text include a long collective prayer (provoked by a surprise attack on the crusaders in October 26, 1218), which is essentially a compilation of references from the Psalms (using the Vulgate references): Psalm 19:10 ("Lord save and care for us and hear us in the day that we call on you"), Psalms 17:6 and 49:15 ("In the day of tribulation and anguish we call on you Lord to quickly hear our prayers"), Psalm 5:2 ("Hear our words and prayers, Lord, and understand our cry"), Psalm 3:8 ("Our king, our God, we have prayed and come to you, lord, hear our voices and prayers. God is salvation and your blessing is on your people"), and Psalm 16:8 ("Protect us under the shadow of your wings").[52] This particular prayer of supplication is reported to have been led by Pelagius, who spoke with tears in his eyes while holding the True Cross in his hand. The prayer itself emphasized the steadfast and collective nature of the soldiers about to wage battle through Pelagius's words of encouragement—"He did not cease to encourage the knights and foot soldiers," his loud and determined voice (*alta voce*) providing a constant reminder that the crusaders were fighting for God. He reiterated that the soldiers needed divine aid and consoled them, telling them that God would protect them if they prayed. And he called on crusaders to remember the words of the Psalms that spoke to their present situation. The petition was successful: "innumerable" Saracens were captured or killed, those in boats were drowned in the water, and there was so much blood and pollution from the putrefying corpses in the river afterward that for several days, the Christians could not use it for drinking or cooking.[53] The *Gesta* describes this as a "great victory" (*victoriam magnam*) for the Christians, whose prayers were clearly answered.

Some of these prayers of supplication were also directed at the natural world, calling on God to exert his power over the elements. The storm of November 1218, when many of the crusaders' supplies and boats were washed away, provoked another moment of despair for the army, who wondered if God had something against them—"Deus est nobis contrarius," they mourned. Again, Pelagius offered words of consolation for all to hear (*omnes audivimus*), asking, "Lord Jesus Christ who, when called by Peter whose boat was endangered, responded 'You of little faith, why do you doubt me?', and immediately called on the wind and the sea and made them tranquil. Intercede for us, dear Father, your army and command the sea and the wind to return to their place who lives and reigns with the father forever."[54] As hoped for, the flood receded, the sun appeared, the crusaders' mood brightened, and some of the supplies were found to have survived the deluge without great damage. A further prayer also relates to the specifics of battle conditions, this time addressing the danger of fire in a battle at the end of July 1219. The Egyptians used fire and sulfur to set alight ladders used by the Christians, and despite pouring the wine and vinegar they had brought with them over the flames (a usual remedy for Greek fire), the Christians were unable to extinguish them. The Christian onlookers prostrated themselves on the ground, crying, "Lord Jesus Christ, king of glory, who has power over all things, hear your servants and free us from these flames and from the hands of these sinful Saracens."[55]

These sorts of prayers of motivation, consolation, and inspiration serve two main purposes relating to remembrance. First, there is a narrative purpose to including these prayers in the description of events. In the *Gesta*, the prayers are inserted at moments when the army is fearful of defeat and death. They provide a narrative hinge between collective despondency and eventual triumph by reminding the reader of the fundamentally divine ordination of events. The prayers seem intended to empower the crusaders in this way; they provide a quasi-liturgical means of bringing about God's assistance when it is most needed through the individual and collective action of supplication. The inclusion of prayer thus confirms the power of continual and reflective spiritual action throughout the Crusade. Prayer linked devotional performance to the memory of why the crusaders were fighting and of God's intercession during the events of other historical and biblical contexts. Such links were particularly resonant in the crusading world after 1187 when, as Gaposchkin has shown, programmatic liturgical supplication had become part and parcel of calls and support for the Crusades.[56]

At the same time, the prayers included in the *Gesta* are used to comment on and enshrine the effective leadership of the Crusade. They therefore secure a particular historical memory of the people and events they describe. For the author of the *Gesta*, the papal legate Pelagius of Albano, who arrived at Damietta in September 1218, is the key voice for these sorts of speeches. As I note in the third chapter of this book, his leadership role in the Fifth Crusade was, for some of the chroniclers and certainly for later historians, controversial. Yet in this text, the work done by the legate to direct military action is represented as reaffirming the essence of the Crusade and the military efforts undertaken by the crusaders. That his words are often represented as direct speech not only endows the legate with a noticeable and communicative space within this text itself but also provides the future crusader with words and ideas to encapsulate and describe the spiritual work of crusading. Thus the words attributed to Pelagius and the prayers uttered in supplication by the Christians at Damietta reinforce the collective effort of crusading and the importance of strong spiritual leadership. The legate was the mouthpiece of some of the distinctive intentions of the Fifth Crusade too, talking of conversion as one of the main reasons the crusaders were in Egypt (*ut gentem perfidam et nequitiam convertere possimus*).[57] According to Oliver of Paderborn, Pelagius also delivered a public sermon during the period after the capture of Damietta, when the army was divided about the next course of action. He reminded them that the Crusade was not over despite the capture of the city and urged them to look forward into the future to reflect on perceptions of their present decisions—they should judge their actions now "lest they be grievously condemned by the Judge of secret things."[58]

The range of ideas expressed by Pelagius and others in the prebattle prayers and exhortations was, of course, familiar to crusaders already. They had heard sermons prior to arriving at the battlefront in which the idea of collective spiritual action was central, and they had been told from the very outset about the right sort of motivations for crusading. As Caroline Smith has outlined, the main themes in sermons that present the Crusade to potential participants during the thirteenth century included pilgrimage, service, the past, the dangers of crusading, martyrdom, and the value of suffering, and she has noted that model sermons used inspirational figures from the crusading past and the biblical past to encourage and motivate people to take up the cross.[59] One of Jacques de Vitry's two sermons to pilgrims, composed after his own participation in the Fifth Crusade had concluded, provides a good example of the sorts of ideas and themes that these crusaders would have heard prior to and even during the Crusade. Jessalynn Bird, who has provided both an edition and translation of this sermon, noted that this sermon "contains the remnants of battlefield exhortations used to reassure the crusading army that their mission was just," and it certainly seems that Jacques drew on his own experiences of the Crusade to reinforce the themes of the sermon.[60] He preaches to future pilgrims and crusaders that "when battle looms, you ought always hasten to confession," as crusaders "should fear the sins of Christians more than the Saracen forces. For our sins make them powerful." Those who prepare properly for pilgrimage to Jerusalem should make confession, receive the body of Christ, and write a will; having done so, they "can go out to do battle untroubled." In the thick of battle, then, such a soldier "does not pay much heed to the weight of his shield amid such danger, but if pleased with the arms which defend him even though they are heavy."[61]

Jacques de Vitry also emphasized renunciation, labor, and sacrifice as key themes. Future crusaders were asked to bring to mind familiar biblical exemplars to help them understand the nature and difficulty of their own actions and service and to draw inspiration from their deeds. Pilgrims would be remembered as having offered "a good example" to others by their actions and aligning themselves with the biblical models. The ever-popular Maccabees were invoked in this context, as were the Israelites, who "used to offer some of each of the year's fruits to the Lord," just as pilgrims offered their possessions and their bodies to God "by spending them on this journey in the Lord's service." As Jacques explained, pilgrims "offer spiritual sacrifices from all of their possessions . . . the wheat of good works, the wine of ardent charity, the oil of joyfulness of mind, the fig of sweet piety and the apple, the odor of a good example and holy behavior."[62] These renunciations were aimed to make pilgrims rejoice at the prospect of the journey, "for whether you live or die you will belong to the Lord." The consolation of sacrifice worked for both those who would survive (they would return with the treasure of remission of sins) and those who would die (they "will cross over to eternal joy"). The right motivation was also important, and those who traveled should do so "in desire and will," not for personal glory but for the glory of God.

The emphasis in the prebattle prayers on providing comfort is also present in Jacques de Vitry's sermon to pilgrims, where he reassures future crusaders that the righteous nature of their actions will strengthen and sustain them. He preaches that crusaders "ought not to fear because you have a just war and unjust adversaries, you possess a good conscience and they do not. There are more allies with you than with your adversaries because you fight with the aid of God, the angels, the saints, the suffrages of the Church triumphant, and the prayers and merits of the church militant." He concludes this part of the sermon by assuring pilgrims that they ought to "be comforted and be strong," for "the Lord loves pilgrims and consoles those who for love of him give up the familiar consolation of their blood relatives."[63] Jacques also situates pilgrimage and battle in different temporal contexts here. The support of past saints, the prayers of present Christians, and the promise of future eternal joy are invoked to simultaneously encourage and give meaning to a crusader's actions.

Other preachers of the Fifth Crusade were encouraged to include examples of the experiences of crusaders who illustrated right intentions and actions. The anonymous *Ordinacio de predicatione S. Crucis*, composed in England sometime after 1216 for the use of Crusade preachers, included material recommended for use in recruitment sermons. Much of the text offers theological and biblical reflection on the figure of Christ on the cross, but at the end of the tract, several "case studies" of crusaders are incorporated so that preachers might have "real" examples of crusaders whose actions were worthy of both remembrance and emulation.[64] These include three brothers, *milites*, who fought in the Albigensian Crusade (which was still probably in progress when this tract was composed), one of whom comforted the others by saying they would be dying for Him who died for humanity. Death and injury are related to the suffering Christ in another exemplum concerning a man who was wounded in four places but, despite the doctor's prognosis that these injuries would be fatal, wanted to go back into combat to procure a fifth wound like Christ. This he did, killing many Saracens in the meantime. The naming of three of these men—Hugo of Beauchamp, James of Avesnes, and Enguerrand of Boves—performs further remembrance work by including the identified individuals in sermons that might be disseminated widely. Hugh of Beauchamp was a hero of Hattin, James of Avesnes had died at Arsuf, and Enguerrand of Boves had participated in the Fourth Crusade. Here was a pantheon of significant and inspirational figures who could motivate others to take up the cross and whose exemplary actions were recorded and perhaps preached for years after their deaths. Alongside biblical exemplars like the Maccabees, the memory of past crusaders was used to inspire crusaders of the future.

Fifth Crusade texts therefore encouraged identification with biblical and historical figures (as had many texts of other Crusades) as discursively central to the performance of crusading.[65] This worked in conjunction with the other modes of identification with the Crusade—making the vow, wearing the cross, and so on—all of which were outward and active performances of belonging. The representation of these acts of belonging and their textual connection to actual lived events communicated powerful messages about the integration of the individual into a larger, meaningful, and enduring spiritual effort. Texts like the *Gesta*, Jacques de Vitry's sermons to pilgrims and the *Ordinacio de predicatione S. Crucis* thus projected representations of the present onto the future remembrance of crusaders and, more importantly, of the Crusade itself.

CONCLUSION

Preparing for war meant facing the very real possibility that one would not return. This was as true in the thirteenth century as it is for modern soldiers, who now write farewell letters to their families to be read in the event of their deaths. Reading some of these modern missives gives us often poignant insights into today's young military: their motivations, their desire to comfort their families and to encourage them to celebrate their lives rather than mourn their deaths, and their wish to attribute a higher purpose to the job they set out to do. In the thirteenth century, preparations for war also included attempts to manage one's memory and to project one's final wishes onto the future. As I have outlined in this chapter, preparations for crusading involved practical as well as personal planning. Crusaders needed to make provisions for the management of their property both during their absence and in the event of their nonreturn. They wanted to provide for their families and kinfolk, and they wanted to secure the safety of their own souls in the hereafter. They tried to ensure the latter by making donations to religious houses and by asking for prayers. In all these ways, crusaders were active contributors to the shaping of their own remembrance and the perpetuation of their names. They did not write farewell letters as we would understand them, but they did put their names in charters and wills, which tell us much about what was necessary planning for what may have been a permanent departure.

These individual attempts by crusaders to shape and manage how they were to be remembered were not the only ways in which future remembrance was generated. The integration of words and actions of consolation in texts like the *Gesta obsidionis Damiatae* also creates an enduring historical memory of events and people. Such words were used within these narratives to illustrate how crusaders needed to continually bring to mind the just nature of the crusading enterprise and the divine support they, as individuals, would receive. Prayers of supplication also reflected widely used themes in Crusade preaching, which emphasized (among other things) trust in God, suffering, and sacrifice—all of which would lead to redemption and eternal reward. On the eve of battle, crusaders could be and were reminded of the higher purpose of their participation in the holy war, and they were offered the consolation that their imminent deaths would stand as a future testament to the glory of God, earning them the glittering and unretractable prize of salvation.

What I have called preparatory memory may therefore provide insights into the nature of crusading temporality. For instance, individual attempts to be remembered were underpinned by a desire to insert one's past deeds into the future through the present action of gift giving or will making. And those who wrote about the historical events of the Fifth Crusade used the promise of the future to communicate the meaning of the present. The multiple temporalities contained in this kind of remembrance work are reflected in how medieval people understood the nature of crusading itself. Participants undertook action in the here and now, drawing on models of biblical and historical precedence, to impact the terrestrial and eschatological future. Time was therefore understood to operate not just in various different modes (historical, biblical, sacred) but simultaneously. Calls to the Fifth Crusade replicated and extended this multivalent sense of time. In *Quia maior*, Pope Innocent III reminded Christians that God was providing them with not just a contemporary "test of their faith" but an opportunity for future salvation. At the same time, he drew on and described history—"Christian people possessed almost all the Saracen provinces until after the time of Saint Gregory"—to elaborate the need for urgent present action.[66] Crusade sermons spoke of bringing Christ into the present by following his instruction to act in memory of him and to identify with his suffering, and even Crusade preachers were told that they bore "the stigmata of Jesus Christ in your hearts."[67] This simultaneity of temporalities was similar to the experience of those going on pilgrimage, which worked concurrently in different times, looking forward and backward and acting in the present. For crusaders and those who wrote about their actions, remembrance—of events, texts, people, and their mission—was the path between these temporalities.

At the same time, preparatory memory shows that processes of identification were the elements of the construction of what we might call the crusading subject. Through the speech acts we find in wills, charters, or narrative sources, we see that the individual crusader was constituted in the context of a collective or community. The suffering that a crusader would endure in imitation of Christ was certainly a very individual and direct identification with Christ's humanity. And for Pope Innocent III, such suffering was "very devout and a heavenly inspiration because by taking the cross you intend to repay in your Christ who on it bore your infirmities and carried your sorrows."[68] Yet this individual bodily identification with Christ's humanity, which many historians have rightly found very pronounced beginning in the early thirteenth century, was played out in the increasingly collective effort of the Crusade. Even Pope Innocent in his letter to Duke Leopold IV of Austria thought that this *imitatio* was necessarily undertaken "under the banner of the victorious cross."[69] Locating oneself "under the banner" in deed and promise defined the crusader. As I noted above, in the early thirteenth century, there was an expansion of who was able to take up the cross as a crusader and benefit from the same spiritual rewards. Preparatory memory was used in this context as one way of describing oneself and others as part of the group.

Remembering war in our era continues to ask for identification with an "imagined community," in Benedict Anderson's words. The interplay of individual and community or national desires to remember and to be remembered still involves the negotiation of complex relationships among the past, present, and future by those who experience war and those who co-opt war memory in the service of the state—perhaps even more so in recent years, as critiques of globalization have caused the West to retreat into the sometimes unpleasantly proclaimed ideological certainties of nationalism. The crusaders of the Fifth Crusade who made wills, disposed of their property, and tried to organize their own burials would not recognize the language of nationalism that has driven so much of modernity's fascination with conflict. Nor would they recognize the media that communicates remembrance of war to vast digital audiences. Those medieval writers, who integrated the language of memory into the prayers and speeches of their narratives of the Fifth Crusade, would not recognize the academic discipline that now exerts and claims much authority over the representation of the past in the texts that call themselves "histories." But they might recognize the power of remembrance in defining groups and their constituent members, and they might appreciate the power of the written word in laying down the trails of future remembrance. In this way, medieval participants in the Crusade perhaps hoped and knew that their stories would transcend the battlefront. It was remembering that would ensure the meaningful longevity of those stories.

In the next chapter, I pursue further issues around the construction of authority in the shaping of the remembrance of people and events. I concentrate particularly on how the eyewitness, through experience and representation, began to determine whose memories are worth recording and why.

CHAPTER 2

Eyewitnessing and Remembrance Work

Heat rose off the sandy banks of the Nile in the summer of 1218 as a group of crusaders prepared to cross the river to capture the Egyptian city of Damietta. Among them was the bishop of Acre, Jacques de Vitry, who in a letter composed that same year reported that the army sat for four long months opposite the city, gazing on it but unable to reach it because of its seemingly unassailable defenses. It was a strange landscape in which they waited, "nothing but sand and salt," although the Nile was known as one of the four rivers of paradise. Frightening monsters called "cocatriz" (crocodiles) lurked in the river's murky depths, waiting "for men and horses and swallowing whatever their teeth capture." As time dragged on, thirsty crusaders started to die on the sand after drinking the "rich, muddy, marshy waters" of the Nile, and others were picked off one after another as the Egyptian defenders of Damietta launched "Greek fire, huge rocks and numerous missiles" from the tower that protected the city. Despair began to pervade the crusader camp, and Jacques described the many thwarted attempts made by the army to break the iron chain that stretched across the Nile, to raise their feeble ladders against the defensive tower, and to launch renewed attacks against the enemy. It was only on August 25, 1218, that the breakthrough came with the help of a newly built siege engine. Damietta was surrounded, and sixty thousand of its citizens were now trapped within the city walls. Over the ensuing months, that population steadily dwindled as hunger and disease claimed thousands of lives. By the time the crusaders finally broke into the city on November 5, 1219, there were only three thousand people left alive inside, of whom scarcely a hundred were fit to defend it, and the ground was strewn with too many corpses for the survivors to bury. Damietta had to be disinfected before the Christian victors could enter, as the awful stench and polluted air of the city were "too much for most people to bear."[1] In a letter Jacques composed the following year, the memory of that landscape of war was still vivid. "I am frail and broken-hearted," he reflected at the end of his description of the battle and siege, "and wish to end my life in peace and quiet."[2]

Jacques de Vitry (born between 1160 and 1170) was a senior ecclesiast who had been one of the Fifth Crusade's most vociferous preachers and who ended his career as a cardinal. He was a seasoned author of hagiographical texts and sermons, and he used his time in the East to begin two historical works, the *Historia occidentalis* and the *Historia orientalis*.[3] His letters are part of an impressive corpus of written material that has long been used by scholars of the early thirteenth century to uncover histories of preaching, travel, the long reach of the Parisian masters, female religiosity, and the Crusades. Jacques himself had studied under Peter the Chanter in Paris but left the world of the schools to live the apostolic life at Oignies, where he developed his spiritual friendship with the holy woman Marie of Nivelles. She persuaded him to go to Paris, where he was ordained as a priest before returning to Oignies in 1211. He composed the vita of Marie after her death in 1213, at a time when he was also preaching the Crusade to the Holy Land. Jacques was elected bishop of Acre in 1216. That year, he went to Italy, was consecrated as bishop by Honorius III, set sail from Genoa, and arrived in Acre.

There are six (possibly seven) surviving letters written by Jacques de Vitry after 1216. These letters are especially valuable documents for the course of the Fifth Crusade, as they cover the period from 1216 (his first letter was written on board the ship that carried him to Acre, and his second was written from Acre in March 1217) to 1221, when the crusaders were forced to surrender. His last four letters were composed from the battlefront (in September 1218, September 1219, March 1220, and April 1221). These four "Fifth Crusade letters" written by Jacques de Vitry in Egypt between 1218 and 1221 are vivid and erudite, often addressed to multiple recipients—including the pope (Honorius III), his former Parisian teachers, John of Nivelles, the beguines of Oignies, the Cistercian nuns of Aywières and their abbess, Leopold (the Duke of Austria), and various unnamed friends—and conform in many ways to medieval epistolary convention, which emphasized the authority of the letter writer to report and represent the information contained within the letter.[4]

Jacques de Vitry's letters offer reasons for how things worked out according to God's plan, underscoring the portentous nature of war with scriptural justification and biblical analogy. They also perform remembrance work. They tell war stories claiming, in their own ways, to be authentic records of events. They represent difficult and dangerous situations in war with a view to perpetuating the memory of those events. And importantly for the purposes of this chapter, the letters are the products of an eyewitness. The letters of Jacques de Vitry were composed in the midst of a time of protracted siege and intermittent combat, when Jacques himself was physically present on the battlefields. They are war reports just as much as they are spiritual justifications for the events taking place; his letters communicate his own experiences and his desire to have those experiences explained and remembered. In this way, these are highly individual texts, composed within the fairly formal narrative framework in which personal memory is created and laid out. But as Alessandro Portelli showed a number of years ago, subjectivity, contingency, and even factual flaws are not, in fact, the limitations of memory but rather memory's strengths.[5] Errors or misrememberings can unexpectedly reveal the desires and interests of the tellers, giving insights into the meaning of their memories. It is the narrated experience of remembering that, for historians, is especially valuable. What we read in the letters of Jacques de Vitry are rich and evocative stories told about the difficult recent past through remembered and individual experience. The kind of remembrance work undertaken in these stories is intended both to communicate individual experience and to make sense of what had happened to people during and as a result of war.

THE MEDIEVAL EYEWITNESS

In Christian theology, the act of "witnessing" meant testifying to the Christian promise and communicating that promise to others. All Christians had a duty to bear witness to Christ, and the example of the martyrs—whose deaths were the result of witnessing their faith—offered a model of witnessing as an act of suffering. The special example of the doctrine of the Jewish witness, constructed by St. Augustine in *De civitate dei*, outlined the theory that Jews survived "as living testimony to the antiquity of the Christian promise."[6] In these ways, witnessing was part of the evangelical and didactic task of Christianity. Christian and Jewish witnesses both communicated and demonstrated the salvific, redemptory, and necessary example of Christ. At the same time, witnessing carried with it the intimation of truth.[7]

This was also the case with early theories of history itself. The connection between the eyewitness and the production of historical truth was, according to Isidore of Seville, based on the authority (*auctoritas*) of the eyewitness. Isidore agreed with classical writers that no one could write a history unless he had been present at an event and seen with his own eyes what was to be written down, "for we grasp with our eyes things that occur better than what we gather with our hearing since what is seen is revealed without falsehood." Thus "what is worthy of remembrance is committed to writing. And for this reason histories are called 'monuments' because they grant a remembrance (*memoria*) of deeds that have been done."[8] Although book 1 of the *Etymologies* concerned grammar, Isidore understood that history is an element of grammar because whatever is worthy of memory is entrusted to letters (*quidquid dignum memoria est litteris mandatur*). For Isidore, then, history possessed a narrative function but was essentially built on memory and had a memorializing and descriptive purpose. People who witnessed things were the ones with the authority to tell of them later, and this would become history. This process was also gendered masculine by virtue of its links to the male world of Latin learning, in which eyewitnesses would transmit and enshrine their memories in text. As a number of modern scholars have shown in relation to medieval historical writing after the time of Isidore of Seville, this conception of the importance of the eyewitness endured and was elaborated on during the great revival of rhetoric and historical writing during the long twelfth century. How eyewitness authority was constructed during this period was specific. In his study of twelfth-century historical writing, Peter Damian-Grint found that *auctoritas* was established by authorial self-naming, frequent recourse in prologues and epilogues to the value of recording history because of the frailty of memory, references to sources, and interjections by the author on the narrative or moral of the history throughout the text.[9]

There was something of a "rediscovery" of eyewitnessing in the history writing of the twelfth century, especially in vernacular verse historical writing and in Crusade chronicles.[10] The authors of the Latin chronicles of the First Crusade placed great emphasis on having been there, on having been participants, or on relying on the words of eyewitnesses as their sources. All these compositional elements built up an authoritative narrative on which later histories of crusading were based.[11] Recently, Elizabeth Lapina has challenged the prevalent view that the privileged role of the medieval eyewitness remained static throughout the twelfth century by linking the Christian concept of witness to the composition of the First Crusade chronicles. Lapina shows how later medieval historians of the First Crusade did not take the truth claims of earlier Crusade eyewitnesses as unassailable and uncontested and suggests that the secondhand monastic chroniclers of the First Crusade "confined in monasteries thousands of miles away from the Holy Land [realized that] true witnesses were not the ones who saw, but the ones who understood."[12] Lapina rightly sees the writing of Crusade chronicles as attempts to integrate Christian theological understandings of the witness with contemporary desires to explain and give meaning to things that had happened in the past. Thus eyewitnessing was only one part of the larger epistemological project of medieval historical writing.

Carol Symes, in quite a different way, has also considered the work of the medieval eyewitness in the context of the first historians of the First Crusade. Symes argues that the testimonies of First Crusade combatants were the basis for the very first communiqués of that Crusade and that they used "available commemorative models and the master narrative of sacred history" for their shape.[13] Many of these earliest histories are now lost to us. But Symes rightly notes that although the monastic chroniclers of that Crusade are typically understood to be its first historians, the lay combatants and minor clerics who participated in the Crusade, equipped with a variety of literacies and ephemeral formats (such as *libelli*, or "booklets") for communication, produced the first texts. Symes makes a crucial, larger argument about the silencing of nonelite literacies and documentation in "official" Crusade histories, both medieval and modern. But she also draws attention to the very important place of memory in the narration of the Crusades' earliest stories. As Symes states, "[All] of these activities—bearing witness to past deeds, preserving ancestral property and rights, telling stories of saints—were regarded as commemorative genres preserved along an oral, ritual and written continuum."[14] Remembering informed and influenced present opinion and policy; it was integral to both the early eyewitness documentation and the later chroniclers who worked those accounts in various ways into their texts.

If medieval people understood the eyewitness to occupy a privileged role in communicating and ascribing meaning to the historical past, then eyewitnesses were always important conduits of remembrance. This has also been borne out in a number of studies of medieval legal records, in which the moral character of the witness and the memories he or she relayed were brought together to constitute evidence for the present, particularly in cases involving reputation.[15] The paths of remembrance laid down by those who could claim to be witnesses were enduring in these contexts and certainly indicate that in medieval legal cultures, memory was considered to be a form of knowing as well as a heuristic tool. Was this the same in other sorts of texts and contexts? In what follows, I am interested in exploring how remembrance was established by eyewitnesses who told their stories using the different genres of letter and administrative inquiry. Eyewitnesses bridged past and present by identifying themselves as central figures in the stories they told, by asserting the material reality of the lived experience in their descriptions of objects and bodies, and by drawing together interior or subjective experience and the external world through integrating emotions into their stories. These stories, which might be described as cotemporal, laid bare the future contexts of remembrance by presenting possibilities for further action in the form of prayer, restitution, commemoration, and even warfare.

THE EYEWITNESS PRESENCE

Eyewitnesses told stories that were directed and legitimated by their own participation in the events they related. This was made clear by the presence of the eyewitness's self, which was integrated into stories by the judicious insertion of the "I" persona into the narrative sequence.[16] Sometimes this was overt ("I saw the pilgrims"; "We drove the sultan from the battlefield"), and other times this was done by inserting the storyteller into the unfolding narrative of action as a third person "telling" device ("He said"; "She remembered"). In the letters of Jacques de Vitry, the eyewitness, named as Jacques himself, does the narrative work of reconstructing and describing events. This is done through the use of the "I" persona (in both the first-person singular and plural) and through the appearance of the narrator at various points during the unfolding narrative. In some legal and administrative texts of the thirteenth century, the eyewitness is described in the third person but is similarly important. In such records, like the famous *enquêtes* of King Louis IX, which asked about the aftermath of war in southern France and beyond, it is the eyewitness who describes the relationship between the large-scale event of war and its impact on the small-scale world of community and family life.[17] Thus eyewitnesses were invested in the task of relaying a narrative that was authoritative because it was based on the individual memories and was itself part of a larger project of remembrance. Overall, eyewitnesses were agents of remembrance by virtue of the stories they told.

Jacques de Vitry identifies himself in the *salutatio*, or greeting sections, of each of his letters by the use of the first person singular and naming himself. In the usual manner of formal medieval letters, Jacques established a relationship between himself and the recipient of this correspondence. "To my most beloved friends in Christ," he writes to his fellow clerics in 1218. "To the most dear abbess" and "To my most beloved brothers in Christ," he writes in 1220, then identifying himself as "Jacques." Quickly, the intimate greeting slides into the reason for writing. Sometimes this is specifically framed by the personal relationship Jacques has with the recipient. In the case of an earlier letter to the masters of Paris and the convent of Aywières, Jacques writes of his wish to imprint himself on their memories: "I wish, however, that all your life your memory of me will remain fresh just as I remember you, and when I manage to find a messenger I will with pleasure impose myself on your memory through my letters."[18] In one letter composed in two stages on September 14 and 22, 1218, Jacques asserts his own authority by noting at the outset that, just as in his other letters, he is telling true things: he tells his recipients that "just as in my other letters I told the truth about what was happening in the Lord's army from the very beginning, in this letter I have decided to inform you about events that took place afterwards."[19] In a letter to the pope composed in March 1220, Jacques begins, "I have thought fit to describe to your Holiness how this happened." In Letter 5, he is more insistent. *Sciatis quod*, he writes—"Know that." The imperative or command form is urgent and confident and signals that what follows is authentic fact.

Inclusive language is extended through the *narratio* section of the letters (the section that contains the main body of the letters' information) by Jacques's use of the collective "we" to describe his participation in the events. The use of "we" was conventional in letters; someone of elevated rank would refer to him- or herself in this way.[20] But the "we" pronoun also establishes a coherent and collective voice for describing the events, especially when Jacques narrates general action and the passing of time: "For months we remained on that island" and "we lost more than a thousand men." Occasionally, it is clear that when Jacques uses this voice, he refers to himself: "When we wrote these letters [*quando hac litteras scripsimus*] on the Feast of the Holy Cross in September, we had not yet crossed the river or besieged the city." And as an individual eyewitness, Jacques himself is very much "there" throughout. This presentness is also established by witness statements such as "I saw," by propositional attitudes expressed in statements such as "I believe," and by statements of cognition such as "I know."

MAKING THINGS REAL

These individualizing statements of authorial direction were supplemented by a number of narrative and thematic strategies. Eyewitness accounts of war are particularly noteworthy for the palpability of the scenes they describe—the communication of the physical or material dimension to things that had happened. Jacques de Vitry's letters—given both his position as a supporter and participant in the Crusade and the epistolary genre in which he recalled and reported events—certainly retain some of the more formal qualities of correspondence and reiteration of the promise of the Crusade. Nonetheless, his eyewitness accounts are also remarkably descriptive, delineating with striking imagery the landscape of Egypt, the course of military engagement, the feelings of the soldiers, and even his own reactions to the Crusade. He wrote particularly about the physical conditions of war, attaching these descriptions to the place of Damietta and its surroundings as well as the bodies of the soldiers. This is evident in Letter 5 to Pope Honorius III, which was composed in two parts, the first in April–May 1219 and the second part in September 1219. This was the time when Damietta was besieged and periodic battles erupted between the defenders of the city and the crusaders. It was a time when the personnel of the army changed, with the departure of Leopold of Austria and others, and it was a period of low morale among the crusader army. Jacques witnessed the stalemate as the army waited out the siege of Damietta, writing to the pope of the situation in which the crusaders found themselves before the walls of the city. The action of the letter begins with the account of the destruction of the fortified tower in the Nile in the winter of 1218–19. The river seemed impassable according to Jacques because the Egyptian defenders of Damietta had stuffed it full of obstacles: there were so many boats and other barriers in the water that they were forced to spend that whole winter trying to cross the river. The water engulfed crusaders who tried to breach the defenses, and Jacques's own boat lost twenty men in the river. Six of them were captured, and the others were killed while battling their way out of the water. Even the Knights Templar, fighting "manfully" (*viriliter*), drowned with about five hundred of the enemy after sinking their boat.[21] That "violent" water even swallowed up Egyptians who fled in fear: "They sank like lead," observed Jacques.[22]

The strangeness of the landscape and the hostile weather confronted the crusaders. In one of Jacques's letters composed in September 1218, he noted enthusiastically that Egypt was a place of biblical resonance because Christ lived there for a time with his mother and that in the very spot where the Virgin had rested was built a church that was now greatly venerated. Marketing the region as a potential pilgrimage site, he also reported that "in this country grows the balsam vine from which chrism is made; it is not to be found in any other land."[23] Yet this was also a place where the river unexpectedly and miraculously rose each year and where he reported that the very water possessed such odd properties that it could be cooled in the heat of the day if placed in white pots. Water was a constant feature of Jacques's Egypt letters: it engulfed people and things and formed an impenetrable barrier to the city. Boats drifted on it, and Saracens were even trapped in it like fish in nets. He said that there was no rain, but water surrounded them. The soldiers were thirsty, but the water they drank was brackish and diseased. Water was among the many perils the soldiers faced, Jacques wrote: "water, fire, the weather and our enemies" all conspired to exhaust and demoralize the men during the stalemate of 1219.

Before and during battle, the bodies of the soldiers themselves marked the special task of crusading and the challenges of warfare. From the moment crusaders made their vows to participate in the holy war, they were understood to be engaging in a unique enterprise that set them apart from other warriors. Jacques de Vitry acknowledged this special path at the start of Letter 5, describing these soldiers as having chosen a new celestial inheritance, as they had left their wives and children and had sold their earthly property. This was literally signified by the marks on their bodies—the cross that was sewn onto their clothing.[24] Their hope was that they would die as martyrs (gaining the "crown of martyrdom," in Jacques's words), although this was not guaranteed. Nonetheless, these new "athletes of Christ" were singular participants in a singular sort of war, and their own bodies told the story of this. Many things killed men on Crusade: Jacques tells us that some "left the tortures of this present life" due to extraordinary weather, all sorts of sickness, and the "great effusion of blood" in battle. Disease proved to be a particular hardship, and Jacques spent some time describing the corporeal tribulations endured. In the winter of 1218–19, during the stalemate before the capture of Damietta, he wrote that "the Lord sent to us an illness that all the arts of medicine could not cure."[25] He remembered that this was a contagious sickness inflicted on a large part of the army without any physical cause: "Thighs and legs swelled and then started to putrefy, and superfluous flesh grew in the mouth, they were in the grip of great pain and sickness until their hearts started to fail bit by bit."[26] Several eminent crusaders are identified as having succumbed to this illness, including Robert of Courçon, the Parisian master who "abandoned his body" and "happily migrated to the Lord." At the same time, the harsh winter wind was "frightful cold," and a sudden inundation of the river from the sea combined to kill more soldiers, wash away their tents and food, and separate the crusaders into two camps. Jacques remembered that the river was full of the cadavers of drowned animals and sick crusaders as their boats drifted away. Others who fled the torrent of water were saved only by the grace of God. Even the horses that survived were enfeebled and emaciated (*debiles et macilenti*).

Jacques was keen to report that the clerical leaders of the afflicted army guided the soldiers well during this trying time. That there was no physical cause to the disease the soldiers suffered seemed to indicate that this was a special tribulation God wanted them to endure. Senior ecclesiasts prescribed more somatic privations, ordering the army to fast on bread and water for three days and process barefooted on Fridays through the camp. They were to cry to the Lord, wrote Jacques, and beg for divine assistance.

Penitence was rewarded when "the Lord took pity on his afflicted people" and orchestrated, according to Jacques, the flight of some of the Egyptian army by reinvigorating the crusaders: the Egyptians felt such terror at the army's renewed efforts that they abandoned their camps, supplies, boats, and animals and fled in the night.[27]

Although their spirits revived somewhat after the sudden departure of part of the Egyptian army, battle conditions continued to test the weakened soldiers. Reinforcements arrived to bolster the Egyptian defenders, and a number of violent assaults on the crusaders were launched. Jacques remembered that the crusaders had taken time to prepare "mangonels, battering rams, ladders and other machines of war" and had devised a plan to tunnel closer to Damietta. They were heartened to hear of continuing political rivalries among the Muslims.[28] But they found themselves subjected to some devastating attacks. Jacques reports these with force: "Know that we have tried with all our energies to take the city often at the cost of injuries from water and land," but "while we were occupied with all this, the Saracens attacked us with such violence that they penetrated our defenses. We drove them back with force and there was a great carnage of horses and men."[29] "We knew," Jacques wrote, "that we would not be able to achieve our aims without tough combat and the decision to engage in this was not made without long deliberations over who would guard the camp, who would come with us, who would direct our vessels across the river to attack the enemy ships."[30] It was with common accord that the army was organized for battle. It left to fight "manfully and courageously" (viriliter et potenter), he said, "on the day of the beheading of John the Baptist."[31]

The soldiers crossed the ditches that they had dug around their camp when the fighting started. Some Muslim soldiers fled before them, but it was deemed useless to follow them as the crusaders were on foot, vulnerable to the heat of the desert and thirst, and would have been "crucified by the weight of their arms."[32] Meanwhile, they were attacked: the Saracens hurled "lances and arrows, masses of weapons, javelins, some attacked us in front and some from the flanks and others from behind."[33] Some crusaders fled in terror, and in their flight, "most of them died of heat and thirst in the desert."[34] The battle continued: "The Saracens attacked us with such violence that they inflicted appalling damage on their bodies. Some of the soldiers could not endure it; others were enraged and threw themselves at the enemy. The Saracens encircled isolated soldiers who did not understand their tactics and attacked them with so many blows from daggers, weapons, javelins and Greek fire that they died."[35] The crusaders lost two hundred men, a notable few of whom Jacques names in his letter to the pope (which I discuss further in chapter 3). He added that even as the crusaders were retreating, "the enemies of Christ [were] all the time killing and tearing to pieces our men, followed us, coming back to provoke us each day." He concluded, "Know that some of our men are now preparing to come home because they have served a year, and some because they are frightened."[36]

This battle account emphasizes the sometimes chaotic nature of hand-to-hand combat, and Jacques does not refrain from incorporating the graphic realities of death in war. It is also interesting that in this section of Jacques's letter, direct biblical references are almost entirely absent. This differs significantly from the first part of the letter, which was composed in the spring of 1219. In the opening section of the letter, Jacques frames his discussion in biblical and prophetic terms, describing the Church in the East as suffering like Job or Lot, wounded, in the shadow of "an eclipse" because of the "perfidy of Mohammed."[37] Jacques piles up quotes from Lamentations, Isaiah, and Ruth to construct the Church as a grieving widow who never ceases to weep. But now "God has turned his eyes to her affliction," writes Jacques, "and in our time has inspired many sons of the Church to have compassion for the sadness of their mother."[38] Quotes from the book of Psalms are incorporated into the letter until the point when Jacques laid the narrative aside for a few months.[39] In September 1219, he returned to the letter, composing the second part, in which the battle scene described above is included together with specific naming of the notable dead. The violence of war and the physical and environmental challenges faced by the soldiers must be read as part of God's plan, given Jacques's initial framing of the Crusade in the first part of his letter. But the absence of direct biblical similitude in this second section means that the immediate physicality of battle was very prominent in his mind, more so than the eschatological commentary that preceded and then transcended the action of warfare, making sense and giving meaning to what transpired on the battlefield.

The integration of physicality and material context into eyewitness accounts went some way toward making the eyewitness experience more palpable and transmitting that experience to others who were not there. It has been broadly argued that medieval war reports that stressed action and danger in battle together with the deeds of brave individual warriors were constructed simply to emphasize and perpetuate chivalric values.[40] I explore aspects of the heroic and antiheroic crusader in the following chapter more fully, but the eyewitness accounts of Jacques de Vitry show that materiality did more than reinforce the virtues of what was always a rather nebulous cultural value. Remembering war through the narrative principles of materiality and physicality also built and communicated the individual experience of the eyewitness in ways that simply describing a sequence of events could not. Materiality (whether an object or body) mediated between the singular interior experience of an individual and the "externality" of the world.[41]

EMOTION

Eyewitness accounts thus aimed to bridge the distance between past and present by individualizing stories and attempting to communicate the palpability of lived experience. Yet one of the most striking features of the accounts explored here is the extent to which they relay subjective or interior reactions to past events. If we understand the outward expression (in word or action) of an inner state to constitute "emotion," then medieval eyewitness accounts should be read as emotional records too.[42] Although historians of the Crusades have been generally slow to integrate the new "emotional turn" into their analyses, the place of emotion in medieval crusading narratives has always been prominent. This has been particularly borne out by Susanna Throop in her groundbreaking study of crusading as an act of vengeance.[43] Throop found that the biblical notion of vengeance both motivated and provided a vocabulary for crusading, deploying righteous anger toward a legitimate cause and enemy. Throop presents vengeance as an emotional, historical, and religious category that also incorporated anger, hatred, and jealousy—often expressed as *zelus*. This idea can productively be analyzed to expose crusading as an act of simultaneous love and violence. Emotions could drive, express, and justify action; and as historians of the emotions have argued, they are also historically specific and contextually meaningful.[44]

In the letters of Jacques de Vitry, we read of fear, hope, joy, sadness, despair, and anger in his reactions to things that occurred. These are emotion words that are recognizable to modern audiences. There are other expressions of interior feeling that will be less familiar to us, phrases like *confractus corde* (fractured or brokenhearted) and words like *dolor* (sorrow that is deeper than mere sadness). These and other terms of emotion carry with them meanings rooted in antiquity and medieval tradition.[45] As cognitive theorists have suggested, emotions are part of a basic human process of perception and appraisal, and the expression of emotion is one way we decide what is right and wrong and what action we should embark on as a result.[46] This moral work done by emotions is highly visible in sources such as narrative legal testimonies, like the thirteenth-century *enquêtes*, where stories of emotional distress were told to illustrate the wrongness of the actions of people in war and to stimulate a positive outcome for the deponents.[47] The inclusion of emotion in the letters of Jacques de Vitry is more selective but nonetheless just as prominent. Especially in his narration of battle scenes and in the conclusions and valedictions to his letters, emotional reflection provides him with opportunities to recall and communicate the events of war.

Fear is one emotion that permeates Jacques's letters, both in relation to himself and to members of the crusading and Egyptian armies. Sometimes fear is represented as a motivational emotion that is inspired by God: "As the Lord sent his fear, a fear that was wrought in us and for us, but without us" (Ecclesiastes 36:2 and Psalm 68:28), writes Jacques, so the Christian soldiers were able to overcome setbacks and act with confidence and to good effect.[48] Other times, Christian soldiers who are individually fearful are condemned for their weakness. In Letter 4, for instance, Jacques opens with a description of cowardice in the army by saying the people were leaving because they were "lacking courage" (*pusillanimes*) or "wavering" (*inconstantes*). They were "seeking consolation in various false excuses to hide their cowardice [*ignavie*]." This letter was addressed to Pope Honorius and to his clerical brethren in September 1218. It was composed before the long siege of Damietta had begun and was written in hopeful anticipation of future successes. The loss of morale that is so plain in his letters written the following year is not yet evident, and the list of achievements of the crusading army to date is proudly recounted. The shaming of recalcitrant soldiers by using words to describe their feelings serves to remind the readers of the unique nature of the soldiers who did not leave the army: "How narrow is the way which leads unto life and few enter through it," Jacques writes, quoting Matthew 7:14.[49] It is worth noting that in a sermon composed after he had returned to Europe to recruit new crusaders, Jacques was

56 WAR AND MEMORY AT THE TIME OF THE FIFTH CRUSADE

particularly scornful of cowards, writing that "they are fearful people not suited for war who will be condemned by the Lord."[50]

Emotion drives the story in this particular letter, and at key points in the narrative, expressions of emotion are included. Jacques reports that after four months of waiting, the army was "about to despair," but then the "fearless" Frisians devised and built a siege engine. This particular group of crusaders was remarkable, according to Jacques, who reported that they fasted and lamented and put their hope in God. "Pilgrims, nobles and commoners alike threw themselves on the sand, covered their heads with dust. Weeping and lamenting," they asked for God's pity.[51] The model actions of the Frisians in what had been an environment of despair was inspirational: "Our men were motivated by the tears and prayers of the pilgrims and strengthened in the Lord."[52] With newfound strength, they leapt through the walls of Greek fire used to defend the Egyptian defensive tower, and eventually the Egyptians surrendered it. The loss of this tower caused "great distress and apprehension" among the Saracens, who were innately fearful in Jacques's view. The sultan's actions are entirely dictated by unrestrained emotion. He destroys a fortress "through fear," he flees "in grief and shame," and eventually all these misfortunes (i.e., crusader successes) "caused the Sultan to die of grief." This is replicated in part in Letter 6 (composed in 1220), where we hear that the Egyptians are "cowardly and panic-stricken."[53]

Yet in a later letter, written after the long siege and eventual capture of Damietta, Jacques was moved to include the terrible cost of battle in both physical and emotional terms: "We lost that day more than a thousand men before we reached our camp; some killed, others weakened by the heat, were taken prisoner when their horses were wounded, while many footsoldiers died of thirst in the heat. Some were so afraid of the just judgment of God, even though this is not known, that they went mad and died."[54] The inclusion of these feelings of terror among the soldiers contrasts those who "journeyed to the Lord happily wearing a martyr's crown" but mirrors Jacques's own despair that he relates in the next few lines: "On that very day I ventured out unarmed, wearing my cape and my surplice with the lord legate and the patriarch carrying the holy cross, and it did not please the Lord to call unworthy, pitiful me to accompany his martyrs; he wanted me to bear labor and grief."[55]

Whereas in the valediction, or closing section, of Letter 4, Jacques notes that he has been kept alive to pay for his sins, in Letter 6, his mood is more despondent. Right at the end of the letter, he returns to the first-person singular, stating that he is now "frail and broken-hearted" and wishes to return to a tranquil life where he can end his days in peace. He addresses this version of the letter not to the pope but to John of Nivelles, a former colleague and now an Augustinian at the abbey of Oignies near Namur in modern-day Belgium. John of Nivelles had a close relationship with Jacques prior to the Crusade. He had been a *magister* at Paris in the late twelfth century and then became the husband of Marie of Oignies, the holy woman with whom Jacques developed an intimate friendship at the priory of Oignies before her death in 1213.[56] Marie had been a great advocate of Jacques's preaching, while her own powerful persona as holy woman had sparked his interest in composing her vita around 1215. Marie and John had decided to dedicate themselves to Christ by living in a spiritual, nonsexual marriage as part of a commitment to the *vita apostolica*. Thomas of Cantimpré described John as an "outstanding preacher of God's word," and it was during the time of his marriage to Marie that he must have become close to Jacques. Jacques wrote Letter 6 to John and Pope Honorius III as well as the convent of Aywières, and it is only in the salutation and concluding sections that the letters differ. Jacques resisted reporting his own interior reactions to what he saw to the pope and the women of the convent, but it seems that he was willing to confide in his friend.

The episode prompting this introspective moment was the crusaders' entry into the city of Damietta after the long siege. Jacques had known, as he wrote to the pope in Letter 5, composed on the eve of the city's capture, that "the trapped inhabitants in the city did not have enough to eat," but nonetheless it was a shocking sight that greeted him when the army broke through in 1219. "The Lord struck our enemies with terrible wounds," he wrote, reporting that there were not enough people left alive to bury the many bodies that lay throughout the streets and in the houses of the city. Shock at what the crusaders found in the city is replicated in the accounts of other eyewitnesses, who wrote their accounts in chronicle form later. Piles of corpses, the dreadful stench of decomposing bodies, and dozens of starving survivors were described by the papal legate, Oliver of Paderborn, who portrayed the state of the besieged city as horrific, with the streets and houses full of the dead and an "intolerable odor" pervading the city.[57] Both Jacques de Vitry and Oliver of Paderborn move on quite quickly in their accounts to describe the Christian colonization of the city,

58 WAR AND MEMORY AT THE TIME OF THE FIFTH CRUSADE

the conversion of the mosque into a cathedral, and the collection of treasure. But Jacques returns to musing on the more traumatic moments of
war and ends the letter with his own emotional state—*confractus corde*,
"brokenhearted."

CONCLUSION

Eyewitnesses to war drew on their individual memories to create remembrance more broadly. They narrated their own life experiences to communicate to others, for various reasons and in a range of genres, what was
important to remember about particular events. This was done, as I have
shown, by individualizing stories, by making experience palpable through
recourse to the material and physical, and by using emotions to bring the
inner world of individuals to the external world of others. The letters of
Jacques de Vitry thus shed light on how medieval people both understood
their past and gave direction to their future.

At the start of this chapter, I suggested that these sorts of eyewitness
narratives might be described as cotemporal, since they bring together the
present telling of past events for future purposes. This cotemporality is also
to be found in new ways of writing about and legitimating the past in the
early to mid-thirteenth century, especially in France. The rise of vernacular
historiography in the later twelfth and early thirteenth centuries, as Gabrielle Spiegel has shown, was due to a new desire on the part of the French
aristocracy to legitimate their past and strengthen their future in the face
of an increasingly centralizing Capetian monarchy. The historical works
that these aristocrats commissioned also gave less coverage to the distant
past, focusing on more recent events in which they or family members had
participated. Eyewitnesses were an important repository of information for
these works, especially for prose histories. As Spiegel argues, "Aristocratic
patronage of contemporary chronicles can be seen as a form of political
action, an attempt to control the subject matter of history and the voices of
the past as a means of dominating the collective memory of feudal society."[58]
This domination was effected through what Spiegel describes as the transformation of historical writing into a "witness discourse" at this time.[59] The
sources I have discussed in this chapter are not chronicles, nor were they
written in the vernacular. Yet they are texts that do similar temporal work.
They shape memory into a language of witnessing that will affect future

remembrance. If there is a new temporality at work in the historical writing of this period, then it is also visible in the remembrance projects of other textual genres of the same time. In this way, Crusade eyewitness narratives may be considered a distinctive example of the broader trends in medieval history writing of the early thirteenth century.

These eyewitness accounts also raise questions about how medieval people understood the notion of "experience" more broadly. As Jacques de Vitry's letters make clear, the narration of lived experience was pivotal to remembering the past. Indeed, the Latin term *experientia* carried with it similar epistemological nuances to the category of *memoria*: it implied not just observation or participation but also the acquisition of knowledge, wisdom, understanding, and even divine learning, particularly in monastic contexts. Experience was a category of knowing.[60] It referred to not just what an individual had lived through in the past but what those things signified and created, what they produced. For modern historians, it is the subject itself that is constituted through experience, while others have suggested that "experience" is not the simple recording of the lived present (a "now"). It is only with the anticipation of future significance that experience has meaning.[61] As Leonard Smith explains, "In terms of simple cognition, experience can achieve some sort of coherence only through recollection." Experience and memory cannot be separated temporally or analytically.[62] This was certainly recognized by thirteenth-century writers. For Thomas Aquinas, *experientia* was the product of sensory data that were stored in the memory and made sense of by reason; it was a retrospective and constructive capacity activated and perpetuated by remembering. This is borne out in the narration of experience in the sources I have analyzed here. For Jacques de Vitry, experience was the product of memory and a prompt for future remembrance.

Finally, medieval eyewitness accounts test some assumptions about the uniqueness of the modern eyewitness of war as an agent of remembrance. As many scholars have made clear, modern cultures give a privileged place to those who actually experienced war, either as fighters or as civilians. Sometimes this privilege serves legal purposes. The testimonial authority of the eyewitness has become important because of the evidentiary value of individual memories, which have been crucial in the war crimes trials of the twentieth century, for instance. This privilege can also serve moral purposes. Collecting statements and testimonies from victims of war is understood to help bear witness to the atrocities that have occurred while also reconstructing in memory the communities shattered by conflict. There are thus legal and social purposes behind the modern historical and political drive to enshrine the memories of those "who were actually there" as authentic and especially valuable.[63] But the medieval examples I have considered here show that eyewitnesses to war in the first decades of the thirteenth century also understood the practice of eyewitnessing to have wider social and political value. Medieval eyewitnesses told stories that privileged individual memory in order to influence future remembrance. Eyewitnesses understood that their stories drew together past and present, established the moral parameters of war, and built a bridge between what happened and what it meant. Again, they did this outside the paradigm of national identity, which has been the driving force of so much of modernity's "memory boom." But their remembrance work was similarly founded on the interaction between the individual and the collective in order to construct experience, provide a hermeneutics of explanation, and stimulate future action.

Of course, remembering war as a moral and cultural imperative does not mean that all stories are of equivalent value, and not all stories are told. This is the case in medieval and modern contexts. The importance of the individual experience I have outlined here can be qualified by a fuller consideration of whose experience is deemed to be worth remembering and whose experience is forgotten. In chapter 3, I consider how the images of the heroic crusader and his counterpoints (such as deserters and prisoners of war) were used to perpetuate forms of remembrance that were both inclusive and exclusionary.

Returning to the shores of the Nile River, we find that the remainder of Jacques de Vitry's war was eventful. The problem of maintaining crusader control over Damietta and the surrounding area was immediately apparent once the city had been captured, and the continued delay of the arrival of Frederick II's imperial forces exposed the vital need for more manpower. The winter and spring of 1220–21 were, as James Powell points out, "devoted to watching and waiting."[64] The crusaders rejected an offer of peace from Sultan Al-Kamil and moved upstream in early July to attack his camp but found themselves disastrously trapped by the newly reinforced Muslim armies and the rising river as the annual flooding of the Nile began. Forced to retreat northward by the end of August, the crusaders surrendered.

Damietta was returned to Muslim control on August 29, 1221, and hostages were given to the sultan to ensure the city's handover. One of these people was Jacques de Vitry. He spent only a short time as a hostage and did not record his experiences. Jacques returned to Acre in September and from there sailed back to Europe.

CHAPTER 3

Remembering Crusaders

> Now the time and the season have come when it will be put
> to the test who are the ones who fear God, for He only summons
> the valiant and the brave: for those who will be faithful, steadfast
> warriors over there, and strong, fine combatants, noble, gener-
> ous, courtly and loyal, may be always unreservedly His; and the
> petty and venal ones will remain behind, since God wants
> the good ones to save their souls over there with fine valiant
> deeds, and this is a glorious salvation.
>
> —AIMERIC DE PEGULHAN

> All our men have one goal and one desire in mind.
>
> —JACQUES DE VITRY

Who is worth remembering and why? In the previous two chapters, I have
mostly considered how individuals shaped their own future remembrance
and communicated their experiences as eyewitnesses and participants in
the Crusade. The evidence of wills and charters, motivational words and
prayers, and personal letters reveals that remembering and being remembered was a core element of crusading activity from the very beginning of
a crusader's identification with the holy war. Crusading was conceptual-
ized as possessing a distinct temporality that drew together past, present,
and future through eschatological ideas and practices of remembrance.
In this chapter, I explore more specifically how individuals and groups of
crusaders were memorialized by others in narratives of the Fifth Crusade.
Texts such as the famous *Historia Damiatina* of Oliver of Paderborn, the frequently cited but still understudied *Gesta obsidionis Damiatae* attributed to

Johannes Codagnellus, and even the northern Italian Crusade song quoted above, composed around 1213, were written for different constituencies, communicated in different ways, and crafted with particular agendas in mind, but all shared the same aspiration of linking the collective activity of the Crusade to the conduct or behavior of individual crusaders and groups.[1] In so doing, these sorts of texts engaged in deliberate and careful decisions about how and why someone ought—or ought not—to be remembered.

As historians of modern war memory have shown, memories are not just the products of shared experiences but narratives often informed by cultural scripts, a "repertoire of useable images, plots and figures" that influence how a person relates his or her memories.[2] Individuals may contest such cultural scripts, yet the very process of communicating memory also involves negotiating the vocabularies already in circulation to talk about the past. The narratives of the Fifth Crusade are especially rich in this regard, as eyewitnesses often had an interest in creating representations of the Crusade for wider audiences than the people to whom they directly communicated their wartime experiences. Authors like Oliver of Paderborn or Jacques de Vitry certainly came to the Crusade already equipped with the well-rehearsed "cultural scripts" or past vocabularies of crusading, holy war, suffering, and martyrdom, and they used those languages to narrate their own experiences, as I have indicated in the previous chapter. But they also meant to fashion narratives that reached beyond their own circles of influence and experiences to create lasting and instructive remembrance of this complex but meaningful Crusade. Bringing together past and present events in service of the future necessarily involved decisions about who was worthy of remembering. This was partly narrated through representations of conduct and behavior on Crusade. This chapter therefore looks more closely at how remembrance is formed and expressed within living memory of an event in order to influence how that event is remembered in the future, performed through processes of what we might understand as "official" memory making.[3]

By the time that the Fifth Crusade was under way, concern about the ideal crusader, the conduct of Crusade, and the relationship between individual sinfulness and the outcome of crusading was very current and had been present for some time. As crusaders attracted criticism for the continued decay of Outremer (a name for the crusader states), their behavior on Crusade had come to embody the idea that individual actions before and during the campaign were critical to the success of this collective endeavor. Those like Emperor Frederick II, who delayed his departure for Crusade, came under particular scrutiny. When Pope Honorius III agonized over the reasons for the failure of the Crusade, he regretted his own willingness to allow the emperor to continually defer his participation.[4] Others were less kind, including the author of the *Chronicle of Ernoul*, whose representation of Frederick veered from conciliatory to critical, attacking him as duplicitous, quarrelsome, and unreliable.[5] Attempts to organize the overall moral character of the Crusade by forbidding the participation of women, banning gambling, and condemning luxurious clothing also became a part of pre-Crusade planning and preaching from the twelfth century. Jacques de Vitry railed against crusaders "who, fatigued from their journey, used to drink until they were dead drunk"; cavorted with the "prostitutes and wicked women in hospices who lie in wait for the incautious"; or valued "horses and worldly pomps."[6] Such warnings against dissolute behavior focused on individual responsibility for righteous participation in the Crusade while also asserting a necessary uniformity to the moral fabric of each crusading army.

Worry about crusader behavior and its effects was also one part of a cultural landscape increasingly reflective about crusading's past. As Nicholas Paul has explained, this was exemplified by significant literary shifts in Crusade writing in the first part of the thirteenth century, when vernacular prose narratives began to be written and crusading romance—in the forms of epic and *chanson*—increasingly became the dominant genre for writing about the deeds of crusading heroes. Paul traces how the "painful birth" of crusading romance that occurred at this time responded to the failure of recent Crusades and reflected continued desires to understand the contemporary Crusades as a part of a lineage of holy war that was populated with distinguished and aspirational individuals.[7] Although Latin histories continued to be written, there seems to have been something of a division between the work done in those texts and the work done in crusading romance. As Barbara Packard describes, "Authors of Latin historical works were now leaving honor, chivalry and heroism to those writing epic literature."[8]

However, many Latin texts of the Fifth Crusade—intended for a literate and mostly clerical audience—do record individuals and groups who were understood to be worth remembering. These individuals were sometimes Crusade leaders, heads of contingents, or ecclesiasts. Most frequently, groups are especially noted—this is the case with the Frisians, who appear in several of the narrative accounts as remarkably effective in battle. Often, we hear simply of Christians or pilgrims. Sometimes groups are collectively critiqued, as in the case of deserters or occasionally captives. Although there may be a dearth of larger-than-life "heroic" figures in the eyewitness texts, it is clear that Latin writers of the Fifth Crusade were still interested in using individuals and groups to tell particular stories about crusading and its meanings.

BEHAVIOR IN COMBAT

Crusade combat stories follow a fairly standard arc. They usually describe proper preparation for battle, emphasize collective purpose and resolve, and conclude with tales of pious gratitude in the aftermath of the battle. How soldiers behaved in battle situations was thus used to motivate others to join the Crusade, to illustrate the justness of the holy war, and—most importantly for the purposes of this chapter—to commemorate particular groups through their inclusion and naming at significant narrative moments. Although the eyewitness accounts of war (as discussed in the previous chapter) were understood to be valuable because of their individualized representations of experience, it is the collective crusading enterprise that was deemed worthy of recording in the narrative texts. Battle stories emphasize the need for commonality and unity much more often than they describe individual acts of bravery or valor. These accounts create a memory of events that require individual participation but depend on the actions of the group for success.

According to Jacques de Vitry, both spiritual and bodily armor were needed once the crusaders arrived in Egypt; therefore, devotional practices were part and parcel of proper preparation for combat alongside the tactical and pragmatic arrangements. These were collective activities, especially processions and prayers that took place before battle. Such community or group liturgical efforts were not unique to the Fifth Crusade, of course—the *Gesta francorum* reports that prior to the Battle of Antioch during the First Crusade, there were three days of processions from church to church throughout the city.[9] More generally, as Jonathan Riley-Smith famously wrote, the Crusade itself could be described rather like a large-scale liturgical procession, a "military monastery on the move."[10] The immediate thirteenth-century context of processional liturgy may also be related to Pope Innocent III's special interest in it, outlined in *Quia maior*, which required that everyone in Europe should take part in monthly processions in support of the Crusade. In conjunction with these processions, he deemed that money should be collected "to be used for the aid of the Holy Land."[11] Such processions were collective prayerful exercises also intended to have a positive impact on recruitment.

The processions that took place immediately before combat on the battlefront could be accompanied by both almsgiving and fasting and sometimes culminated in the rites of confession and Mass. Other processions performed a supportive function for the armies who witnessed them. During the early attempts by the army of the Fifth Crusade to attack the chain tower at Damietta, these processions seem to have been an especially important element of the collective action. The crusaders were said to have held firm during the battle for control of the tower, encouraged by the "pilgrims, nobles and commoners" who were watching them, lamenting and praying.[12] Indeed, in some reports, the prayerful work done by witnesses influenced the battle's outcome. Oliver of Paderborn reports that on the day before the Feast of St. Bartholomew in 1218, the pilgrims and clerics made a "procession barefoot to the Holy Cross with devotion on the part of our people" while the "clergy, barefoot, walked as suppliants on the shore."[13] Watching the efforts of their fellow crusaders, "their faces streamed with tears of sorrow as they protested the pity they had for those who were enduring peril in the depth of the river and the loss of all Christendom."[14] The Italian author of the *Gesta obsidionis Damiatae* also described these barefoot pilgrims, who knelt and prostrated themselves on the ground for an hour in supplication, tears streaming from their eyes as they petitioned, "Domine misere! Adiuva nos!"[15] That their prayers were answered was evidenced by the appearance of the Holy Cross over the chain tower; on witnessing this, the weeping pilgrims recovered and gave thanks, and the battle for the tower was renewed with the successful capture of a number of prisoners.

The weeping reported to have accompanied these prayers is noteworthy. Tears and the act of crying contained a range of spiritual meanings for medieval people: tears indicated identification with the suffering Christ, linked the experience of inner anguish with external response, and could be seen as a sign of holiness—a gift from God. As such, tears could have a personal salvific effect. One twelfth-century text even delineated four very specific sorts of spiritual tears: tears of compunction, compassion, contemplation, and longing for heaven (*lacrimae peregrinationis*).[16] Crying made piety visible and created a fluid path to God; tears were the link from the locus of emotion, the soul, through the vehicle of the body to the outer world. Tears were streams or rivers, and they flowed especially during prayer.[17] Crying while in prayer was also understood by Christian authors as a participatory act in a temporal sense; for someone like the twelfth-century Cistercian Aelred of Rievaulx, for instance, the recluse for whom he composed his *Regula* would, by weeping, effectively transcend her immediate environment to share fully in the experience of biblical history and the suffering of Christ.[18] This temporal work of weeping was also shared by crusaders. Tears were an indicator of the value of hope over mere military strength. Those who "put their trust in God alone" externalized their own inner transformations and reminded others that the Crusade was spiritual work.[19] When tears were shed by the papal legate as he heard crusaders pray that they not die in this place and when all wept in 1219 as they prayed that God not let them perish at the hands of the cruel Saracens, their tears did not simply signify fear or despair; they signified hope in God.[20] Weeping was a demonstrably collective physical and emotional act that set up the conditions for proper conduct during fighting.

Fighting is mostly described as a collective act, although descriptions of combat also provide eyewitnesses opportunities to pay special attention to those with whom they had close relationships. The Fifth Crusade contingents were quite separate, as noted by the author of the *Eracles* continuation of William of Tyre, who reported that "the Christians" were divided into various "cantons" that mostly lodged separately but presumably came together at times in combat—the French, the Pisans, the Templars, the Frisians, the Genoese, the Hospitallers, and others.[21] The Frisians and German groups are especially noteworthy (especially in Oliver of Paderborn's text), and the respective narratives communicated the effective outcome of unity of purpose by elevating these groups with whom they particularly identified. In Oliver of Paderborn's lengthy description of the attack on the tower in August 1218, he reported that after the prayers and tears—"the devotion of the people and the raising of their hands to heaven" (*ad hanc populi devotionem et elevationem manum in celum*)—God worked his "divine

68   WAR AND MEMORY AT THE TIME OF THE FIFTH CRUSADE

kindness" (*divina pietas*) to inspire one soldier in particular to break the stalemate: "A certain young man of Liège was the first to ascend the tower; a certain young Frisian holding a flail by which grain is usually threshed, but which was prepared for fighting by an interweaving with chains, lashed out bravely to the right and to the left, knocked down a certain man holding the saffron standard of the Sultan and took the banner away from him."[22]

The Frisians were also singled out by Jacques de Vitry, who particularly noted that although they were excellent tacticians, they trusted God above their military and strategic prowess.[23] The Frisians' reward for proper spiritual preparation for battle and proper conduct within battle was managing to avoid the ravages of the three-day storm in November 1218 that flooded the crusader tents and caused some of the ships and many of the supplies to drift away down the Nile. Oliver of Paderborn reported that "the Lord spared the labors of the Frisians and the Germans for whom the tower had been captured." And for the author of the *Gesta obsidionis Damiatae*, this storm was a highly symbolic and spiritual event. Quoting from Matthew's gospel, Johannes Codagnellus has the papal legate Pelagius pray for divine intervention to calm the waters and the wind; again with tears, the crusaders (described in this text as Christians, not Frisians) watched as a *sol splendidissimus* appeared in the skies above the river.[24]

There is an element of self-congratulation in Oliver of Paderborn's account of the superior military and spiritual strength of the Frisians and Germans. These were some of the first crusaders to set out from Vlaardingen in May 1217, and this was the group to whom Oliver himself had preached so effectively and to whom crosses had miraculously appeared in the sky in 1214.[25] They had already undertaken battles against Muslims in Portugal en route to the Nile delta, defeating them successfully after the siege of Alcácer do Sal in October 1217, alongside a number of German contingents. Oliver of Paderborn himself played a significant role in the strategic construction of the "siege engine," which supported a scaling ladder for climbing into the chain tower and resulted in its successful capture.[26] It seems that a number of these Frisians and Germans sailed for home soon after the capture of the tower in the summer of 1218, so Oliver's privileging of this group in his account may also be due in part to a desire for their participation in a key moment of military success to be recorded for posterity. More significantly, Oliver continued to preach the Crusade once he returned from the Holy Land; he was in Cologne in 1222 and by 1224 was commissioned as a Crusade preacher. It is from this time that we see the three separate redactions of the *Historia Damiatina* being produced and a number of manuscripts being circulated. Some twelve surviving manuscripts are thirteenth-century ones.[27] There is no doubt that Oliver drew on his own participation in and knowledge of the events of the Fifth Crusade to influence future crusaders—especially those he hoped would participate in the Crusade of Frederick II. His elevation of both Frisians and Germans must be seen as a part of his mission to muster Crusade support among these particular groups.

Similar privileging is seen in the *Gesta obsidionis Damiatae*, which singles out the Italian contingents for special mention. They possessed *magne fortitudinis*, and they were the first to launch one of the many attacks on the city in July 1219. It was with the efforts by *prudentissimos viros Romanos et Latinos* that the siege of Damietta finally ended.[28] The author of the *Gesta*, Johannes Codagnellus (ca. 1172–1235), was a notary from Piacenza, who was one of the early thirteenth century's most prolific Italian chroniclers and was especially well known for his *Annales Placentini*, composed in the 1230s, which dealt with Frederick II's campaigns in Italy. His historical writings are highly urban centered; indeed, Paul Magdalino observes that Codagnellus "saw Italian history as whole simply as city resistance to invasions."[29] Codagnellus's focus on the Italians at Damietta is not surprising in the context of his own audiences. The *Gesta* appears in two manuscripts of the thirteenth century, one of which also contains his entire opus (Paris, Bibliothèque nationale de France, MS Lat. 4931). Although it is not one of his more widely read historical accounts, it gained a local circulation alongside his reworking of Otto of Freising's *Gesta Frederici*.[30]

Having narrated proper preparation and conduct within battle through emphasis on unity of intent, these writers then emphasized the right sort of behavior to mark the conclusion and aftermath of battle. Thanks were to be given to God along with acknowledgment of the divine determination of the outcome of events. Both the *Gesta obsidionis Damiatae* and Oliver of Paderborn unsurprisingly report that the great Christian victory was God's work through the miraculous power of his divinity. Immediately after the chain tower was captured, Jacques de Vitry also tells us that the crusaders gave thanks to God, and in a later letter, he notes that the military victory was not merely the result of human effort, but "the Lord was reserving victory for Himself alone. . . . We trust Him who miraculously opened the gates of Egypt to Christian rule, illuminating the darkness and spreading his Church to the ends of the earth."[31] The clerical authors communicating this trajectory of preparation, action, and gratitude were not just enshrining what was, after all, a conventional explanation for battle success here. They were also creating a narrative in which their own preaching efforts (in the case of Jacques de Vitry and Oliver of Paderborn, at least) were shown to have been successful. They provided textual evidence that the right sort of conduct led to the desired outcome—at least at the outset of this particular Crusade—and in so doing provided a template for future successful action.

INDIVIDUALS AND NAMING

Individuals are listed as especially worthy of memory not just if they died in battle or as part of the supporting army of pilgrims on Crusade but if they had a relationship with the author or his audience. This sort of personal connection with the dead is evident in the letter composed by Jacques de Vitry in September 1218. He urges the recipients of this version of the letter—in this case, his "beloved friends in Christ"—to pray for his dead companions (*pro sociis nostris defunctis*), among whom are a number of his colleagues from Acre. In this version of the letter, Jacques, who identifies himself in the letter's salutation as *Iacobus divina permissione Acconensis ecclesie minister humilis*, lists both the names and the statuses of these men with whom he had recently worked, including the archdeacon Walter of Tournai, who "was the instrument of our Lord for many good deeds in the city of Acre"; dean Constant of Douai; cantor John of Cambrai and his nephew, Reinier, *pastore* at the church of St. Michael; and master Leonius, who taught theology at Acre.

The last moments of Reynald of Barbichon, who was the former treasurer of the Acre church, are reported in more detail: he "received the viaticum on bended knee before the altar after hearing matins in the night of Whitsun and the celebration of Mass in the day. At the end of Vespers he ordered a bed to be set up for him in a small tent next to our chapel and that night he gave him the rite of the anointing of the sick. Continually pronouncing the name of He who he had faithfully preached in life, just before dawn he migrated to Him, praising and thanking God."[32] The naming of such individuals meant not only that others were informed soon after their deaths but that their names and connection with Acre (and the work they had done there) became, through text, part of the story of the Crusade. Moreover, Jacques presented to his audience examples of good deaths—men like Reynald of Barbichon provided evidence for the steadfastness of faith and an ideal (and idealized) transition between this world and the next. Jacques also singled out the English *magister* and cardinal Robert of Courçon, "a cultivated and devout man, affable, liberal and generous, full of the zeal of God and burning with desire to see the liberation of the Holy Land."[33] Courçon died in the epidemic that followed the winter of 1219 and claimed the lives of up to one-third of the crusading army. Courçon's name (and those of noble others) is worthy of inclusion in the "book of life," according to Jacques, who not only was part of the same Parisian circle (made famous by Peter the Chanter) but had possibly received his commission to preach the Crusade from Robert himself.[34]

These named men were mostly nobles who often possessed significant personal or institutional power. Of two hundred men who died or were taken prisoner on the Feast of the Beheading of John the Baptist (August 29, 1219), Jacques de Vitry named the bishop-elect of Beauvais; Walter the king of France's *camerius* and son, the Viscount of Beaumont (Jean D'Archies); Lord Andreas d'Epoisse; and Lord Andreas de Nanteuil (the brother of the bishop-elect of Beauvais). The dead were described as "knights of the Temple and the Hospital," "other pilgrims," *alii nobiles viri quidam capti, quidam interfecti sunt.*[35] Such deaths on Crusade sometimes meant martyrdom; Oliver of Paderborn observed that dead soldiers were "vigorous and well-armed, wounded in body to the advantage of their souls, crowned with a glorious martyrdom."[36] Only a few of these individuals were named in his text and explicitly connected to martyrdom: "The count of La Marche and the count of Bar and his son, brother William of Chartres, master of the army of the Temple, Hervé of Vierzon, Ithier of Toucy, Oliver son of the king of England and many others of the knightly order and common people ended their days at Damietta. Many martyrs for Christ, more confessors of Christ, being delivered from human cares at Damietta, went to the Lord."[37] And Jacques de Vitry also identified those who died in the attack on the chain tower as receiving the "crown of martyrdom."[38]

Episodes like those of August 29, 1219, provided opportunities for the narrators of contemporary texts to also connect the meaning of events with biblical history. The *Gesta obsidionis Damiatae* narrated that John the Baptist sought beheaded companions, which was why, on his feast day, the fate of so many Christians was decapitation. These men included Templars, thirty Germans, thirty-two Hospitallers, and others *sine numero*.[39] This is the only place in the *Gesta* where the author includes a long list of names and specifically links them to martyrdom. "Listen dear brothers and sons," he wrote, "how Christ receives his holy martyrs." He wrote that one German, who was thought to be dead, opened his eyes and saw a great multitude of angels floating over the battleground, intoning words from Revelation above all the corpses—"Here are they who came from great tribulation and they have washed their robes in the blood of the lamb (Apoc. 7, 13)." Here, martyrdom is implied in the connection between the particular saint and the fate of the Christians. The Palm Sunday attack of May 31, 1219, provided similar opportunities. For Oliver of Paderborn, this event was a chance to remind his readers of the important place of the Duke of Austria in battle—we are told that he "for a year and a half had fought faithfully for Christ, full of devotion, humility, obedience and generosity" while also bestowing money on the Teutonic Order and the Templars. On Palm Sunday, the Duke of Austria with the Germans directed the defense of a bridge, which was under sudden and vicious attack by a "fearful and innumerable army of horsemen and foot soldiers." The significance of the day of this attack was noted, as Oliver lamented that on that day, "We were not given the opportunity of carrying palms other than crossbows, bows and arrows, lances and swords and shields." Although for Oliver it was the Duke of Austria who led the action, he also reported that women supported the army by bringing them water and stones, while priests tended to the wounded and "persisted in prayer."[40]

For Johannes Codagnellus on the other hand, the Duke of Austria was not important enough to mention. What was important in his account was the symbolic significance of Palm Sunday; he writes that the Egyptians knew that this was a day of Christian celebration and thus were determined to attack. The huge toll of this attack on the army is described, and the dead were said to carry palms to the Lord. As the Psalmist said, "The just will grow like a palm tree, they will multiply like the cedar of Lebanon" (Psalm 92:12: *Justus ut palma florebit, sicut cedrus Libani multiplicabitur*). There are no words, wrote Codagnellus, to describe the misery, anguish, and illness suffered by the Christian army "for the love of Christ" and "for the Christian faith."[41] This sort of language reflects early thirteenth-century emphasis on Christian sharing of Christ's suffering and is replicated throughout the *Gesta* account in sometimes quite graphic language or in conjunction with lists of the dead, but at other times—as in the Palm Sunday battle—it serves as a way of stressing the transcendent meaning of the events.[42]

Thus the actions of individuals were commemorated in text by the inclusion of their specific names, especially in the context of particular trials and death. Going into battle appropriately, supported by tears, right intent, collective purpose, and trust in God, would ensure not only victory but also remembrance. The naming of soldiers was important in communicating their memory to others who might have familial or social relationships with these individuals while also providing models for emulation directed at future crusaders. We know that Jacques's letters, for instance, reached a variety of audiences—monastic, papal, and clerical—while Oliver of Paderborn's subsequent preaching activities after the Crusade would suggest that his representation of Damietta and its fallen soldiers as a discrete and important episode in the history of the Fifth Crusade was deliberately constructed to move others to action.

DESERTERS AND PRISONERS

The major moments of triumph during the Fifth Crusade, such as the capture of the chain tower and the successful capture of Damietta, allowed those who narrated the events to fit them into the trajectory described above. Of course, this Crusade also involved a long and difficult siege and stalemate, eventual surrender, and withdrawal from Egypt in 1221. These realities had to be accounted for in the narrative reports too, and the efforts to create some sort of transcendent meaning for these events will be discussed more fully in the following chapter. Here, the ways in which individual and collective actions were represented as contributing to the ongoing and then ultimately unsuccessful crusading effort offer further insight into the construction of remembrance of these events.

Desertion and captivity were reported in the narrative accounts to reinforce the messages that upholding the crusading vow was fundamental to the success of the Crusade and that collective action and support were crucial to military and spiritual victory. Including these "difficult" moments as part of the transmission of the Crusade story also contrasted "types" of crusaders worth (and not worth) emulating. From the beginning of the Crusade, there were concerns about commitment to the crusading vow and the potential problem of desertion. One of Jacques de Vitry's sermons to crusaders and potential recruits described those who were fearful and timid as "so weak and rotten that the cross cannot be sewn onto them; like old pieces of cloth that are worn out by age and are no longer useful for anything, they cannot hold a seam. They are fearful people who are not suitable for war and they will be condemned by the Lord."[43] Writing to Pope Honorius III in September 1218, Jacques condemned men who left the Crusade early in similar terms, describing them as cowardly and lacking in stability (*pusillanimes et inconstantes*), particularly since they left without having accomplished their vows. Such criticism was repeated by Oliver of Paderborn, who dismissed the sailors and pilgrims leaving Egypt in September 1219 before the capture of Damietta as "betrayers of Christianity" whose "love of themselves was greater than their compassion for their brethren."[44]

Medieval law codes distinguished between flight from battle—sometimes justified—and desertion from an army, which was more heinous, especially if it was accompanied by defection to the enemy. The thirteenth-century *Las siete partidas* recommended banishment and the loss of half their property for noblemen who deserted a king's army (thus causing him dishonor in defeat) and death for those of lesser rank who did the same. Those who fled from battle before it was over, causing ranks to be broken, or who deserted to the enemy were traitors—their houses should be demolished, their possessions should be confiscated, and they should die. Indeed, "the desertion of their lord, while engaged in battle with his enemies [is] such a grave matter . . . that . . . neither wives nor children should welcome men of this character to their houses, or live with them from that time forward."[45] The pragmatic reality of battle sometimes mitigated such dramatic action, though. The rule of the Templars, for instance, allowed soldiers to leave the battlefield "if no Christian banner was left flying as a rallying-point." However, bodily mutilation was still a punishment for some during the Crusades. Richard I declared at Messina in 1190 that runaway soldiers would lose a foot.[46] A papal edict pronouncing anathema on deserters was in place from the First Crusade and was reissued during the Second Crusade by Paschal II.[47]

There is certainly some evidence of desertion throughout the Fifth Crusade, but again, the audiences at whom the texts were directed had an influence on who was singled out in this regard. For instance, Oliver of Paderborn records a time of particularly low morale in August 1219, when the long siege of Damietta had caused division among the leaders of the contingents and dissension among the soldiers—"The foot soldiers reproached the cowardice of the horsemen, [and] the horsemen made light of the risks of the foot soldiers when they went out against the Saracens." On August 29, the disastrous attempt to engage in open combat resulted in a massacre of soldiers, which was preceded by the desertion of others. Oliver of Paderborn names these groups of deserters: the knights of Cyprus "showed their timidity" (*timiditatem suam ostenderunt*), but it was the Italian foot soldiers who "fled first" (*Italici pedites primo fugerunt*). Despite the pleas of Pelagius and the Patriarch of Jerusalem (who carried the cross), these men left behind others to be captured or killed.[48] He also accused the Italians of just wanting to make a name for themselves by going on Crusade, and he reminds his readers that it was through God's power alone that the city of Damietta would be captured.[49] The naming of deserters seems to be quite a parochial narrative choice, illustrated by the fact that the *Gesta obsidionis Damiatae* says that the Italians were especially brave and that the Pisans were the first to arms.[50] Both Codagnellus and Oliver of Paderborn describe this day as one of particular tribulation, a *dies irae* and a day of "divine rebuke."[51]

There were numerous reasons why desertion was considered problematic. It set a poor example for others, it brought shame and dishonor on families back home, it damaged the military capacity of the army, and it flew in the face of the collective effort of this special army of Christ. Most alarmingly, it meant that someone who had had the chance to share in the agonies of Christ refused that glorious opportunity—such people were betrayers of Christianity, according to Oliver of Paderborn. In this way, desertion also abrogated the spiritual vow made by crusaders to fulfill their obligations in order to benefit from the remission of sins. For Jacques de Vitry, there were clear reasons why individuals fled in the face of battle, all of which had to do with their resolve. Some were "weak-hearted" or "faint-hearted," and one band of knights advanced with "pride and elation" rather than with tears and devotion, showing they were motivated by seeking wealth. This meant that even before battle broke out, their discipline collapsed and some of them "turned around and fled," leaving the others ("some of our steadfast knights") at a disadvantage.[52] That desertion must have been taken seriously at least some of the time is clear from a Coptic Christian observer who commented that two crusaders condemned for cowardice at Damietta were hanged.[53] Public censure of deserters seems to have been occasionally practiced during the First Crusade, such as when ropes were hung over the walls of Antioch after the capture of the city as a "monument of shame" to those who had deserted during the city's siege. One contemporary observer of that Crusade, Ralph of Caen, noted that these ropes were left as temporary memorials to cowardice.[54]

One feature of the Fifth Crusade was the coming and going of contingents throughout the campaigns. The leaders of some of these groups were sometimes criticized for leaving the Crusade too early, and some were accused of too short a time on Crusade or of desertion. Andrew of Hungary attracted opprobrium and the threat of excommunication for leaving the Crusade only three months after his contingent left Split. He participated in the skirmishes for Mount Tabor but never continued to Egypt "to the great detriment of the Holy Land," according to Oliver of Paderborn. John of Brienne, who left the Crusade around Easter of 1220 for more than a year, was another who attracted some criticism from contemporaries by leaving the Crusade early. Oliver of Paderborn noted that John had a claim to the throne of Cilician Armenia and, with one eye to the main chance, prioritized that rather than the Crusade. For this, Oliver saw John as something of a deserter: "When the year was changing, when kings usually set out for war, John king of Jerusalem, left the camp of the faithful . . . acting contrary to an agreement which he had made at Acre when [the armies] were about to sail to Egypt, that he would not desert them so long as he was alive and free."[55] Jacques de Vitry also described John of Brienne as abandoning the Crusade with almost all his knights, the Master of the Temple, and most of the brothers. For John, the word *deservit* is used; for the Templars, *recussit*.[56]

Although desertion was represented in the texts as dangerous and shameful, captivity had a more complex set of meanings. The liberation of Christian captives was one principal reason the Crusade was preached: in *Quia maior*, Pope Innocent III described Christians who were "imprisoned by the faithless Saracens in a cruel prison and endure the harsh yoke of slavery," asking, "Perhaps you do not know that many thousands of

Christians are held in prison and slavery . . . and they suffer countless torments?"[57] These captives suffered by virtue of their faith, so their liberation was thought to be one of the Crusade's great acts of brotherly love. Further, by the time of the Fifth Crusade, those who busied themselves redeeming captives in other ways were thought to be performing an act of great piety. Yves Gravelle found that the redemption of captives was also a means for individuals to identify with Christ, who said, "I was naked, and you gave me clothing. I was sick, and you cared for me. I was in prison, and you visited me" (*nudus et operuistis me infirmus et visitastis me in carcere eram et venistis ad me*; Matthew 25:36). Thus the act of liberation served spiritual purposes for both captive and ransom-negotiator alike.[58] In this way, orders like the Order of Santiago, the Trinitarian Order, and the Mercedarians of the midthirteenth century in the Iberian Peninsula worked under the assumption that prisoners were not unworthy per se; the act of releasing these suffering captives (through ransoming) could work for mutual benefit.[59] This was a view shared by others at the time of the Fifth Crusade, including songwriters such as the highly anticlerical Huon of Saint-Quentin, who encouraged crusaders to remember that Christ "paid our ransom with His blood" and that there was an urgent need "to avenge those who are over there in prison for God's sake."[60]

Shame could nonetheless still be attached to the condition of captivity. William of Tyre notoriously wrote that knights should choose death rather than captivity, and he wrote in disgust of noble fighters who "surrendered without resistance like the lowest slaves, utterly regardless of the shameful yoke of slavery and the ignominy which would cling to their names forevermore."[61] William of Tyre's history had emphasized the liberation of the Holy Land as the central purpose of the crusaders' presence there. Therefore, it was not only a matter of personal dishonor for a crusading knight to allow himself to be taken captive but a sign of a more serious dereliction of the knight's primary obligation to protect and defend his Christian brethren and to free Christ's patrimony. The notion that the crusader himself was at fault for his capture and imprisonment was also articulated in explanations of captivity as divine punishment for sin. For instance, William of Tyre believed that on the First Crusade, Bohemond of Tarento was captured because of his sins.[62] Such connections between captivity, sin, and divine punishment reflected broader criticisms of the crusaders, their motives, and their actions, especially beginning in the mid-twelfth century when, after the fall of Edessa in 1144, more attention was paid to the reasons for misfortune in these holy wars.[63] In *Quantum praedecessores*, Pope Eugenius III lamented that "because of our sins . . . demanded it, there has occurred what we cannot make known without great sadness."[64] Responsibility for failure was increasingly perceived to lie with individual and collective sin, and captivity could also be interpreted in this way.

The narrative texts of the Fifth Crusade differentiate between those taken captive during the Egyptian campaign, those who were used as hostages while the surrender agreement was taking place, and Egyptian prisoners. The crusaders in the first category were sometimes named alongside those who were killed in battle, such as the bishop-elect of Beauvais and his brother, Andrew of Espoisse; Walter the king of France's chamberlain and his son, the Viscount of Beaumont; and Odo of Chatillon.[65] These men were clearly worthy of being remembered according to the authors who recorded their names, and their inclusion among those lists of martyrs elevates them to significant status. For authors like Oliver of Paderborn, the captivity of such men and the death of others was the cause of "gloom but not despair. For we know that this affliction was the punishment of [general Christian] sin."[66] The senior Christians who were used as hostages during the truce negotiations included Jacques de Vitry and Oliver of Paderborn. From Oliver's subsequent letter to Sultan Al-Kamil, it seems that his time in captivity was not onerous, and he acknowledges the sultan's kindness and benevolence before outlining the reasons why he should convert to Christianity.[67] Other Christian prisoners were kept in less pleasant conditions, as Oliver himself reports, noting that some "followers of Christ" were found in chains in a fortification captured by the Seljuk sultan of Iconium at the time of the siege of Damietta. In his 1221 letter to Al-Kamil, Oliver also pleaded with the sultan to release Christian prisoners—presumably those of lower status who were not part of the negotiations and who still languished in captivity in Egypt—and restore the holy places to Christian ownership.

The texts also describe Egyptian prisoners being paraded in front of Crusade leaders. John of Tulbia and Johannes Codagnellus told of enchained soldiers being brought before the Duke of Austria and John of Brienne, revealing to these leaders that an apparition of white knights led by a red knight had blinded them as they tried to defend the chain tower. Here, the prisoners are used as witnesses to God's divine will and the celestial support of the army. Jacques de Vitry also told of how four hundred of the "best and richest" prisoners from Damietta were to be exchanged "for our men who had been taken by the enemy."[68] Others, especially children, were given to members of the Orders and sent to the Holy Land or France—Jacques de Vitry himself says that two infants who were sent to John of Nivelles had been "saved when Babylon burned."[69]

LEADERSHIP

Guy Perry's study of John of Brienne most recently describes the various candidates for the leadership of the Crusade, noting that Pope Innocent III meant to decide on the Crusade's leader before the contingents mustered at Brindisi, Messina, and Cyprus prior to departing for the Holy Land. These musters did not occur, and Innocent himself died before the Crusade began. John of Brienne's position as nominal leader was therefore a result of decision-making on the ground (previously, Count Simon of Saarbrücken had been chosen as leader "before the King . . . arrived" at Damietta).[70] John of Brienne's leadership was based entirely on his status as King of Jerusalem and was not, as Perry points out, constitutionally strong by the time of the Fifth Crusade—his marriage to Maria of Jerusalem had initially secured his position, but once she died in 1212 (in childbirth), the kingdom was left with a minor heir and John as anointed king. The baronial disaffection with this situation festered throughout the Fifth Crusade, although it is clear that John's skill at garnering support from important groups and individuals (such as the Patriarch of Jerusalem and even Frederick II during the Crusade) prevented any serious challenge to his status until 1225.[71] Thomas Smith's work on Pope Honorius III has also recently nuanced our understanding of the relationship between the pope as the overseer of the Crusade from afar and those—especially Pelagius and John—who variously directed the Crusade "on the ground."[72]

Although the "leadership question" has framed earlier historiography of the Fifth Crusade, this is not the main concern of this book. However, in relation to textual decisions about remembering individuals, the leaders of the Crusade are still an important group to note. As with the representation of other individuals, the narrative strategies to describe Crusade leaders were very much determined by the contemporary authors themselves and their intended audiences. This did lead to some polarizing differences in representation. But it also informs the modern reader about which qualities of Crusade leaders were understood to be particularly worthy of recording and which behaviors and decisions were not. Focusing on this question rather than apportioning blame for why the Crusade failed reveals that the medieval authors most often emphasized individual piety and participation in collective action. In this way, the representation of Crusade leaders followed a pattern similar to the representation of crusaders overall.

Crusade leaders were meant to embody the spiritual virtue of crusading, and these qualities were overtly included in texts. Oliver of Paderborn, as we have seen, reserves high praise for the Duke of Austria, who in his eyes was "full of devotion, humility, obedience and generosity."[73] The *Gesta obsidionis Damiatae* notes with approval that John of Brienne was a "distinguished king, noble, prudent and of great faith and discernment" (*rex vir egregius, nobilis, prudens, magne fidei et discretionis*), but it is really Pelagius whom Johannes Codagnellus singles out as directing the spiritual integrity of the Crusade and overseeing its most successful moments. His text represented Pelagius as the provider of motivational and consoling pre-battle guidance. He directed prayer and led in the penitential weeping and lamenting that preceded combat. According to Codagnellus, he also took the lead in the general confession of the army in February 1219. For other authors, Pelagius attracted a more measured response. Oliver of Paderborn likewise recognized that Pelagius executed the office of legate "skillfully and vigilantly," but he seems to have thought that Pelagius's support of some military strategies was not always wise. He noted, for instance, that the legate "supplied copious funds" to the Pisans, Venetians, and Genoese for an attack on Damietta but reported disapprovingly that these soldiers only "wished to make a name for themselves, going forward with trumpets and reed pipes and many standards." Oliver observed that this attack was fruitless, writing that "so it was truly understood that by divine power alone would Damietta be delivered into the hands of the Christians."[74] Vernacular texts tend toward anticlerical representations, and the *Chronicle of Ernoul* goes as far as to say that it was a shame that a man like Robert of Courçon died at Damietta while Pelagius survived.[75] Other sources recognized the importance of military prowess among Crusade leaders: one of the Old French continuations of William of Tyre tells us that the Christians were successful in their victory of October 1218 (before Pelagius arrived) because the Lord saved them "by the hand of good king John," while Jacques de Vitry later unsurprisingly praised Pelagius for his cautious and farsighted general oversight of the "Lord's business."[76]

The dispute over the distribution of Damietta and the two peace offers made by Sultan Al-Kamil provided some moments for those who wrote about these events to comment on leadership in the context of the Crusade's mission. The sultan approached the Christians in late 1219, offering the city of Jerusalem, the True Cross captured at Hattin, Christian prisoners, money to repair the walls of Jerusalem, and various fortifications except Kerak and Montréal in exchange for the Christian army leaving Egypt entirely. For Jacques de Vitry, it was Pelagius who was the voice of caution and calm during the dissension among the Christians that followed this quite extraordinary offer (one that the legate refused). Once Damietta had been captured, conflict between John of Brienne and Pelagius over the distribution of the city festered for a couple of months following November 1219, and the arrival of various members of Frederick II's circle in 1220 and 1221 had the effect of isolating John.[77] On the other hand, John of Tulbia reported that Pelagius's division of the spoils of Damietta caused such dissension that the Christians rioted, and shockingly, the legate's life was endangered. Again in 1221, a peace offer was made by the Egyptians in advance of the disastrous Christian move toward Cairo. Those who describe this period oscillate between condemning John outright for abandoning Damietta and reporting his wisdom in resisting the ill-fated move to Cairo on his return. Oliver of Paderborn wrote that John was "wise" in suggesting that the peace terms be accepted in 1221 in order to avoid further loss of life, but both the pope and the emperor refused to accede. At the same time, however, Oliver castigated John for promising a speedy return to the Crusade but staying away for a year—"Forgetful of the past he turned to the future," Oliver wrote with disapproval. Jacques de Vitry, on the other hand, had more general anxieties—he was mostly worried that all the crusader leaders were responsible for the failure of the troops to keep faith.[78]

These sorts of representations indicate that, just like the naming of crusaders as worthy of memory, it was leaders' participation in the collective effort of the Crusade that was the most important. This collective effort did not necessarily mean military success, since God would decide that. Rather, it meant good guidance, both spiritual and military, and the ability to negotiate all the different groups that made up this rather motley set of crusading forces. As with individual crusaders worthy of memory, personal and institutional relationships at least partly account for the ways in which Crusade leaders were represented. Both John of Brienne and Pelagius had their own attachments and obligations, and Perry is right to point out that the "papal-Hohenstaufen rapprochement" was the real problem on the ground in Egypt rather than the personal relationship between these two individuals. The authors whose letters and histories survive to report and record what they considered the most important events of the Crusade sometimes also take sides along these lines. But more often than not, it is the pious commitment to the Crusade and all its eventualities that all authors—whatever their own allegiances—understand to be worthy of permanent record. In this way, the representation of leadership does not just speak of the events of the Crusade but also sets up the more enduring notion that good leadership under the umbrella of God's overall leadership was the most important story to tell. In terms of remembering, this tells us that there are clear links between the representation of events, the choice of individuals to tell particular stories about the past, and the didactic or purposeful functions of remembrance.

CONCLUSION

Combat stories narrated the proper way to get ready for battle (with spiritual and penitential preparation), the best way to conduct battle (with the prayerful help of others), and the appropriate way to conclude it (with thanks to God). All participants in the Crusade were deemed collectively worthy of remembrance if they fitted in with this scheme or could provide a useful counterpoint to illustrate the dangers of not abiding by its rules. The individual conduct of soldiers and Crusade leaders was dependent on spiritual integrity and pious resolve just as much as it was marked out by military capacity or, in the case of leaders, the ability to guide and oversee the resolve of others. Again, remembering individuals was attached to the work of the larger group.

The narrative strategy of individualizing war stories that I discussed in the previous chapter in relation to Jacques de Vitry's own letters is thus more overtly deployed in other texts with the purpose of illustrating the higher ideals of the Crusade. When individuals or groups like the Frisians are named in the narratives, they serve to communicate to particular audiences the "right" way to conduct a Crusade. As I have mentioned here, the authors of the main narratives—Oliver of Paderborn, Johannes Codagnellus, and others—were keen to relay the memory of these groups to those audiences who would relate to them most directly. But we can also see that the recording of names and deeds co-opted the memory of crusaders for didactic and spiritual purposes. The cultural scripts brought to bear on the stories these men chose to tell (the narrative arcs, the images, and the biblical or historical allusions) located crusaders in a larger story that transcended the Fifth Crusade itself. Remembrance of individual crusaders was subsumed by the more important work of communicating piety, right conduct, and collective commitment to the service of God.

In answering the question "Who was worth remembering?" we might therefore reply, "Everyone and no one." War memory privileged the collective, although ties of kinship and association between individuals were certainly integrated into its communication. Models of exemplary conduct were named, and the highly individual spiritual work of prayer, for instance, meant that the behavior of each individual crusader was represented as critical to the Crusade's outcome. But the dominant form of remembrance that we find in the narratives of the Fifth Crusade is crafted around the collective. Indeed, some have termed "official" memory as being written there. The historical texts that organize remembrance of the Crusade draw on and perpetuate hegemonic narratives of purpose, conduct, and results that are intended to illustrate the worthiness of the Crusade.[79]

At the same time, it is also clear that there is a complex set of interactions between what Wulf Kansteiner called "memory makers, memory users and . . . traditions of representation."[80] Remembrance projects in the thirteenth century were not solely top-down impositions of general "collective" memories, nor were they solely the creation of those with lived experience of events. Rather, we see in the case of the Fifth Crusade that remembering was understood to be dynamic and relational as well as instructive. Those who claimed authority to create "official" or dominant memory also understood the importance of the individual experience in illustrating the power of the collective. That the individual did not dominate historical narratives of the Fifth Crusade must be understood in the contexts of traditions and choices of representation and the intentions of memory-makers themselves. In this regard, it is necessary to understand something more of representational choices and authorial intention. In the following chapter, I consider the explanatory force of remembrance and the construction of a transcendent meaning for war.

CHAPTER 4

Remembering Loss

> Since He now saw that we had been sufficiently purified by penance and a fountain of tears, He mitigated the cruelty of our enemies to such an extent that they sent messengers to us, who were wasting away with hunger, to treat of peace and concord with us.
>
> Let all posterity know that in view of the critical point of our necessity, we made an excellent bargain.
>
> With great sorrow and mourning we left the port of Damietta, and according to our different nations, we separated to our everlasting disgrace.
>
> —OLIVER OF PADERBORN

Along with Jacques de Vitry, Oliver of Paderborn is the most well known of the Fifth Crusade's participants and supporters. Born around 1170, Oliver was master of the cathedral school at Paderborn by 1200 and then head of the cathedral school at Cologne shortly thereafter. Alongside Jacques and Robert of Courçon, Oliver was designated a preacher of the Fifth Crusade, traveling to the Low Countries from 1214 to 1217 and then departing for Acre in mid-1217.[1] Oliver of Paderborn's remarks about the end of the Fifth Crusade in Egypt capture something of his desire to acknowledge and explain the Crusade's disastrous conclusion and to construct the story of the Crusade as part of God's plan. Oliver was not alone in trying to make sense of the loss of Damietta, the loss of many lives, and the loss of morale at various times during the Crusade and then afterward. A letter written to the Earl of Chester in 1222 also spoke of the great misery and suffering of the crusaders as they tried to move upstream, reporting that "in this condition our people agreed to a truce," an outcome for which "we were much grieved." Another letter (from Peter Montacute, a Templar) in 1222 reported how the crusaders were little more than a "famished army" by the time Damietta was given up and were consequently forced to agree to "a confirmed truce for eight years."[2] In offering explanations for the outcome of the events, these writers were also quite careful about how they represented the Crusade. Oliver of Paderborn, who had been so instrumental in Crusade preaching and who, as we saw in the previous chapter, also played a decisive military role in the events, was keen to craft a story about this recent past that would concomitantly shape future understandings of the Crusade and create a lasting set of mostly more positive meanings about what had occurred.

By writing their narratives, men like Oliver of Paderborn tried to ensure that the Crusade would be remembered as possessing a meaningful nature and purpose that transcended the immediacy of events. In this chapter, I discuss the explanatory function of remembrance—that is, how attributing meaning to a past event fixes (or attempts to fix) how that event will be remembered in the future. In the case of the Fifth Crusade, some narrative texts sought to formalize remembrance of the Crusade by relating it to transcendent discourses of time and space. Both Jacques de Vitry and Oliver of Paderborn suggested an apocalyptic immanence was part of the Crusade—through the integration of prophecy in their narratives, they looked back in biblical time to situate the act of crusading as part of an eschatological story that foresaw the eternal future. These and other writers also reflected on how the Crusade mirrored (or at least emulated) Christ's suffering. The messages of sacrifice and suffering in their texts reassured crusaders and others of the significance of their own actions in the present and the importance of the act of crusading in general. At the same time, communicating the transcendent meaning of the Crusade became material and visible. In the case of the consecration of mosques as Christian holy spaces after the capture of Damietta, for example, we see very clear and overt evidence for a systematic memorial project that was meant to eradicate the Muslim past and inspire future ritual reflection and celebration of the Christian victory. Together, such narrative and material strategies brought together and manipulated different temporalities—biblical time, Christian time, historical time, and future time—to explain and give meaning to the Crusade and to construct its memory.

Historians of war have frequently discussed the creation of meaning around conflict in terms of the particular demands of the modern state.

George L. Mosse, for instance, discusses how a widespread desire to find a higher meaning in the carnage of the First World War came to be transformed into what he calls "the myth of war experience," where "the memory of the war was refashioned into a sacred experience" tied to the cult of the nation.[3] Ashplant, Roper, and Dawson also identify the construction of memory in terms of hegemonic narratives about war that are created by nations intent on organizing its commemoration; they describe this process as the creation of "official" or "dominant" memories to shape future stories about war, drawing on inherited tropes such as sacrifice, duty, and loyalty. These tropes are historically specific, as are the national contexts in which they are rehearsed and disseminated. But the idea that meaning for war could be linked with its immediate and ongoing remembrance is something that was clearly shared by the medieval clerics who wrote about the Fifth Crusade. They used text and space to maintain myths of transcendent meaning for the conflict in which they had played a role. And they were concerned with explaining not only what had happened on Crusade but why. Explaining and remembering were thus very closely linked.

Before I turn to how "explanatory" remembrance was expressed, it is important once again to recognize that the construction of remembrance about the Crusade was directed by mostly clerics to specific groups and individuals—clerical and monastic, in the main—and only then further afield. In the case of Jacques de Vitry, his letters went to Pope Honorius III, his former Parisian teachers, John of Nivelles, the beguines of Oignies, the Cistercian nuns of Aywières and their abbess, Duke Leopold of Austria, and various unnamed friends. As I discussed in the second chapter of this book, these letters privileged Jacques's status as an eyewitness to the events in order to communicate his own experience and authorial authority. In the case of Oliver of Paderborn, his account of the capture of Damietta was also initially composed in epistolary form (as two letters that were then later compiled into a more extended chronicle).[4] The account of the Fifth Crusade that we now know as the *Historia Damiatina* was the third of Oliver's writings composed on Crusade and sent to Cologne, and it formed, in effect, the last part of what was supposed to be "a complete history of the Holy Land from Adam to Oliver's time." The *Historia Damiatina* only found its form as a coherent chronicle after the outcome of the Crusade was known.[5] The subsequent and complex dissemination of these texts is similarly important to at least acknowledge. The twenty-three manuscripts

88   WAR AND MEMORY AT THE TIME OF THE FIFTH CRUSADE

of the *Historia Damiatina* attest to its circulation, for instance. And because Oliver, like Jacques, continued to preach the Crusade after he returned from the Holy Land, we might assume that at least some of the content and tropes of his *Historia* may have found new audiences via preaching.[6] In other words, the content of some of these well-known narratives of the Fifth Crusade was still being shaped (through redaction and reception) after their authors returned home to environments where new demands for explanation were being made.

PROPHECY AND TIME

Constructing meaning for all Crusades involved placing them in a larger spiritual and temporal context. This is particularly evident in the rhetoric of Crusade preaching and participation, where prophecy and the idea of apocalyptic immanence were embedded right from the start. Indeed, Jay Rubenstein has argued that the idea that the first crusaders were bringing about the last days was not just one reason the call-up was so successful but the principal reason.[7] Matthew Gabriele usefully notes that for some crusaders, what had been prophesied in Revelation was thought to be in the actual process of the transformation to the Apocalypse—that is, what was foretold was thought to be actually occurring at that time.[8] Evidence for a relationship between the Crusades and the Apocalypse may be found throughout the twelfth century, although references to eschatological ideas are not necessarily consistent or explicit in all Crusade texts. But when such allusions do appear, they certainly communicate that, as Nicholas Morton recently wrote, "something truly momentous was happening."[9] Guibert of Nogent, for instance, reported that Pope Urban II spoke at Clermont in 1095 of the nearness of the time of the Antichrist, and almost a century later, Roger of Howden described Richard I of England's meeting with Joachim of Fiore at Messina in 1190, during which Joachim explained the relationship between Saladin and the end of days.[10] The appearance of celestial phenomena and the occurrence of miracles and visions en route confirmed the cosmological and eschatological nature and consequence of crusaders' actions. Elizabeth Lapina found that the chroniclers of the First Crusade who recorded celestial phenomena such as comets and fire in the sky—from west to east—were using these signs and cardinal points to communicate the broader "logic of sacred history in its entirely, stretching from the Fall to the second coming . . . chroniclers suspected that this spread of Christianity from west to east was to bring about the end of time, which the spread of Christianity from east to west a thousand years earlier had failed to do."[11] The events of the Crusade and the actions of crusaders were hoped to cause the heavenly Jerusalem to descend, bringing together sacred and terrestrial space and ushering in a new age.

Later Crusades were also sometimes narrated as either the precursor to the sequence of events leading to the last days or the actual fulfillment of apocalyptic prophecy. During the Fourth Crusade, for instance, Pope Innocent III's letters of November 1204 and January 1205 to Latin clerics in Constantinople described the capture of the city as a precursor to the Second Coming of Christ and a sign of the immanent beginning of the "Sabbath Age."[12] Innocent's vision of the coming together of East and West derived in part from the contemporary *Expositio in apocalypsim* of Joachim of Fiore, whose commentary on the ages of history described Muhammad as the fourth head of the seven-headed dragon and Saladin as its sixth head. It outlined how the Saracens would persecute the Church during the fourth age and the sixth age, which would precede the eventual Sabbath Age, or age of the Holy Spirit.[13] In the Fifth Crusade, these dimensions were also sometimes present in the preaching and dissemination of the Crusade message. In *Quia maior*, Pope Innocent III again spoke of God's present sign "that the end of this beast [i.e., Islam] whose number according to John's Apocalypse counts 666, of which now almost six hundred years are completed, approaches."[14]

But the eschatological dimension of crusading was not only a rhetorical device designed to underscore the transformational nature of the Crusade or to provide extra stimulus for Christians to participate in the urgent recovery of the Holy Land. Rather, prophecy and the intimation of the beginning of the last days could also be of tremendous pragmatic and military impact. This is especially and famously true for the Fifth Crusade, when the course of events was twice determined by prophecy—or, at least, it was represented as doing so. Oliver of Paderborn reported that "before the capture of Damietta there came to our attention a book written in Arabic" that prophesied the events of the recent crusading past, including the successful capture of Damietta, and predicted future successes for the Crusade, which would capture all of Egypt. This book, known in Röhricht's modern printed edition as the *Prophecies of Hanan*, was summarized by Oliver in a section of the text (numbered 35 in Hoogeweg's edition) immediately after his account of the end of the siege of Damietta (chapter 32) and his description of the meaning of that event (chapters 33 and 34). In chapter 33, the city of Damietta is represented as a woman who has been punished for uncleanliness and who has now cast out "the adulterer whom you kept for a long time [and who has] returned to your former husband." The city's surviving infants were cleansed by Jacques de Vitry "in the sacramental waters of baptism," and Oliver intoned that "you who first brought forth bastards now shall bear legitimate sons for the faith of the Son of God."[15] This short chapter is followed by another, which commends Cologne for providing more aid for the Crusade "than the rest of the German kingdom." Significantly, this chapter, immediately preceding the description of the prophecy, tells that "our illustrious emperor and king of Sicily is being eagerly awaited by the people of God for the happy consummation" of the Crusade.[16] In this way, the circulation of a series of predictions about the Crusade—some already proven to be true—occupies a meaningful place in Oliver's narrative. It ties together the immediate history of the Crusade with prophesied future events, situating them in the present situation of Frederick II's imminent (or thought to be imminent) arrival and what arguably marked the high point of the entire Crusade and the promise of an even more glorious future.

Things were different in the crusader camp by the time Oliver recorded another prophecy, sometimes known as the "Book of Clement." As James Powell has narrated, by 1221, the stalemate that followed the capture of Damietta had both sapped morale and caused friction among the crusader leaders. It was at this time that another peace offer was made by Al-Kamil (in the spring of 1221). This is the context in which the circulation and meaning of another prophetic text should be understood. Oliver summarized the content of the book. He reported that the text was also written in Arabic and that it was read aloud at Pelagius's command "in the hearing of the multitude" with the assistance of an interpreter.[17] The book began with the creation of the world and ended "in the consummation of time," and it contained prophecies already fulfilled, including the capture of a "watery city" in Egypt together with another Egyptian city. It also told of two kings, one from the East and one from the West, who would come to Jerusalem in the year when Easter fell on April 3. The latter event would occur in 1222, the following year. Again, Oliver connected the prophecy to current events. Just prior to his inclusion of the discovery of the prophecy, he tells of the imperial coronation of Frederick II in 1220, the rising of the river Nile, and the connection between the king of the Persians (i.e., Genghis Khan) and King David, son of the mythical Prester John.

Jacques de Vitry's letter of April 1221 to Pope Honorius contains one of the most well-known of the accounts of the mythical Prester John (who is sometimes conflated with King David). The tale had, by the time of the Fifth Crusade, been in circulation for more than half a century.[18] This myth was current from 1145 through the writing of Otto of Freising, who included in his history of the world the story told to him by a bishop of Antioch about the Christian king *presbyter Johannes*, who was from the family of the magi and and who held an emerald scepter. A letter purportedly from Prester John began to circulate around 1165 (addressed to the Byzantine king Manuel Comnenus), in which it was claimed that he ruled over the Three Indies. This letter was translated into European vernaculars and circulated widely. Jacques de Vitry's letter includes the story of Prester John (in this text known as the *Historia gestorum David regis Indorum qui presbyter Johannes a vulgo appellatur*) in the context of both the stalemate after Damietta's capture and a moral and spiritual reinvigoration of the crusading army.

Just prior to his description of the Prester John myth, Jacques wrote of the Lord's army newly burning with spiritual fervor, having been cleansed by expelling prostitutes from the camps and forbidding drinking—it was as though the Lord's host had become a monastery, he wrote approvingly.[19] The inclusion of the prophetic history of Prester John at this point of Jacques's narrative constructed the episode as an impetus to action in a time of new spiritual determination and as a harbinger of a larger and more widespread promised victory. Again, it was connected to the hoped-for arrival of Frederick II, which would bring a great force in August of that year to rout the Egyptians.[20] The truth of the prophesied events to date was supported by other prophetic works that were being circulated at that time; Jacques de Vitry had also received three short texts in Arabic from Bohemond of Antioch (including the "Book of Clement"), which he translated in abbreviated form in the same letter. Those texts predicted the taking of Damietta, victory over the pagans, the Judgment, and "then the end" (*inde iudicium et finis*). These were "joyous rumors" (*rumores iocundos*) that inspired renewed confidence, faith, and hope among the Christians.[21]

Most historians have considered the prophetic elements of the Fifth Crusade in functional terms, specifically in relation to the subsequent decision of the legate Pelagius to move the troops upstream to Cairo, thus precipitating the failure of the Crusade overall. More recently, and in relation to Jacques de Vitry's *Historia orientalis*, Jan Vandeburie suggested that Jacques had placed the "events of the Fifth Crusade in an apocalyptic setting" to give a "sense of urgency to the reform of the Church and the recapture of Jerusalem."[22] This can also be seen in one of Jacques's later sermons to potential crusaders, one of which opened with a theme from the book of Revelation—"I saw an angel rising from the sunrise carrying the sign of the living God, and he called in a powerful voice to the four angels whose duty was to devastate the land and sea: Do not devastate land and sea nor the trees, until we have signed the servants of our God on their foreheads."[23] Others, especially later authors, related the growing importance of conversion and mission to the representation of the Crusade as eschatologically significant.[24] We might also consider the prophecies as authorial strategies to both explain and give meaning to the broader landscape of events. This is done through the interplay of the different temporalities contained in the prophetic "genre" and the careful inclusion of prophecy in these particular eyewitness narratives. The Crusade is represented as a part of a set of prophecies that would ultimately precipitate the last days: Oliver of Paderborn and Jacques de Vitry both collapse time in order to show that the Crusade (the present) was part of a prophesied sequence (outlined in the past) that would lead to the Apocalypse (in the future). That the Crusade did not ultimately match the prophecies or their imagined outcomes mattered less than its temporal representation as part of a larger and more important Christian story.[25]

THE VALUE OF SUFFERING

Despite these promising prophetic signs, the Crusade was not able to fulfill its early promise, and the death toll in Egypt was high. Some crusaders and pilgrims were killed in battle, others died from outbreaks of disease and illness, and others disappeared into captivity. Although some of these men were consciously identified and named in the narratives of the Crusades in order to praise or disparage individual and collective behaviors, suffering and death on Crusade also provided medieval commentators with opportunities to inform and edify present and future audiences about the value and meaning of the Crusade itself. Often the narratives emphasize the suffering that was endured by those who participated in the Crusade, looking back to Christ's suffering in order to express the hope that crusaders, by emulating and sharing in this pain, could look forward to eternal life. At the same time, emphasis on suffering was meant to shift the explanation for the Crusade's failure from being a military defeat to being a divinely ordained outcome with individual and collective rewards.

Suffering in imitation of Christ and for Christ brought together the corporeal reality of warfare and the spiritual motivations that justified it. In the case of bodily pain, crusaders were told that suffering cleansed them and was the outward demonstration of their individual commitment to God's work. The physical wearing of the cross identified crusaders with Christ, of course, but in some cases, this was also reinforced by stories, especially from the First Crusade, of the divine imprint of the cross on a crusader's flesh.[26] The idea that crusaders' suffering imitated Christ's suffering did not mean that the pain was considered precisely equivalent, however. In Pope Innocent III's 1208 letter to Leopold, Duke of Austria, he famously compared the suffering of Christ to the somewhat easier work of the Crusade, reminding the duke that "you receive a soft and gentle cross; he bore one that was sharp and hard. You wear it superficially on your clothes; he endured really in his flesh. You sew on yours with linen and silk threads; he was nailed to his with iron and hard nails."[27] But remembering Christ's suffering was integral to understanding the transformative potential of the Crusade for each individual. The *Ordinacio de predicatione S. Crucis* was very clear about the need for crusaders to understand that taking up the cross required a complete inner and outer conversion and that imitating the suffering Christ was part of the process of salvation. Christ provided a model for crusaders to imitate, according to this text, which focused Christ's body and wounds.[28]

Bodily pain and suffering while on Crusade are also narrated in the texts that sought to explain the course of events. The long period of stalemate between the taking of Damietta and the decision to move toward Cairo was a particularly despondent time for the army. Sporadic skirmishes and the outbreak of this disease combined to send morale plunging, and those who wrote about this period draw particular attention to the physical suffering of the army. The flesh-eating disease that swept through the crusader camp, killing many (including Robert of Courçon), was described by Oliver of Paderborn quite graphically: "A sudden pain attacked the feet and legs and at the same time corrupt flesh covered the gums and teeth . . . a horrible blackness darkened the shins and . . . very many went to the Lord with much suffering."[29] Crusaders drank fetid water and died of dysentery from the very start of the Crusade, while Jacques de Vitry also told of the contagious illness sent by God, which "no art of medicine could cure" and caused the limbs of the soldiers to swell and putrefy. But all this illness and suffering was an expiation of sin, according to Jacques, and the deaths that ensued were, he thought, a gift to God.[30] He wrote that this was an illness without any physical cause; rather, it was divinely inflicted upon the army as a healing and spiritually effective instrument of God's will.

Other descriptions of suffering in combat offer a similar transcendent and consoling meaning for injury and death. The beheading of crusaders on the day of the Feast of the Beheading of St. John the Baptist in 1219 was a time of terrible suffering for the Christians, who were also forced to listen to the Egyptians "cum cimbalis, tubis, tamburiis et vocibus exultantes" (with cymbals, horns, drums and cries of joy) as they celebrated their victory. For Johannes Codagnellus, this was a time of lament. But it was also a moment to talk about martyrdom and the promise of comfort in eternal life. It is at this point that he narrated the story of the thought-to-be-dead German soldier who opened his eyes to see a great man in white and a crowd of angels hovering over his dead companions and citing Revelation— "Here are they who have come from great tribulation and washed their robes in the blood of the lamb."[31] The dreadful deaths of the Christians are strategically positioned in this episode to make prominent the more eternal message of consolation. Oliver of Paderborn equated the suffering of the army with its corruption and sinfulness but also thought that God's mercy mitigated and corrected human fault. Describing the flooding of the Nile in the summer of 1221, which precipitated the end of the Crusade, Oliver wrote that some of the crusaders were "struggling wretchedly in the mire" while others drowned after having drunk too much wine during the night. Hunger eventually forced them into "a lamentable peace" with the Egyptians, according to Oliver. But he wrote that the "astounding thing, a thing to be handed down to the knowledge of the future," was that although the crusaders "fell into danger," it was so that God could exercise the "mediation of mercy." "Although we may be sinners," wrote Oliver, "nevertheless carrying His Cross we have left homes or parents or wives or brothers or sisters or sons or fields for the sake of Him who shows anger placidly, who judges calmly, who chastises lovingly, having the blows of the father, but the heart of a mother."[32]

The relationship between suffering and martyrdom is, despite the example of the heavenly angelic host congregating over the bodies of the dead, not quite as frequent in the Fifth Crusade texts as one might expect. Although Bachrach suggests that the Crusades generally resulted in a renewed emphasis on martyrdom as the explanatory framework for death in combat, other historians have noted that thirteenth-century writing on the Crusades does not make martyrdom especially prominent. For instance, Caroline Smith has suggested that martyrdom remained a contentious issue during the thirteenth century, and there seems to have been some deliberate ambiguity about its achievability simply on the basis of how one had died. In other words, certainty about whether someone was a martyr or not seems have been premised on the context of the virtue of a life rather than simply circumstances of death. And Barbara Packard speculated that the rise of heresy and the desire to prevent false prophets from assuming spiritual status through the performance of suffering may also account for early thirteenth-century reticence to describe more Crusade deaths in terms of martyrdom.[33] In the context of the Fifth Crusade texts, we can see that suffering is occasionally specific—narrated as injury, hunger, or disease—but that it is a mostly capacious category, only occasionally connected to the specific condition of martyrdom. Mostly, physical suffering is deployed in the texts as a way of reminding the reader of God's higher purpose and the exercise of his mercy.

As Oliver of Paderborn intimates, suffering could also be expressed as a mental and emotional condition. Crusaders are often represented as recalling their personal pasts during the crusading present, emphasizing the anguish of separation and distance, while mental suffering is also frequently included in both the vernacular texts and clerical writings. As noted in the second chapter of this book, Jacques de Vitry was concerned to include the emotional nature and consequences of being an eyewitness to conflict. At the same time, his letters indicate that he was also interested in locating his experience at least partly within the framework of suffering. Mostly this was done through the inclusion of his reactions to his travels, especially his constant statements about missing and needing his friends. His first letter, composed just prior to the Crusade proper, states that although he had started his sea journey to Acre in good health and high spirits, with his companions and affairs intact, he nonetheless requested that his friends immediately pray for both his safety and that "God should guide him to the port of Acre and then to the port of eternal beatitude."[34] Jacques was quite overt about his mental state:

> Between various pains and continual fatigue and many disagreeable things that plague my travels, I have for the only remedy and consolation the memory always present of my friends; thanks to them my spirit is sustained and because of whom, fortified by their prayers, my soul is preserved from complete weakness. But the same remedy brought by memory that cures my wounds is sometimes source of new wounds in my heart . . . my spirit is so occupied by the thought of my friends and acquaintances that almost all the other preoccupations are no more than boring; therefore the taste for prayer and the desire to read evade me because of all this concern.[35]

The memory of his friends providing him comfort but engendering distraction is repeated in a subsequent letter when Jacques again describes being continuously afflicted by tribulations and exposed to daily danger. The one thing that provides him comfort, Jacques writes, is remembering his friends in his prayers.[36] Quite frequently, Jacques notes that he is in good physical health but that the journey itself is something of a mental and spiritual test. On the way to Acre, for instance, a near miss with another boat saw panic erupt on Jacques's ship. Some of the sailors took pity on him and tried to get Jacques to evacuate to a smaller and safer boat, but he refused because he did not want to set a bad example (*malum exemplum*) and wanted to face the same dangers as the others.[37] The idea that the journey was a continual but meaningful trial is extended in both Jacques's letters and other sources to describe the emotional and mental hardship of the act of crusading itself, which necessarily separated a crusader from his home and loved ones. Jacques himself, despite his own expressed feelings of sadness about being so far from his friends, nonetheless talks with admiration about those who left their families, children, wives, and possessions to take the pilgrimage to eternal salvation. In his fifth letter home, Jacques genders the Church feminine to describe her as a wounded and weeping widow, who "in our times has inspired many of the sons of the church to sympathize with the sadness of their mother" and to take up the cross.[38]

The pain of separation from family and friends while on Crusade was not limited to Jacques de Vitry, of course. One of the key features of the many French and Occitan "Crusade songs"—composed in the twelfth century in the genre usually described as *chansons de departie*—is the trope of the knight leaving behind his lady.[39] One song composed by the so-called Châtelain d'Arras, probably around 1213–17, when he intended to leave for the Fifth Crusade, laments that "I have to go to where I shall suffer pain, to that land where God was tortured; there I shall have many heavy thoughts, when I shall be far away from my lady; and be well aware that I shall nevermore be happy until the hour when I shall have her close. Lady, have mercy! When I return, I beg you for God's sake to take pity on me."[40] For this singer—like Jacques de Vitry—the separation from loved ones is represented as certainly painful but concomitantly as an opportunity to express resolve: "I go off to the kingdom of Syria without a heart: it remains with you, it is its sweetest gain. Worthy lady, how will my body survive alone? If I have yours (your heart) for company, I shall be constantly more joyful and fight better: thanks to your heart I shall be bold in battle."[41] A song by Aimeric de Pegulhan written around 1213–15 provides a similarly reassuring message, singing that "a man should not fear to suffer death in God's service, for He suffered it in ours so that those who follow him over there to Mount Tabor will be saved along with St Andrew. No-one should be afraid of this carnal death on the journey; he ought more to fear spiritual death where there will be weeping and gnashing of teeth, for St Matthew shows this and guarantees it to be true."[42]

Other crusaders expressed similar sentiments. One song, composed by Hugues de Berzé before he went on the Fourth Crusade (sometime between September 1201 and June 1202), confronted the pull between love of God and love of his lady. "A crusader in love," he wrote, "must well ponder whether to go towards God or to remain here, for no-one, once Love has taken hold of him, ought ever to assume such a heavy burden: one cannot serve more than one lord; but since a noble heart that aspires to high honor cannot avoid doing this, you ought not, my lady, to blame me for it." And in another verse, he reiterated, "Ah, lady, there is no more room for indecision!—I have to leave you without delay; I have gone so far that I cannot turn back. But if staying behind were not a base and shameful thing, I would go and ask true lovers for permission to remain; yet you are of such great worth that your lover ought not to fail in his duty."[43] These sorts of sentiments were social and moral "touchstones," in Routledge's words, for knightly behaviors.[44] These songs were often produced by and for the aristocratic men who were active crusaders, such as the northern French knight, the Châtelain d'Arras. At the same time, Crusade songs were highly stylized; the trope of the heart far from home, the themes of praise and blame, and the integration of courtly love motifs were formulations common to many of these songs. The expression of suffering and separation in these lyrics thus brings together the rhetorics of suffering and love that were integral to the meaning of crusading itself. Indeed, as Lisa Perfetti recently suggested, the crusader's suffering in the songs "testifies to the deep-seated appeal of sacrificial desire as a way to demonstrate virtue in courtly culture."[45]

Prominent in such representations of emotional and physical suffering is reflection on the past. For the clerical authors of the Fifth Crusade texts, remembering Christ's suffering alongside the purpose of individual suffering while on Crusade was a clear narrative strategy linking the eschatological story with contemporary action. Remembering family and friends in letter and song was not so much an opportunity for writers and singers to express their own "real" feelings as it was a chance to communicate the great personal sacrifices crusaders were making by leaving their loved ones and familiar landscapes behind and the great devotional commitment to Christ that crusading entailed. In so doing, the individual difficulties of the act of crusading were explained as both necessary and exemplary. Suffering in the present brought individual and collective future reward. At the same time, recourse to biblical explanation could mitigate what must have been a traumatic set of experiences—if not for those who endured them, then for those who later heard or read about them.

BUILDING THE FUTURE BY REMEMBERING THE PAST

Once the crusaders had captured Damietta and entered the city, one site became of particular interest—the central mosque.[46] Oliver of Paderborn tells us that once the city had been cleared of bodies and disinfected, the mosque of Damietta was consecrated as the Cathedral of the Holy Virgin by Pelagius on the Feast of the Purification on February 2, 1220. Altars dedicated to St. Peter, St. Bartholomew, the Virgin, and the Holy Cross were added to the building, which seems to have been of grandiose scale. Oliver wrote the following:

> The mosque of Damietta, through the invocation of the holy and undivided Trinity, was converted into a church of the blessed

and glorious Virgin Mary. Being built in square form, we can see almost as much of its width as we can of its length. It is supported by one hundred and forty-one marble columns, having seven porticoes, and in the middle a long wide-open space in which a pyramid ascends on high in the manner of a ciborium; beyond the west side a tower rises in the manner of a campanile. Four main altars are built in it: the first under the title of Blessed Mary; the second of Peter, the Prince of the Apostles; the third of the Holy Cross; the fourth of blessed Bartholomew, on whose feast the tower in the river was captured.[47]

Spatial claims over Damietta were then extended: the houses of the city were divided up among the various crusading groups, and the remaining population was ransomed, enslaved, or in the case of some five hundred infants and children, baptized and given away—some to Jacques de Vitry's friends.[48] The occupation of the city was similarly recorded in other texts, which also noted that Damietta's "high church, formerly the chief mosque," was assigned a new archbishop and that various lords and princes were given "rich and handsome residences within Damietta."[49] The *Rothelin Continuation* also reported that the churches that had been mosques were furnished with rich adornments and that "great care and determination, great thought and judgement did the king apply to these things and to others by which the service of Our Lord should be maintained in the city of Damietta and in that land, and the Christian faith be upheld and respected."[50]

The conversion of the main mosque into a cathedral was particularly meaningful, as it not only demonstrated the present occupation of the city but also represented the displacement of Islam from Damietta's spiritual landscape and the growing intent of thirteenth-century crusaders to convert the wider population of Egypt and beyond. At the same time, it seems that the mosque was always intended to serve memorial purposes. The ceremony of consecration conducted in the old mosque was also a memorial service of thanksgiving, conducted by the papal legate. Jacques de Vitry reported that it was an emotional affair, "with tears and intense popular devotion" evident in the crowd that filled that great basilica, and the Divine Office was repeated "day and night without a break" throughout the city.[51] The gathering in the basilica commemorated a moment of military and spiritual victory by providing a moment for thanks, by ritually cleansing the city of its past pollution (both physical and spiritual), and by delineating the building itself as a new venue for ongoing remembrance. The mosque was now the seat of an archbishopric and the center of the newly Christianized city, the lordship of which was formally entrusted to the king of Jerusalem.

Like Jacques de Vitry, Oliver of Paderborn reported in his chronicle that the aftermath of the siege was horrific to witness. He provided a graphic account of the corpse-strewn streets of Damietta, the suffering of its inhabitants, and the decimation of the population. He linked the fate of the people to prophecy, quoting Isaiah—"Instead of a sweet smell there shall be stench, as rotten carcass shall not have company in burial"—and numbered the dead at eighty thousand. The conversion of the mosque is narrated in some detail in Oliver's account. He particularly emphasized the scale of the mosque itself and discussed its interior architecture, describing the installation of new altars. Oliver's account of the newly converted mosque is striking for a number of reasons, not the least of which is his overt attempt to connect the visual dimensions of the structure with familiar European and Christian architectural forms. The campanile-like tower, the ciborium-like pyramid—these are described in ways that not only resonate with Western observers of the built environment but also render the old mosque as a space devoid of any non-Christian visual history. The observer (in this case, the reader of Oliver's text) is invited to see a Western structure in a newly Christianized landscape—not an unfamiliar building in an unfamiliar world.

Recent work by Amy Remensnyder has shown how consecrations of mosques as churches during the medieval and early modern periods were always acts of eradication intended to "remove the stain of Islamic idolatry."[52] This was effected by similar rituals throughout the Iberian Peninsula and beyond, including a procession around the exterior of the building, prayer, sprinkling the walls and floor with holy water, and waving thuribles of incense throughout the space. Thirteenth-century commentators on the ritual of consecration noted the particular symbolism of sprinkling the holy water: Jacobus de Voragine, for instance, was clear that there were three reasons for this liturgical effort—to drive out the devil, to purify the space, and to remove all maledictions.[53] Likewise, the specific dedication of the mosque to Mary was particularly important. As an inviolate and chaste figure, Mary symbolized an enduring purity; as a figure of intercession, Mary was also redemptive. This meant that any capture of a church dedicated to the Virgin was a particularly heinous violation, as William Durand explained in the later thirteenth century. In his *Rationale*, he wrote that consecration "appropriates the material church to God ... it is endowed and becomes the proper spouse of Christ, which it is a sacrilege to violate adulterously."[54] In the specific context of Damietta too, the presence of Mary in the biblical history of Egypt meant that she had a particularly meaningful association with the region and so offered it, in theory, her special protection.

We know little of the conversion of other specific sites in Damietta, with two exceptions. To recognize the special role played by the English in the siege, two mosques were allegedly turned into churches dedicated to Edmund the Martyr and Thomas Becket, respectively. The English sources for these churches are keen to stress the links between the martyrdom of Edmund and Becket and the crusaders' defense of the faith. A miracle of retribution occurred against a man who insulted Edmund in the Damietta church, for instance, and the wall paintings in the building (now destroyed) depicted the death of the saint at the hands of the Vikings.[55]

Both Jacques de Vitry and Oliver of Paderborn represented the capture and Christianization of Damietta as an act of territorial entitlement based on biblical association. The building stood as a reminder to the remnant of the Muslim population that their world had now changed; eyewitnesses such as Jacques and Oliver were keen to assert that the city would be forever Christian. The cathedral was also a place where military and spiritual victories were commemorated, and it provided a practical material environment for thanksgiving, ritual observance, and ongoing commemoration of the events of 1220. Of course, this was not to last. It was only a year later that the crusaders were forced to evacuate Egypt entirely after their failed attempt to move to Cairo.

Yet the occupation of Damietta, no matter how brief, had larger implications for later Crusades. A letter composed by Sarrasin in June 1249 during the Seventh Crusade states, "The day after the Feast of St Barnabas the Apostle, the king [Louis IX] led the entry into Damietta, had the main mosque and all the others in the city dismantled and rebuilt as churches dedicated to the glory of Christ."[56] Once again, the most significant site of Islamic worship in the city was given a new purpose, and once again the other, smaller mosques dotted throughout Damietta were also Christianized. Sarrasin's letter hints at the material violence that accompanied these acts: not only were these buildings overlaid with a new religious identification, but they had first been "dismantled." It is not clear from the letter what this entailed in practical terms, and there is no evidence that the buildings were completely razed to the ground by these later crusaders (although according to another eyewitness, the inhabitants of the city set fire to it as they abandoned it).[57] Rather, it would seem that the practice of stripping the liturgical furnishings from the mosques, as had been done during the Fifth Crusade, was repeated. The pulpit, for instance, was removed, as were the bells, which seem to have been distributed beyond Damietta for other uses.[58] The stripping of the mosque seems to have been galling for the Muslim population of the city. As late as 1282, it was still remembered that the Franks had taken the pulpit from the great mosque at Damietta "and cut it up and sent a piece to each of their kings." Ibn Wasil wrote that once the Muslims retook the city, they refused the Franks permission to take with them some "enormous masts for the ships" until the damaged pulpit was returned. This was not done, and Ibn Wasil noted that the Franks were forced to give up their claim to the masts.[59]

The public liturgies of cleansing performed in 1220 were replicated in 1249. One eyewitness recorded that all the Crusade faithful returned to the cathedral, "having shed in their rejoicing tears of gladness and devotion" in a barefoot procession led by the legate (Eudes of Châteauroux), while chanting the *Te Deum laudamus*: "Where the Christians long ago had been in the habit of celebrating Mass and ringing their bells, he purified the place and sprinkled it with holy water before having the Mass of the Blessed Virgin celebrated."[60] It was with wonder that Gui of Melun reflected that only three days earlier, this building had been the site for the glorification of "the most filthy Mahomet . . . with abominable sacrifices, cries from on high and the blast of trumpets." In vivid contrast to the noise and chaos of Muslim worship, according to Gui, came the order of the Christian consecration ritual, accompanied not by shouts but by gentle weeping, with the building cleansed not with blood but with holy water. Gui represents the whole city as washed clean with the arrival of more Christians "in the manner of a lake which is broadened as it is flooded by torrents."[61]

But it was Louis IX who laid claim to the city and its surrounds. He was reported to have brought with him "ploughs, mattocks, drays and other farming equipment" and allegedly told the sultan that "I made a vow and an oath to come here . . . but I took no vow or oath to leave; nor have I set a date for my departure. That is why I have brought with me the tools of cultivation."[62] Louis certainly knew the symbolic value of consecrating the Damietta mosque. He issued a foundation charter in November 1249 in which he represented the occupation of the city as a gift from God and the act of consecrating the cathedral as an act of gratitude. Rejoicing that Damietta had been "utterly purged of the pagans' filth," Louis reclaimed complete possession of the city for Christianity, asserting that Damietta had been received from God's hand "emptied of enemies."[63]

The mosque itself was surrounded by various buildings, which Louis granted to the archbishop of the cathedral ("Two towers together with the neighboring dwellings, the structure which was known as the 'Mahomerie' and the courtyard that adjoins these towers"). The newly installed canons of the cathedral were granted "the compound that extends from the stone stairway ascending to the walls . . . as far as the street lying between the two houses which the Patriarch holds and the house of St Lazarus, along with all the dwellings and the courtyards included within it." This occupation of urban space also involved administrative responsibilities and fiscal benefits. The archbishop and chapter, for instance, were granted the right to levy tithes "on all leases in the city and diocese of Damietta that would accrue to its lord." This included tithes on mills, baths, fisheries, ovens, money-changing and minting, port dues, weights and measures, bird snares, and salt springs—"in general all the revenues of the city." The archbishop was to receive two-thirds of this revenue and the canons and ministers one-third. More gains were contingent on the whole of Egypt being "liberated from the infidels," including the fiefs of ten knights who would serve the archbishop in perpetuity and the grant of ten thousand besants of annual revenue to the archbishop, canons, and ministers of the cathedral. These were confident promises, and Louis expected that once he returned to France, whoever was in charge of Damietta would ensure they were carried out: "We desire and command that if the above assignments are not made over by us to the same church in whole or in part before we depart from this side of the sea, whoever governs the country in our stead is bound to make them over in their entirety as detailed above."[64]

A new discourse underpinned the conversion of the Damietta mosque in 1249. This was the notion that the crusaders of Louis IX's army were *retaking* Christian property that was rightfully theirs. The formality of the charter did not only indicate how the urban landscape was to be possessed and administered; it indicated how the king understood Christian occupation of the city to be legitimate. This is entirely in keeping with territorial claims increasingly made by crusaders beginning in the mid-twelfth century, when recovering lands gained and then lost during previous Crusades became sufficient motivation and justification for new holy wars to be launched. Damietta was no exception. Although the aim of Louis IX's own Crusade was to recover Jerusalem, its policy to destabilize Egypt first was both a military decision and a spiritual one. Remembering the occupation of Damietta during the Fifth Crusade—just as Jacques de Vitry and Oliver of Paderborn would have hoped—was part of Louis IX's Crusade motivation and justification.

CONCLUSION

This chapter has sought to look at how both narrative and material strategies formalized "official" memories about the past. By including the tales of prophecy in their texts, authors like Oliver of Paderborn and Jacques de Vitry located future understandings of the Fifth Crusade in the context of a more important and eternal Christian story, one that transcended the immediate historical moment. Biblical Christian time is deployed in their texts to communicate very deliberately the enduring and fundamental importance of undertaking God's work. At the same time, themes of suffering and separation were included in these texts to demonstrate the great sacrifice that individuals made as crusaders and to remind future crusaders of the innately purposeful nature of taking up the cross. These written attempts to communicate and explain the meaning of the Crusade despite—or perhaps because of—its unwelcome outcome sought also to determine how the Crusade would be remembered in the future. It may have failed in its intended military sense, but it succeeded in providing evidence of God's will, individual and collective devotional commitment, and the exercise of divine mercy. Moreover, it succeeded in creating what crusaders in the future would understand to be Christian territory in Egypt. The careful physical and material efforts to alter the landscape of Damietta were also part of this formalization of memory. By colonizing the sacred space of the city, performing liturgies of cleansing and thanksgiving, and occupying its houses, the soldiers and clerics of the Fifth Crusade constructed Damietta itself as a site of memory and made visible the domination of Christianity over an Islamic landscape.

Formalized discourses of remembrance absorbed individual and collective experiences into a framework of explanation that privileged the communication of the broader purposes of crusading. Men like Jacques de Vitry were quite clear about the immediate goal of the Fifth Crusade; he wrote that the crusaders were all present so that "in the promised land the Lord's vineyard [will] be increased, the churches repaired, the infidels ejected, the faith restored, the walls of Jerusalem our enemies destroyed be built, that he will be pleased with the sacrifice of righteousness, with burnt offering and whole burnt offering, and we will worship where his feet have stood."[65] But how crusaders and the Crusade were to be remembered demanded attention to more inventive and careful discursive strategies. Such strategies needed to address multiple audiences in the present and in the future, explain the Crusade and encourage others to emulate its participants, and even provide solace to those who might have expected a grander success after 1219. In shaping such memory, the meaning of the Fifth Crusade became part of an ongoing and uplifting story of Christian history, even despite its pain and failures.

CHAPTER 5

Places of Remembrance

Memorials claim a collectivity of memory.
But places are always connected with elsewheres.

—DOREEN MASSEY

Where the "gold-bearing" Tagus River joins the western sea lies the ancient city of Lisbon.[1] According to its medieval visitors, this was a very fine city, built on a steep hill that overlooked the treacherous but alluring Atlantic Ocean. Legend tells that Lisbon was founded by Odysseus after his departure from Troy, although by the thirteenth century, the city was more famous for its cathedral treasury that housed the precious relics of St. Vincent. Medieval Lisbon was also a place founded on more recent stories of war and battle, in which remembrance of crusading was embedded and encouraged. Captured by a group of German, Frisian, and Anglo-Norman crusaders in 1147 and then handed over to King Afonso Henriques, this most glorious Christian city had been taken from its Muslim rulers and "cleansed": in the words of an observer of the Siege of Lisbon, its pre-Crusade population had been so dense that "each man was a law unto himself" and so disparate that "the basest element from every part of the world had gathered there, like the bilge water of a ship, a breeding ground for every kind of lust and impurity."[2]

During the Siege of Lisbon in 1147, the bodies of those who had died were buried in cemeteries, and after the capture of the city was complete, two commemorative churches were built to honor São Vicente de Fora of the German troops and Santa Maria dos Martiros of the Anglo-Normans. At the cemetery of São Vicente de Fora, miracles were reported to have occurred in 1147 around the graves of the fallen German and Frisian soldiers, especially the tomb of Henry of Bonn, a leader of the German contingent.[3] These miracles were reported back in the German lands and in Portugal itself and retold in the foundation history of São Vicente de Fora, which was composed in 1188 to give the newly founded monastery a venerable and appropriate past.[4] In 1217, a group of German and Frisian crusaders stopped at Lisbon on their way to the Fifth Crusade. They had already "sought out the shrine of the glorious St James in Compostela" but came to São Vicente de Fora to pay their respects at the tomb of the fallen soldiers of seventy years earlier.[5] In particular, they wanted to see the tomb of Henry of Bonn. One account reported, "To the east outside the city is a venerable cenobium where a beautiful palm tree rose into the air from the sepulcher of the martyr of Christ and leader of the Christian peoples lord . . . Henry. Seventy years ago along with his squire he ended life in Christ and is now canonized by divine revelation in earthly and eternal glory."[6]

The 1217 visitors to Henry's tomb were men who had no direct memory of the events of the 1147 siege and capture of Lisbon. But a shared language of attachment drew them into a landscape of remembrance that stretched across decades and from the edge of the western sea to the gray north. These new crusaders from a different generation found both inspiration and solace at Lisbon. Looking back at their successful crusading forebears and looking forward in hope to their own Crusade to Egypt, the 1217 crusaders understood São Vicente de Fora to be a sacred place of remembering, a reminder of the triumphs of long-gone soldiers and a promise of the domination over Islam that they hoped to achieve for themselves.

As I have argued in previous chapters of this book, medieval people's remembrance possessed a spatial logic that was both mental and material—the real and the imagined were often elided. For crusaders in particular, whose preachers told them that they were liberating Christ's patrimony from unjust occupation and that their encounters with sacred places were commemorative acts, the links between imagined and real locations were always clear and often connected by remembrance. Preaching the Fifth Crusade, Jacques de Vitry reminded crusaders that they were physical pilgrims but their journey was a transcendent exercise in interior virtue: "Pack your baggage for exile," he stated. "You ought to migrate from place to place, that is from virtue to virtue." He warned the crusaders that only the wicked "change their homeland but not their behavior, [such people] hasten across the sea changing the skies above them but not their souls."[7]

Crusader journeys were interior and spiritual just as much as they were physical and terrestrial. They were justified and animated by the memory of biblical history, claims to ownership of place and the crusaders' physical relocation from one place to another.

Yet Crusade places were also consciously remembered and commemorated as locations of conflict and war, where battles had been fought and where soldiers had died. Such places included the city of Lisbon, which was particularly meaningful to quite a small and specific group of northern Europeans. Here was a memorial site that had been constructed to commemorate a military success that itself signified spiritual triumph. Gathering around the tomb of Henry of Bonn, visitors to São Vicente de Fora were presented with the evidence of crusader martyrdom and God's will in material form—a monastic attempt to stabilize remembrance and promote this historical episode of war as a reminder of the dominance of the universal Church and the collective character of crusading itself.

Places of remembrance may well intend to create stable repositories of meaning, but meaning shifts depending on individual and collective encounters across time. This is especially true of places associated with remembering war. In a modern context, physical monuments such as war memorials never tell an uncomplicated story of war, its victories and losses, even if that is their claim. Such places are politicized, often exclude difficult wartime stories, and are used to build national narratives and perpetuate national myths: they frequently assert a cohesive historical representation and collective contemporary reception that sometimes has no place for exceptions, nuances, and pieces of the past that complicate a single narrative. And how people encounter those places is also contingent on both individual subjectivity and temporal context. Places of remembering can connect the living with the dead and the past with the present and provide locations for grieving, but they do so in multiple ways, for diverse audiences, and at different times.[8]

If modern places of war remembrance reinforce collective identity, collapse the past and present, and even perform therapeutic work, then what did medieval places of war remembrance do? In this chapter, I explore how places of crusading remembrance were created and manipulated rhetorically and physically in the early thirteenth century. Ownership of specific topographies was asserted in texts that justified crusading by linking particular territories with Christian history. At the same time, the material culture of remembrance, especially the built environment, came to assert the ownership of places and their stories most visibly. Sites like São Vicente de Fora claimed and perpetuated war remembrance by both sacralizing a physical topography and inviting encounters with that topography across time.

CLAIMING PLACES

Every Crusade was underpinned by the fundamental claim that a particular place was being unjustly occupied by an invader and that it was the collective duty of Christians to reclaim that territory (often expressed as Christ's patrimony). What exactly constituted Christian territory was mostly very clear to crusaders: it was the land where Christ lived and died, Christian lands "polluted" by heresy or invaded by non-Christians, and (increasingly) land won on previous Crusades that had now been lost. Such places were remembered because it was understood that they had been legitimately and collectively possessed by Christians in the biblical or historical past. In the case of Lisbon, for instance, it was increasingly asserted that the city (and its surroundings) had been Christian territory since late antiquity, held by the Visigoths until they were pushed north by the invading Moors. The discourse of "reconquest" that was eventually shaped to justify Christian expansion in the Iberian Peninsula was premised on a territorial claim to place that saw historical possession as deeply entwined with religious legitimacy. The author of the *De expugnatione Ulixbonensi* wrote that the Siege of Lisbon was justified as an act of vengeance against those (i.e., Muslims) who had despoiled the Church, made captives of priests, and stolen Church property. He declared that among the motives that made this a just war was that it was fought to recover property. And in a speech ostensibly directed to the Muslim defenders of the city, the archbishop of Braga stated, "You are holding our cities and landed possessions unjustly—and for three hundred and fifty-eight years you have so held them—which before that were held by Christians."[9] Such words indubitably justified the attack on Lisbon on the grounds of prior ownership.[10] But they also established remembrance of past possession as the marker of the significance of place.

The ideological development of the notion of Christian property and legitimate ownership owed much to St. Augustine. Material possession, according to Augustine, was part of an ideological scheme in which property ownership was a civil right based in natural law but the right to retain property was a matter of *divine* law. Augustine wrote that God had given the right to own property only to the just and that those who were not just did not have the right to material possession.[11] This theology of ownership conferred by divine law on the just also argued that the right or just use of property was necessary for possession to be retained and that property could be confiscated if it was not being used justly. The idea that Christian property was being despoiled was incorporated into Crusade preaching as part of the justification for war: Pope Urban II was said to have told his audience at Clermont in 1095 that the Turks had not only seized "more and more of the lands of the Christians" but "devastated the kingdom of God." Gregory VIII lamented in *Audita tremendi* (1187) that "the infidels invaded and ravaged everything so that it is said that there are very few places left which have not fallen into their hands [and] those savage barbarians [have been] using all their force to profane the Holy Places." Innocent III reported in *Post miserabile* (1198) that "the sepulcher of the Lord has been profaned by the unrighteous and has thereby been made inglorious" (quoting Isaiah 11:10).[12] Tales of unjust and unrighteous use of Christian property by non-Christians was brought together with reminders of collective Christian obligation to recover for Christ his patrimony. And as Jonathan Riley-Smith points out, the idea of the Holy Land being the hereditary patrimony of Christ was powerfully communicated: crusaders were told that they themselves were part of the Christian family whose property was being violated by its illegitimate occupiers, while dozens of Crusade sermons and *excitatoria* included the mournful words of Psalm 78: "O God, the heathen have come into thy inheritance."[13]

Connections between Christian places and Christian ownership were rhetorically consolidated in 1213 with the issue of Pope Innocent III's great crusading letter *Quia maior*, which instigated planning for the Fifth Crusade. *Quia maior* framed the impending Crusade as a test of faith for a Christian community, in which "evil now abounds and the charity of many has become cold." The Crusade would provide an opportunity and reason for salvation, and its great outcome would be the liberation of the Holy Land. The image of the holy places in captivity was sharpened by the depiction of the crusaders' "brethren in faith and the Christian name . . . imprisoned by the faithless Saracens in a cruel prison and [enduring] the harsh yoke of slavery." Freedom for them would come with spiritual freedom for those who traveled to the Holy Land to rescue them, while the more precise territorial justification for war followed. Innocent reminded his readers that "indeed the Christian people possessed almost all the Saracen provinces until after the time of St Gregory" and decried the loss of Christian sites in the Holy Land. He wrote of the "faithless Saracens" building a fortress on Mount Tabor, "where Christ showed the nature of his future glorification to his disciples. By this they think that they may be able to occupy the nearby city of Acre quite easily and then without resistance invade the rest of the land."[14] *Quia maior* also asked all Christians to remember the loss of these Christian sites during a new monthly procession (for men, though women could participate in a separate one), in which prayers for the restoration of the Holy Land were sung and fasting and almsgiving were also encouraged. When the rite of the Mass was celebrated, Christians were instructed that after the pax, they were to prostrate themselves on the ground while Psalm 78 was sung by the clergy and then followed by a prayer for the liberation of the Holy Land.[15] This new collective ritual element to Crusade participation was certainly an individual act of penitence, but it reflects some deeper connections between remembering and place, expressed in terms of both ownership and obligation.[16]

Others who participated in the Fifth Crusade also made the connection between place and remembering by stressing the links between particular topographies and biblical history. This is especially evident in the accounts of the Crusade written by the senior ecclesiasts Oliver of Paderborn and Jacques de Vitry. Both men had preached the Crusade prior to joining it themselves, and both were noticeably concerned with communicating the events of Christian history in their accounts of the regions through which they traveled. Although Oliver's account of the capture of Damietta is his most well-known communiqué from the battlefront, his lesser studied writings are important sources of information about holy places and how they were meant to be remembered in the context of early thirteenth-century Crusade history.[17] The *Descriptio terre sancte*, for instance, was written for the participants of the Fifth Crusade and for future pilgrims who might wish to know more about the lands in which Christ walked. This text derived from (and mostly copied) an earlier account by Eugesippus-Fretellus and was framed as a narrative of actual and potential Christian redemption, describing locations that were then attached to biblical and occasionally more recent history. Beginning with Hebron, the ancient home of the

Philistines, as Oliver notes, the area is identified as the place where the four "most reverent fathers"—Adam, Abraham, Isaac, and Jacob, together with their wives, Eve, Sarah, Rebecca, and Leah—were entombed and the region where the "promised land was first explored." Linking this site with the history of creation itself, Oliver turns to significant locations in the vicinity, noting the Valley of Tears (where Adam wept for a hundred years over the death of Abel), a field where the earth is red, a hill near where Abraham lived, and the oak tree (*ylex aut quercus*) under which he was visited by angels. He also mentions some significant rulers of the area, such as David.[18] This sort of description then continues throughout the text in a narrative that culminates in a long account of the significant sites of the Passion of Christ.

Because Oliver was writing in the midst of the Fifth Crusade, his account of the holy places also incorporates some references to moments in crusading history. He notes in the *Descriptio* that pilgrims could see the castle of Montreal that was established by the first Frankish king of Jerusalem to protect the land that the Christians had subjugated.[19] And he records that the "most noble city of the Phoenecians," Tyre, was known for the marble seat on which Christ sat when he performed miracles of healing (Matthew 15), "unharmed from the time of Christ until the expulsion of the people from the city, but later robbed of the French and Venetians [in 1124 during the capture of the city]."[20] Relics are also mentioned, especially those with some European or Byzantine connection: Oliver repeats the legend that Christ's foreskin was brought by an angel to the Emperor Charlemagne at Aachen and then placed later in a church at Charroux in France.[21] And he places some emphasis on the relic of the True Cross, which had been lost to Saladin at the Battle of Hattin in 1187. These relic objects underscore the materiality of possession in crusading discourse. The loss of relics such as the fragment of the True Cross was used to motivate continued military action and to forge links between the crusaders and the places they encountered.

Christian claims to the Holy Land and its significant sites are extended in the *Historia de ortu Jerusalem*, which was probably composed in February 1220 or 1221 and relies heavily on the *Historia scholastica* of Peter Comestor. This text describes the long genealogy of rulership of Jerusalem from Old Testament kings to Frankish kings while also including Egypt as part of Christ's patrimony. Oliver wanted to place Frankish kings in a direct line of descent from the rulers of the Old Testament and was especially interested in telling his readers that it was the Germanic kings who were the most recent inheritors and members of this genealogy. Listing biblical rulers from Cain and his descendants, focusing on the Books of Kings and integrating classical figures such as Darius, Xerxes, Alexander in Egypt, and various Romans, Oliver delineates the long history of territorial claims on the Holy Land. He tells of the coming of Islam (*heresy Machometina*)— "which lasts, alas! to this present day"—and mourns the capture of Jerusalem before turning to the Frankish claims to rulership. This is a carefully constructed list of names that would certainly have resonated with his German readership. Beginning with Pippin, the first Frankish inheritor of the *imperium*, Oliver lists the Merovingian and Carolingian rulers before stating that now the *imperium* had transferred to the Germans. In the year 1096, Duke Godfrey (of Bouillon) with "a multitude of those signed by the cross, overcame the holy city of Jerusalem held for so long by the Saracens." The end of this text thus invokes the memory of the successful First Crusade as a motivation for the participants of Oliver's own Crusade and a reminder that the linear trajectory of possession of the holy places continues through the instrument of crusading and its personnel.

Statements of territorial ownership made by those who preached the Crusade—high-ranking ecclesiasts such as Oliver of Paderborn or Pope Innocent III—reveal how remembering the recent and distant past was understood to be an important way of forming collective and meaningful attachments to particular places. Those attachments were made even more evocative by the historical narration of their threatened or actual loss. In Oliver of Paderborn's *Historia regum terre sancte*, which was compiled in the Egyptian city of Damietta while the siege of the city was in progress, this is apparent. Unlike his other commentaries of the holy places, Oliver's *Historia* is an abbreviated history of the Crusades, beginning with the sermon of Pope Urban II at Clermont in 1095. Drawing heavily on Fulcher of Chartres for the early period and William of Tyre for the more recent past, Oliver declared that many things worthy of remembering (*res dignam-emoria*) occurred during the First Crusade in particular. These "worthy" things included the names of the leaders of the First Crusade as well as signs of divine intervention like the miraculous sign of the cross appearing on drowned pilgrims or the appearance of Christ in a vision to the men of Antioch.[22] But they also included moments of awful defeat, such as the fall of Edessa (1144) and the loss of Jerusalem itself in 1187. Given that Oliver wrote in the midst of the Fifth Crusade, he was also concerned with encouraging rousing military success. As he narrated the various twelfth-century conflicts in the Holy Land, he told a story of both past triumph and future encouragement. Again, the German emperors are singled out as potential sources of inspiration, including Frederick Barbarossa (chapter 98), Henry (chapter 108), and Frederick II (chapter 111). At the same time, Oliver reported the loss of holy places and things and the death of so many crusaders who fought "manfully" (*viriliter*) for the defense and liberation of Christ's patrimony. He included a short section toward the conclusion of the text on the internal threats to Christendom in the form of pagans and heretics in Livonia, Estonia, Prussia, and the region of Toulouse.[23]

Oliver was also aware of the places that were immediately pertinent to his audience, and he spends some time describing Saladin's successful defense of Damietta in 1169. The strategic value of this topographical information was germane, as was the following information on Egypt, which was thought to be about to fall to the Christians. Egypt itself was a generally meaningful locale both for Oliver and for other writers of the Fifth Crusade. The Crusade's presence there was a pragmatic decision aimed at gaining territory that could lead to access to (and possibly negotiation for) the Holy Land of Jerusalem. Egypt also provided a spiritually valuable objective, which integrated sites once frequented by Mary, Moses, and other Christians into Christian possession. The deliberate familiarizing of the Egyptian environment is also emphasized in a later portion of Oliver's *Historia Damiatina*, where he described the land surrounding Damietta in terms of its biblical associations. He noted that a church dedicated to the Virgin stood between Cairo and Babylon (Alexandria) some three days from Damietta, which was the place where Mary and Christ stopped to rest. He tells about a garden located one mile from Cairo in which Mary was said to have washed the clothes of the infant Christ. The garden now contained a tree from which balsam emanated: "The master of this garden is a Christian," wrote Oliver, "having Christian and Saracen servants under him."[24] Others, including Jacques de Vitry, were also keen to connect the occupation of Egypt to a longer tale of Christian ownership described in the biblical past. Although this landscape—where the undulating Nile seemed almost magical in its power to simultaneously flood and fertilize—was certainly strange to these writers of the Fifth Crusade, it was also a place that was profoundly recognizable and constantly animated as a sacred space in the collective Christian imaginary.

Also of strategic and discursive interest was Mount Tabor in the Holy Land, near the Sea of Galilee and famous to Western and Eastern Christians as the place of the transfiguration of Christ, who had appeared there to Peter, James, and John, bathed in shining light (Matthew 17:1–9). It had a significant history of Christian ascetic activity during the crusading period. Hermits lived in caves there—apparently one from the time of the First Crusade—and ecclesiastical sites had been constructed beginning in the twelfth century, churches dedicated to the Transfiguration, Moses, and Elijah. A Benedictine monastic house had been established right at the start of the twelfth century ("the monastery of the Holy Savior of Mount Tabor"), which was protected first by the pope and then by the patriarch, its privileges upheld by successive twelfth-century popes. Although a massacre of the monks threatened the existence of the monastery in 1113, it was reestablished and became a place of burial and pilgrimage. An orthodox monastery existed there too. Mount Tabor was raided by Saladin in 1187, prior to Hattin. Once a truce between the barons of Acre and the Ayyubids expired in 1210, Mount Tabor was again under threat. Al-Adil started fortifying it (as it is next to the main road from Egypt and Syria), and this new set of fortifications was, of course, Pope Innocent's immediate impetus for launching the Fifth Crusade. The crusaders attacked the Muslim fortress there, and although it held up, the Muslims nevertheless decided to destroy it to prevent it from falling into Christian hands in the future.[25]

Christian writers thus understood the importance of Mount Tabor in spiritual and military terms. Due to its close distance to Acre, Pope Innocent III worried in *Quia maior* that having built a fortress there, "the Saracens . . . think that they may be able to occupy the nearby city of Acre quite easily and then, without any resistance, invade the rest of this land." The mountain is often represented by medieval pilgrims as a particularly paradisal location, verdant and lush, rising from its flat desert surrounds like a ladder to heaven. Mount Tabor contrasted with the rocky, dry terrain of Mount Sinai, the scene of another revelation (of Yahweh to Moses).[26] Oliver of Paderborn thought that "Christ Our Lord reserved this triumph of the mountain for Himself alone, since He ascended it with a few disciples, pointing out there the glory of future resurrection"; this was why the attack on the mountain by John of Brienne and others was not successful at the outset of the Crusade.[27] In his *Descriptio terre sancte*, Oliver briefly concentrated on the biblical resonance of Mount Tabor, noting that this was where God announced during the Transfiguration "hic est filius meus dilectus" to the apostles and locating the site itself four miles from Nazareth.[28]

The passage of time did not diminish medieval people's connection with the places identified as part of Christ's patrimony. If anything, texts that claimed holy places as Christian territory augmented subjective and collective attachments to place. By claiming possession of places theologically and historically, preachers of the Crusade drew on and encouraged remembrance of terrestrial locations as part of Christian eschatology. In so doing, Christ's patrimony could be extended in both idea and reality. Although concepts of ownership were not always uniform across Western Christendom, papal and clerical discourse did invite and communicate a common understanding of what constituted Christian territory that was founded on both imagined and historical relationships with the past.

MAKING SACRED PLACES

After the monastery of São Vicente de Fora in Lisbon had been founded to commemorate the actions of the crusaders of 1147, the initial memories of eyewitnesses to the siege of the city were written down to encourage others to view this monastic foundation as a place of crusading remembrance. These miracle stories were transmitted across the decades to the crusaders of the Fifth Crusade, who visited Portugal in 1217 due to the foundation history of the monastery of São Vicente composed around 1188. In this text, the eyewitness accounts were integrated into the story of the monastery's establishment and the articulation of that monastery as a sacred space. Integral to its sacrality was the monastery's connection to the memory of the Second Crusade.

The foundation history of São Vicente de Fora is known as the *Indiculum fundationis monasterii S. Vincentii*,[29] and it was written in Lisbon by an anonymous author. It recounts the events around the Siege of Lisbon and claims to have interviewed eyewitnesses who participated in the events in order to offer an account of how the monastery came to be established. The text opens by locating the circumstances of the monastery's foundation in the context of holy war, describing Afonso Henriques as a "courageous extirpator of the enemies of the cross of Christ" who conducted annual expeditions against the "Saracens." The *Indiculum* reports that in 1147, his "chosen band of strong men whom the Lord had sent, raised by zeal . . . from the northern parts of diverse people" arrived by boat to participate in the Siege of Lisbon.[30] They were experienced soldiers, "fearless," willing to follow Afonso's orders and united in purpose, but they were divided ethnically: the English camped on one side of the city and the Germans on another. Nonetheless, the crusaders together fought bravely for the love of Christ, according to the author, and their interment in the separate burial sites of São Vicente and Santa Maria recognized them as martyrs.

The miracles narrated in the *Indiculum* established the centrality of the German and Frisian crusaders—described generally as *christicolae* and ethnically as *Franci*—in the Siege of Lisbon by attaching the location of these marvelous occurrences to the tomb of Henry of Bonn, one of the leaders of the Crusade. Henry himself remains a rather shadowy figure whose subsequent reputation as a brave and pious martyr derives entirely from the *Indiculum*. In this text, he is described as a "knight of Cologne named Henry born in a town some four leagues outside Cologne named Bonn, a man steeped in nobility and custom who died in the fight for the city."[31] He, like the others who died during the siege, was a martyr "precious in the eyes of God" (*in conspectu Domini preciosam existere*). The site of Henry's grave was the proximate location for instructive miracles wrought by "divine work." These miracles occurred while the siege of the city was still taking place.

The first miraculous event was a healing first reported in the Anglo-Norman and German accounts. In the *Indiculum*, this miracle became a little more descriptive. It was said that two young men, deaf and mute from birth (*duo iuvenes ambo surdi, ambo muti a nativitate*), were watching Henry's tomb one night when they had a vision of the martyred crusader holding a palm frond, who asked them to stand guard. *Mirabile dictu*, wrote the author of the *Indiculum*, the two youths were suddenly able to talk and hear as if they had always been able. Everyone who heard of this miracle was thus convinced not only of God's wonder but also of Henry of Bonn's rightful status as a martyr of Christ (*habentes de cetero militem Henricem utpote dilectum martyrem Christi*).[32] Another miracle also located at Henry's tomb described the death of one of Henry's arms bearers and his interment at some distance from Henry's own tomb. At night, the guard of Henry's tomb was confronted by the figure of the dead Henry, who, calling him by name, insisted that his comrade be moved to lie next to him. This occurred three times until Henry, now angry, finally got his way, and his comrade was moved to his rightful place next to his lord.[33] The third miracle that was explicitly attached to Henry's tomb told of the miraculous sprouting of a palm tree at the head of Henry's grave, which had grown from fronds laid down at the tomb after his burial. Pilgrims and locals came to see this marvelous tree, which was said to exude magical healing properties. They wore its fronds around their necks and ground them into powder, which they drank to cure illness.[34]

Although the imagery of the palm fronds has been the most frequently noted element of these miracles, especially their associations with both pilgrimage and martyrdom, the sacralizing of space also occupies an important symbolic role in these tales. The particular location of the cemetery and the tomb of Henry of Bonn are constructed here as fecund and holy sites around which it was appropriate for a monastery to be founded. The building of the monastery itself occupies the subsequent chapters of the *Indiculum*, and Afonso Henriques himself is praised as the pious patron of this holy location. The miracles, then, work to activate the site as sacred space in similar ways to other medieval cult sites. At the same time, the miracles suggest that sacred space is carefully delineated: access is allowed to pilgrims seeking healing, the arrangement of space is meaningful, and miracles are visible only in the location itself.

These points are underscored by another miracle, first reported in the *De expugnatione Lyxbonensi*, which recounts the discovery that the bread used for Mass was bloodstained:

> A portent appeared among the Flemings. For on a Sunday after the completion of mass, a priest observed that the blessed bread was bloody, and, when he directed that it be purged with a knife, it was found to be as permeated with blood as flesh which can never be cut without bleeding. And afterwards it was divided into fragments of the same bloody appearance and it has now been seen for many days after the capture of the city. And some interpreting it, said that this fierce and indomitable people, covetous of the goods of others, although at the moment under the guise of a pilgrimage and religion, had not yet put away the thirst for human blood.[35]

As Stephen Lay has pointed out, the version of this miracle that appears in the *Indiculum* is less critical of the northern crusaders and rather more elaborate:

> It happened that people who went into battle, after the solemnities of the Mass, desired to fortify themselves with the *eulogia*, that is, the blessed bread. This became a daily habit. When the priest wanted to break the bread into pieces to distribute them to each person, and already had got a knife to cut the bread, behold a thing of wonder: the sliced bread was bloodied and the blood was still exuding from it. Then the priest and all who were present were seized with sudden astonishment and then at the sight of this thing, were alarmed. When the cause of this was investigated, it was discovered that the bread had been made with stolen flour that a dying man had sent to distribute to the poor. When at last it was revealed in the camp, all came to see the spectacle and seeing what had happened, they returned full of wonder, not doubting that divine assistance was with them, full of faith, they praised and glorified God, who alone who makes miracles.[36]

The bloodlust of the crusaders in the earlier version is now absent, and the tone of the miracle is less cautionary and more celebratory. Lay is correct to read the *De expugnatione* version of this miracle as illuminating some fundamental tensions around crusading motives, suggesting that the *Indiculum* version is more concerned with setting up the conditions for martyrdom. Lay also interprets the "dying man" who donated the flour to have been a crusader, although there is no evidence for this in the text—the phrase *quidam moriens* is simply too general to denote a crusader or even anyone necessarily associated with the army.

There is, however, a little more to the *Indiculum* version of this miracle that may shed further light on this foundation history as a memorial document. First, the motif of bleeding bread is a clear reference to the sacramental theology of the Eucharist, in which the hidden presence of Christ in the sacrament is occasionally made visible in the form of blood and sometimes flesh, as famously demonstrated in the sixth-century Mass of St. Gregory. By the twelfth century, the ideas that the body and blood of Christ could be present in the bread and wine of the Mass had a long and venerable history. As Steven Justice has recently demonstrated, this remained a logically problematic claim for medieval Christians, even as stories of the appearance of Christ and his fleshly qualities proliferated throughout the high Middle Ages.[37] Peter Lombard's *Sentences* named the Eucharist as one of the seven sacraments in 1140, and by the time the *Indiculum* was composed in the 1180s, the word *transubstantio* was in use, although it was not yet conclusively articulated as part of Eucharistic theology until 1215.[38] Indeed, the later twelfth century was an important moment in the enshrinement of the notion of the real presence, and it is perhaps not surprising that it should be included as a foundational moment in the history of a new monastery such as São Vicente. The suffusion of the "blessed bread" in the *Indiculum* miracle evidently took place in the context of the Eucharistic ritual: the bread was consecrated by the priest, who dispensed it, and the crowd interpreted the presence of blood as a sign of God's presence and miraculous power. The Eucharistic ritual itself was, of course, innately commemorative, as Christ's words in Luke 22 instructed.

At the same time, the detail that the bread had been made with stolen flour is an interesting inclusion in the text. This may be read in a number of ways, most obviously that the substance of flour itself might be understood to represent the body of Christ. Christ referred to himself as a grain of wheat (John 12:24), and twelfth-century commentators on the sacraments understood that it was important to make the host from wheat alone because "if it is made from another grain it cannot be offered; what we have said [about the nature of the sacrament] makes sense by the change whereby in substance it is transformed into God's body."[39] Other writers echoed this sentiment. Even Abbot Suger, writing of the "anagogical window" at St. Denis that showed the apostle Paul turning a mill, considered that "by working the mill, Paul, you take the flour from the bran. You make known the inner meaning of Moses' law. From so many grains is made the true bread without bran. The perpetual food of men and angels."[40] The "inner meaning"—the flour—is the redemptive truth of Christ's presence. The sustaining nature of Christ, represented in the artisanal images of the mill, grinding grain, and the production of flour, may also be seen in representations of Mary and the infant Christ with a mill grinding grain. As Caroline Walker Bynum points out, in such representations, the body of Christ, ground but fleshly, was also meant to communicate ideas of both fertility and redemption through sacrifice.[41]

Importantly, the miracle also stresses that the dying man had intended the flour to be distributed to the poor in an act of charity, but it had been stolen, a fact that was revealed by its spontaneous bleeding. This bloody revelation also discursively connects to better-known bleeding host stories, mostly related to anti-Jewish rhetoric that told of stolen hosts dripping blood to reveal both the sacrilegious theft and the omnipresence of Christ. The proliferation of these stories from the twelfth century is well known, and they were used to illustrate the threat posed by outsiders, especially Jews and heretics, to the mystical body of the Church.[42] It is interesting to note that similar imagery can be found in the *Historia Albigensis* of Peter of Vaux-de-Cernay, who was writing of the Albigensian Crusade between 1212 and 1218, just prior to the Fifth Crusade. The *Historia Albigensis* tells of a miracle that occurred near Carcassonne. Readers are told that a group of heretics were harvesting their crops on the day of the Nativity of John the Baptist. One of these men looked down at his hand and saw that the bundle of corn he was holding was bloody. He thought he must have cut his hand but realized that this was not the case and there was no injury to his flesh. When this heretic called his companions, they too found that their bundles of corn were covered with blood although their hands were unhurt.[43] This episode is inserted in the *Historia* to show that the antisacramental stance of these southern heretics was unjustified. But it was also a reminder—as was the miracle of the bloody bread at São Vicente—that Christ was not only present everywhere but was specifically with the crusaders themselves. In both texts, blood is thus evidence of the sacrality of the crusaders' work and Christ's revelation.

In the specific context of the foundation history of São Vicente, it is significant that this miracle is included just prior to the account of the final defeat of the "pagans," the building of the monastery, and its subsequent growth. The author describes the miracles as invigorating and inspiring the crusaders, who were moved to fight with renewed vigor and ultimate success. Like the soldiers of the First Crusade, who found inspiration and renewed energy in the miraculous discovery of the holy lance at Antioch in 1098, the 1147 crusaders were fortified and encouraged by the real presence of Christ to overcome the defenders of the city. The *Indiculum* praises Afonso in particular and includes an account of the conversation between the king and the bishop that ended with the declaration that the bishop would be in charge of the church of Santa Maria and the king would oversee the basilica of São Vicente.[44] That the site of São Vicente de Fora was now a *loca sancta* was underscored in the foundation charter issued by Afonso, a copy of which was inserted into the *Indiculum*.[45] The charter made clear that the monastery had been established because of the success of the war against the Muslims (*Mauri*), thereby connecting the site forever with the memory of the Crusade.

Three principal German and Frisian eyewitness accounts of the crusaders' stay in Portugal during the course of the Fifth Crusade in 1217 mention São Vicente de Fora and its significance. These are brief accounts, to be sure, but they demonstrate that the site of São Vicente was still meaningful enough to be mentioned particularly. The eyewitness author of the *Gesta crucigerorum Rhenanorum* simply noted that Lisbon had been constructed by Odysseus after the fall of Troy and was now known for its devoted veneration of St. Vincent the martyr. He reported that the crusaders were in the city for some time (*aliquot dies*) before assisting with the capture of the fortress of Alcácer do Sal.[46] The anonymous author of the *De itinere Frisonum* is a little more informative. This text, composed during and after the Fifth Crusade, records that relics of blessed Vincent were housed in a silver sarcophagus in the church of São Vicente de Fora. This text offers a little more detail on the tomb of Henry of Bonn. The author reports that the palm tree over the grave of Henry of Bonn still remained to be seen by visitors to the city and describes Henry as a *princeps milicie christiane*, noting that seventy years before, he had died and was recognized for canonization "by divine revelation." Henry's tomb is described in relation to the landscape, describing that it lay in a "venerable cenobium where a beautiful palm tree rose into the air." Henry was a "martyr of Christ and leader of the Christian peoples," who had died seventy years prior, "and is now canonized by divine revelation in earthly and eternal glory."[47] This source was eventually included in the *Chronicle* of Emo, which was composed starting in 1219 at the monastery of Floridus Hortus in the northern province of Groningen.[48] Again, the city of Lisbon is briefly described, and the palm tree is particularly mentioned in almost exactly the same words as the *Itinere*.[49] The third relevant text composed during the Fifth Crusade is the idiosyncratic poem of Goswin, *De expugnatione Salaciae carmen*, a text of 230 verses that narrate the taking of Alcácer do Sal.[50] Although this poem does not explicitly mention Henry of Bonn, it certainly references the Siege of Lisbon and its relation to current events. At the end of the poem, it states that with the capture of Alcácer do Sal, "light shines again on Lisbon after seventy years."[51] The text's insertion into the *Chronica regia coloniensis*, along with other texts relating to the Fifth Crusade (including Oliver of Paderborn's own account), demonstrates both its interest to the church at Cologne and its perceived significance as a record of events in this region's history.

Moreover, the integration of miracles into the texts that describe the soldiers of the Fifth Crusade's experience in Portugal connects the activities of the 1217 soldiers with a longer history of God's work. In an account reminiscent of the portents during the Siege of Lisbon in 1147, miracles were said to have indicated to the crusaders that victory was ensured and imminent. According to Goswin's poem, a cross appeared in the sky—*quod splendet in aere*—just as crosses had appeared in the sky over Friesland during the preaching of the Fifth Crusade by Oliver of Paderborn. Reinforcements suddenly arrived when the crusaders' fortunes were at a low point. Finally, the Muslims suddenly found themselves blinded by a hail of arrows fired by a heavenly host of knights all clad in white.[52]

These short texts intimate that the memory of the 1147 Siege of Lisbon and the deeds of Henry of Bonn had, by 1217, entered the realm of what we might describe as cultural memory. In other words, seventy years after the events of the Second Crusade, there were no longer any who had personally experienced the siege or the initial establishment of the monastery of São Vicente de Fora. Those memories had been, via the accumulation of stories about the site, including the *Indiculum*, transformed into a more generalized commemoration of the place and its value to pilgrims generally and to crusaders in particular. The formal cenobium, the beautiful palm tree, the silver sarcophagus, and the enshrinement of Henry as a saint all created an environment of remembrance now far removed from the violent war that established the site—even if these things all hinted at the sacrifice, martyrdom, and miraculous events of that more distant past. Whereas the foundation history had sacralized this space in the context of monastic beginnings with a view toward creating a lasting memory of the particular location of Henry's tomb at São Vicente de Fora, the texts produced outside this specific monastic environment now spoke of space in a different way. Remembering was still attached to the same location, but the details of the miracles were no longer told, and sacrifice and redemption were not narrated by blood. Sacred space was now a more generalized phenomenon where meaning could be reshaped according to current interests.

CONCLUSION

Monasteries like São Vicente de Fora were not just places of remembrance in the medieval imagination. They were built environments that encouraged direct encounters through pilgrimage while also asserting a dominant story about the past. This can also be seen in religious sites not associated with crusading culture: monastic foundations such as Battle Abbey in England, for instance, commemorate the Norman invasion while also providing visible evidence of the connection between military victory and God's grace.[53] Sometimes building places of remembrance was also a way of eradicating other stories of the past, as discussed in regard to the cathedral of Damietta during the Fifth Crusade. In a triumphalist effort to sacralize the built environment and to make permanent the memory of the Crusade's finest hour, the cathedral was intended to embody and display a past free of Islamic history. As crusading increasingly took place in theaters of war outside the Holy Land later on in the twelfth century, places of war became more diverse. This did not mean, however, that they were less "sacred" or important in the mental landscape of crusaders and their descendants. On the contrary, in the first half of the thirteenth century, there were renewed and careful efforts to connect the fundamental territorial claims of the Crusade with multiple locations. Places were sacralized and built to assert old claims of possession and to display new successes. The communities that kept places of remembrance did so with specific local agendas in mind, but they also decided which stories would be attached to these sites or consigned to oblivion. In so doing, places perceived to be on the fringes of the crusading enterprise—São Vicente de Fora or even the port city of Damietta—could be fashioned as significant topographies of remembrance for local communities and for future crusaders.

CHAPTER 6

Coming Home

The Materials of Memory

> Minds joined by the Holy Spirit cannot be separated by geographical distance; those things that are imprinted on the minds of friends by the seal of love do not easily disappear with the passing of time.
>
> —JACQUES DE VITRY

> Such "testimonial objects" carry memory traces from the past, to be sure, but they also embody the very process of its transmission. They testify to the historical contexts and the daily qualities of the past moments in which they were produced and, also, to the ways in which material objects carry memory traces from one generation to the next.
>
> —MARIANNE HIRSCH

In 2015, a team of scientists from the Société archéologique de Namur in collaboration with the Belgian Fondation Roi Baudouin embarked on a forensic project called CROMIOSS (Études croisées en histoire et en sciences exactessur les mitres et les ossements de l'évêque Jacques de Vitry). This project is intended to find out whether a number of bones held in a reliquary casket at the Musée de Namur belong, as has long been assumed, to Jacques de Vitry. Jacques died in Rome in 1240, but some of his remains—bones and teeth—were collected in a reliquary box and sent to the priory of St. Nicholas at Oignies, where Jacques had requested he be buried. These body parts are now the subject of scientific analysis, along with one of

Jacques's miters, which was also left to the Oignies priory. Recent updates on the findings of the CROMIOSS team indicate that the bones certainly belong to a man of about 165 centimeters in height who died sometime during the thirteenth century and who was about sixty years old when he died. It seems highly likely that these are indeed Jacques de Vitry's bones. The miter is still under examination, and the expectation is that DNA from it can be matched with the bones. It was one of a number of objects given to the priory by Jacques over the course of his life and willed in his death, thus it is hoped that definitive scientific connections can be established between it and Jacques himself.[1]

As the Belgian scientific team understood, objects like the bishop's miter tell stories of connection between people and places. They bridge space and time by embodying and expressing the many associations that exist between individuals and communities. In so doing, they carry material traces of memory from past to present. Indeed, the importance of material culture in communicating memory is especially evident in the context of the Crusades. Crusaders on pilgrimage carried with them objects from home and brought back souvenirs from the Holy Land as tiny as stones or as large as reliquaries. Those on the home front, especially women, were gifted and cared for rings and reliquaries, cups and crosses.[2] Objects like these affirmed kinship and ancestral identity and perpetuated family associations with the crusading movement, as Nicholas Paul discusses.[3] Such objects also created and communicated a sophisticated temporality that brought together past and present in highly individuated ways. They linked people, places, and earthly and eschatological time, and those who possessed or viewed objects associated with crusading became witnesses to and participants in a trajectory of sacred history. Thus objects provided tangible connection to and evidence of the distinctive spatial and temporal qualities of the Crusade.

This chapter elucidates these broad points by focusing on a parchment miter, a portable altar, and ivory and glass relic containers. These were objects that were given to the priory of Oignies by Jacques de Vitry and that now form a part of the famous treasury at the Musée de Namur. My aim here is to consider how these objects connect Jacques de Vitry's life before, during, and after the Crusade and what they might tell us about the material qualities of remembrance at the time of the Fifth Crusade and its aftermath. These three objects express personal links between Jacques de Vitry and the community of Oignies, especially his close relationship with the holy woman Marie of Oignies, who had died just before Jacques set off on Crusade. The items were not just valuable objects to add to the treasury at Oignies in order to further the priory's prestige but also deliberate and meaningful conduits of connection between Jacques's own past, present, and future remembrance. The Namur objects, their collection, and their meanings thus provide a fruitful way of linking the multiple stories of Jacques's experiences as preacher, friend, member of the Crusade, and senior ecclesiast.

JACQUES DE VITRY'S RELATIONSHIP WITH OIGNIES

Jacques de Vitry's association with the Augustinian priory of Oignies began in a formal sense when he joined the community of regular canons before Marie of Oignies's death in 1213. The priory itself had been founded in 1187 by Giles de Walcourt and his brothers, while a female "wing" was simultaneously established to accommodate their mother. With the arrival of Marie of Oignies and her husband, Jean, both of whom were committed to a life of continence, poverty, and prayer, the small priory grew in reputation and drew visitors, including the young Paris-educated Jacques de Vitry. Jacques moved to Oignies in 1210, and after his ordination in 1211, he remained there until 1213. It was during this period that his spiritual friendship with Marie deepened. On her death, Jacques wrote the hagiographical *Vita Marie Oigniacensis*. As the previous chapters of this book have narrated, Jacques's life after he left Oignies was eventful. It was only well after his return from the Fifth Crusade that he made a few visits to the priory—one around 1226–27, when he consecrated a new church there and had Marie's body moved from the cemetery to a new sepulcher placed near one of the church's altars.

But it is clear that Jacques's connection with both Oignies and Marie of Oignies remained strong throughout his life even when he was not physically present at the priory. It was his wish that his body be buried near Marie, and before he died in 1240, he sent money, textiles from the East, books, personal ornaments, and relics to the community, probably also including the gemstones that were later incorporated into the famous metalwork of Hugh of Oignies, whose reliquaries and liturgical objects remain the most well known of Namur's treasures.[4] The 1243 charter that records Jacques's testamentary gifts and donations notes his body as being among the items received by the priory. Listed too are relics, books, textiles of silk, liturgical objects, money, and other items that added significantly to the priory's treasury and allowed its charitable works to continue.[5] We know that Marie of Oignies herself was particularly devoted to collecting and protecting the priory's relics, and there seems to have already been in the priory's possession items of value. Jacques de Vitry reported in the *Vita Marie Oigniacensis* that Marie's enthusiasm stretched to guarding the community's relics at night.[6] But it was the great variety of objects given and willed by Jacques de Vitry himself that elevated the priory's collection to one of the most significant in the Low Countries.

Most of the treasury objects still held at Namur were described in two seventeenth-century inventories: one from 1628, compiled by Arnold de Raisse (or Rayssius), and the other in 1636, compiled by Moschus. The latter almost entirely replicated de Raisse's list. These inventories are the earliest formal inventory listings of the Namur items, so we do not know exactly the composition of the treasury in its entirety in the 1240s. Nonetheless, it is evident that the items came from a variety of locations and that some of Jacques's personal possessions were still among them in 1628. The objects directly connected with Jacques in de Raisse's inventory are a miter of parchment and another of silk, a flagellum, episcopal rings, a missal, a foot reliquary, and a portable altar. Dozens of other items held in the treasury included relics of saints, items associated with Marie of Oignies—some of her clothing and a walking stick—and the liturgical ornaments and reliquaries created by Hugh of Oignies.

We know only a little about how these sorts of objects were encountered within the priory itself during the thirteenth century. Thomas of Cantimpré, writing the continuation of the life of Marie of Oignies in the 1230s, tells us that on feast days, relics and vestments were brought out and laid on the altar, with a burning candle in front of the relics.[7] On one unfortunate occasion, the candle set fire to the precious objects and ruined them; Thomas reports that Jacques's subsequent gifts of "every episcopal vestment, with many other garments of fine linen, as well as all the altar vessels with the divine utensils of its ministers, all crafted of gold and silver" had been predicted by Mary, who had consoled the prior of Oignies after the fire with the promise that the incinerated items would be miraculously replaced in the future. The personal connection between Jacques and the priory's material culture is also seen in his devotion to a finger relic of Marie, which he carried in a silver reliquary around his neck and eventually gave to the future pope Gregory IX.[8] This is a relic that had saved one of Jacques's mules during a tempestuous river crossing in 1216: the basket in which it was contained miraculously kept his mule afloat as he tried to cross a raging torrent. Another basket carrying Jacques's books was lost to the river.[9]

THE PARCHMENT MITER

The first object I consider here is a parchment miter given to Oignies by Jacques de Vitry.[10] This episcopal headdress exhibits conventional thirteenth-century style: miters of the eleventh and twelfth centuries were initially rounded with two lappets, or long ribbons of fabric down the back, but in the thirteenth century, they had "horns," or peaks on the sides or front and back, like this miter belonging to Jacques. As Ruth Mellinkoff's study has shown, the change in style of these "horned" miters was visually and spiritually linked to the iconography of the "horns of Moses." The horned miters thus signified a "helmet of salvation."[11] Miters were mostly made of linen or silk and painted with patterns, and sometimes they were decorated with beads or embroidered. They were seen by congregations during Mass and processions, and they were the sartorial expression of a bishop's senior ecclesiastical authority. In the later thirteenth century, William Durand commented in his *Rationale divinorum officiorum* that two-horned miters should also be interpreted as representing the two Testaments. When a bishop donned the miter, "it is so that he may live as he is worthy of an eternal crown."[12]

Jaroslav Folda was correct to state that "everything about this miter [at Namur] is unusual"—its material, its iconography, its place of production, and its putative meanings. The choice of its material is by far its most distinctive element. In July 2016, the CROMIOSS team at Namur confirmed that the parchment of the miter is vellum—calfskin—a material most commonly associated with manuscript production. Parchment, a particularly hardwearing and pliable material, was sometimes used for clothing during the Middle Ages, including small items such as pilgrim badges, which, although mostly metal during the period of the Crusades, came to be also made of vellum in the later medieval period (partly because they could easily be sewn into private prayer books). Parchment was used for

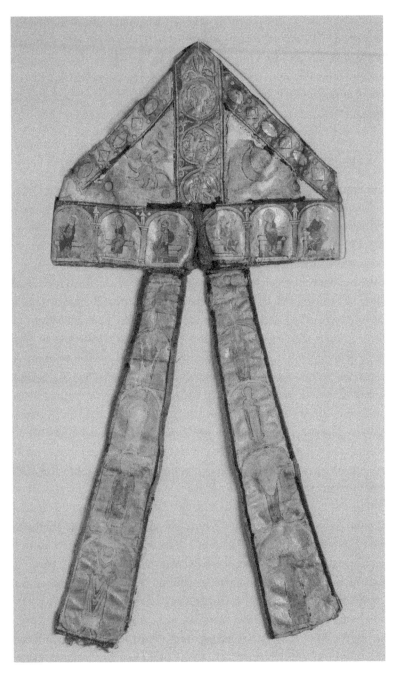

FIGURE 1   Parchment miter (front). Société archéologique de Namur. Photo: Namur, SAN / Guy Focant, Vedrin.

FIGURE 2 Parchment miter (back). Société archéologique de Namur. Photo: Namur, SAN / Guy Focant, Vedrin.

the stiff lining of dresses or to dress sculptures (rather like dolls' dresses), such as those found at the Cistercian convent of Wienhausen in northern Germany.[13] The only other uses of parchment I have found in episcopal miters are quite different from the one owned by Jacques de Vitry. One miter now held in Copenhagen is of a later date and recycles pages from a thirteenth-century manuscript in the lining rather than using vellum as the dominant fabric of the headdress.[14] Another fifteenth-century miter from Minden in Lower Saxony (and now held in the Berliner Kunstgewerbemuseum) uses parchment for its lining.[15] And a third example dated earlier than the others (ca. 1325) and held in the Germanisches National Museum also uses parchment to stiffen the miter in its lining.[16] The parchment miter of Jacques de Vitry is thus not just unusual but apparently unique in its deployment of parchment as the object's material and visible surface of display.

Folda's argument that the miter was commissioned by Jacques in Acre before he left the Holy Land in 1225 is compelling. An older historiography claimed that the miter was of French production, but as Folda has shown, its decorative style and iconographic program suggest a highly personal link with Jacques himself and his work in Acre. In particular, the sun and moon iconography of the parchment miter has been connected to the same iconography on the portable altar (which I explore below), the evangeliary in the Namur collection made by Hugh of Oignies, and Jacques's own seal, which used the same images.[17] Likewise, the inclusion of the evangelists resonates with Jacques's own role as a preacher of the faith. If Folda is correct that Jacques commissioned the miter, it is also probable that it was for his personal use. This begs the question of whether the miter was actually worn or was a display object. Further forensic work may answer that question more definitively, but it is not beyond the realm of possibility that this miter was a useable object, given the use of vellum in other clothing that was evidently worn, its lightness and portability, and the fact that decoration appears around the entirety of the object, which would suggest it being viewed "in the round."

Parchment possessed a range of cultural meanings that might help us understand why this particular material may have been used in an episcopal context and how it might have been received at Oignies after Jacques's death. For St. Augustine, the animal skin from which books were made could be likened to both the garments that Adam and Eve wore before the expulsion from the garden and the word of God itself, which stretched out over the firmament like a skin. For Adam and Eve, garments of animal skin signified not only sin but also mortality, sin's bodily consequence. And the word of God as a skin across the heavens indicates both revelation and the "firmament of [God's] authority."[18] The idea that animal skins were, as Jane Burns puts it, "metaphorical clothing for the words of the Scripture" meant that they could simultaneously conceal God's word by physically wrapping it and reveal it through its visibility and tangibility.[19] In other words, the body of words in a book and the animal body or skin that covered it become the same; a textile cover might merge with the object that it covers.[20] Thus the fleshly reality of parchment or vellum was not obscured either theologically or visually; it was understood to express larger Christian truths.

In the visual culture of medieval spirituality, skin was symbolically rich. Images of the punctured skin of the incarnated and crucified Christ, the flayed St. Bartholomew holding his skin like a coat over one arm, the mortification of the flesh through flagellation in monastic culture, and the miraculous preservation of the skin of saints as relics all abound in a range of media throughout the Middle Ages.[21] The suffering body was particularly resonant for crusaders, who not only shared in Christ's suffering via their participation in the holy war but faced the reality of bodily pain and the disfiguring consequences of combat. Their wounded bodies were visible reminders of both their individual experience and their imitation of Christ's suffering, and in some cases, they were especially praiseworthy. For instance, one knight who was entrusted with delivering a letter on behalf of one of the Hospitaller knights in 1178 was described in these terms: "Because the bearer of the letter suffered dangers with us, and in Christ's name gave his strength and his blood, so that his mutilated and lacerated body has left him incapable of working and useless for combat, we ask every single pious person to consider his needs, so that by your generous alms and his work and our prayers, he may complete his journey to the community of martyrs."[22]

Thus the material and metaphorical connotations of skin, both human and animal, depend very much on its own fleshliness and on its association with other corporealities. In the case of Jacques's miter, we might understand the vellum from which it was made and that he wore to contain a number of meanings. The theological tradition that argued that parchment and the words it contained were collapsed into the same thing might be extended to suggest that the miter signified Jacques himself. As the preaching embodiment of God's word, Jacques de Vitry literally wore the word of God and represented the fleshly delivery of the incarnated Word.

But of course, the miter is also a performative object that is portable and public. As a symbol of ecclesiastical status, it is also a strong visual statement of personal authority for whoever has the right to wear it. As Thomas of Cantimpré wrote, the bestowing of an episcopal miter showed that "the earthly imperium" had been entrusted to Jacques.[23] In the case of Jacques's parchment miter, this is particularly communicated in the iconography of its decoration, which includes twelve seated apostles under arches (six on the front of the miter and six on the back); three medallions on the front in a vertical section that contains Christ, the Virgin, and a bishop; and the four evangelist symbols in the interstices that display seated or winged human figures or winged animals.[24] The lappets show ten saints, half of whom are women and two of whom carry palms as pilgrims to Jerusalem. The inclusion of the bishop in this way is "an ambitious program that placed the bishop . . . directly in the line of latter-day apostles," and in so doing, the miter narrates a story about the place of a bishop as part of the evangelical tradition and lineage of Christianity.[25]

Jacques de Vitry's own preaching was famously effective and engaging, and his gifts in this regard had been personally encouraged by Marie of Oignies: Thomas of Cantimpré said that Jacques's gift of preaching was such that "scarcely any mortal could equal him in expounding the Scriptures and destroying sins." The Cistercian Pierre of Vaux-de-Cernay remarked on the efficacy of Jacques's preaching in the south of France and in Germany in 1211–12, which inspired many to join the Crusade.[26] Jacques himself understood both the missionizing promise and the burden of preaching in practice. He found it extremely difficult to communicate to the population of Acre when he first arrived there in November 1216 and had to rely on an interpreter "who knew the Saracen language" to deliver a sermon and to explain to another group "the words of eternal life." When he discovered that some of the Acre community "refused to come and listen to [his] sermon," he reported, he "went to them and expounded the word of God to them in the street, in front of their houses."[27] Eventually, Jacques did achieve preaching success in the city, although he recognized that many other places "desperately need our preaching." He took to the road in early 1217, preaching in Tyre, Sidon, Beirut, Byblos, and Tripoli, as well as the fortresses of Crac and Chastel-Blanc, Tortosa, and Margat. He made a particular effort to deliver sermons on the borders of Christian-Muslim territories so that his words might reach both groups.[28] He was in all senses an active preacher, and this formed much of the work he did while on Crusade.

Jacques de Vitry's status as preacher was also informed by the scholarly training he had received in the Parisian scholastic milieu of the early thirteenth century. Indeed, his combined identities as a scholar and preacher came together in the years after the Fifth Crusade, when he produced his collections of model sermons and exempla during the time he made his visits back to Oignies. Among the exempla is a tale that brings together some of the connections between Jacques as scholar, the parchment miter, and Jacques as preacher in a rather unexpected way. The tale concerns a Parisian student who died and appeared to his master in a parchment cloak that was covered in small letters. The master asked what the meaning of this parchment garment was, and the student told him that the letters represented all the sophisms and curiosities with which he had wasted his time as a student and that the cloak weighed him down tremendously—"more than if he carried the tower of St-Germain on his back." When the master extended a hand to comfort his former pupil, a drop of sweat from the student's brow dropped onto his hand and punctured it like an arrow. The master then abandoned the schools to live the life of a monk, saying, "I leave croaking to frogs, cawing to crows, vanities to the vain; I go to the logic which does not fear the conclusion of death." He continued to live near the schools, however, showing everyone the hole in his hand, as Jacques de Vitry saw himself when he was in Paris.[29]

This extraordinary tale appears in a number of exempla collections, some of which predate Jacques's own writing, so we know that it was not Jacques's own invention.[30] But its reiteration and glossing by Jacques de Vitry must be read in the light of Jacques's own personal experience as a scholar who left Paris to live a life still informed by letters but that was now dedicated to spreading God's word as both a preacher and senior ecclesiast. The parchment garment in the story is a weighty piece that prevented the student from understanding and living the liberating life of the faithful; the heaviness of the cloak and the chaos of its tiny letters convey their uselessness. But Jacques's own parchment garment, the miter, does something different. It is pictorial, hierarchical, and personal. It conveys a sense of its wearer as both a "scribe of the Lord" and a communicator of the Word through preaching. Without writing, it still functions as something of a mnemonic cue and as a memorial text. It asserts Jacques's authority and status while reminding the viewer of the many identities he inhabited throughout his life, from a scholar to a member of the priory, preacher, pilgrim, and bishop. In bringing all those aspects of Jacques's life back to the priory in a material, even fleshly form, the miter also brought Jacques himself back to the religious house that had been so transformational for him.

THE PORTABLE ALTAR

A small portable altar now at Namur, dated to the early thirteenth century, is another remembrance object connected to Jacques de Vitry.[31] This altar is usually described as a Mosan piece (as the Mosan style is characterized by the use of brown glaze) that was owned by Jacques and probably taken with him when he set out for Acre in 1216. It appears in Rayssius's

FIGURE 3 Portable altar, detail. Société archéologique de Namur. Photo: Namur, SAN / Guy Focant, Vedrin.

inventory of 1638, but it seems to have arrived in Oignies around 1243 and was probably part of the many gifts Jacques bestowed on the priory in his will. The portable altar is a fairly small item of 22 centimeters height, 17.5 centimeters width, and 2.5 centimeters depth.[32] Its consecration stone is gray marble, and the top face is covered with a champlevé enamel plaque engraved with an image of Christ on the cross between St. John and Mary. Christ and St. John both wear a red enamel nimbus, while Mary's nimbus is blue. Between the figures are a sun and moon on either side of the top of the cross, and trefoil and quatrefoil insertions appear on both sides and above the cross. These openings allowed the relics inside the altar to be glimpsed. We know about the relics that were once inside the altar thanks to the text around the its perimeter, which identifies them: "Reliquie sunt in hoc altare: De lancea dominis; de stipite domini; de sancto petro; de sancto andrea; de sanctobartolomeo; de lingno domini" (The relics in this altar are: from the holy lance, the bonds of Christ, from Saint Peter, from Saint Andrew, from Saint Bartholomew, from the Lord's cross). The other face of the plaque is bordered with more writing, which says, "De sancto matee dei martir sancti laurencii; de sancto vincentio; de sancto nicolao; de ioseph abarimacia; sancto bernardo abate; de s. Cecilia" (From the holy martyr of god Saint Laurence, from Saint Vincent, from Saint Nicholas, from Joseph of Arimathea, from abbot Saint Bernard, from Saint Cecilia).

This portable altar is in some ways quite a conventional liturgical object in its dimensions and function. All portable altars took the form of a rectangular piece of (mostly) stone that had been consecrated, on which Mass was celebrated.[33] They were not large items, and dimensions range in height and depth—some are box shaped, while others simply consist of the flat stone. The oldest surviving portable altar is from St. Cuthbert's shrine (Durham), dated around the late 680s. This particular object is made of oak, but the most common materials are marble, stone, or slate. Lisa Bailey has noted that the extensive use of these objects in the early medieval period can be inferred from references to Mass being said in a variety of locations—including prisons, private homes, army camps, and so on—even during the very early Christian centuries, but the first surviving textual reference to portable altars as objects themselves can be found in sixth-century Gaul.[34] In the eighth century, a traveler to the Holy Land mentions seeing a portable altar stored in Bethlehem at the Church of the Nativity, so it seems that the portable altars eventually became a part of the liturgical possessions of some Christian churches.[35]

Portable altars were also occasionally controversial in the early medieval period. There seems to have been some anxiety about both the need for solid evidence of their consecration and the fact that their very portability transgressed clear divisions between sacred and profane space.[36] But portable altars were also useful and indeed necessary for traveling priests and missionaries, and a trail of legislation supporting and regulating their use developed from the Carolingian period. This included instruction on their consecration by a bishop and the precise materials from which they had to be made. The solidity of the stone or marble was related to the solidity of faith, the rock upon which the Church was built, and Christ's stone tomb. In these ways, they were, as Éric Palazzo described, at once the Church in miniature and a representation of the itinerant Church.[37] These small objects were associated with the ark of the covenant, with Christ's body, and with the holy sepulcher.

Portable altars soon came to be seen as sacred and precious objects in themselves. This was partly because of their important liturgical functions and partly because of the relics they often contained, which were sealed into the altar. They also came to be highly decorated, and most of the surviving high-medieval altars were produced in the Rhine, Meuse, and Saxon regions from the twelfth century on.[38] These portable altars are noteworthy for their metalwork and enamel; one particularly famous example is the Stavelot portable altar (ca. 1160), now held in the Musées royaux d'art et d'histoire in Brussels, which contained a piece of the True Cross. Inscriptions on portable altars were common starting in the eleventh century: sometimes, as with Jacques de Vitry's portable altar, they communicated the list of relics inside the altar, and in other instances, inscriptions named the donor or quoted scriptural phrases.

Chronicles throughout the crusading period tell us many times that Mass was said before battle. In locations where there was no church, a portable altar could be employed for the Eucharistic service in tents, fields, on the march, or outside the walls of besieged cities. Robert of Reims mentioned altars among the liturgical paraphernalia of the First Crusade; William of Puylaurens described how soldiers were comforted before the Battle of Muret in 1213 by receiving communion and confessing their sins. At midnight before the Battle of Las Navas de Tolosa in 1212, the soldiers celebrated "the mystery of the Lord's passion, and making confession and receiving the sacraments, they took up arms and advanced to the field of battle."[39] During the Fifth Crusade, exhortations before battle often took place in the context of liturgical activity—the *Gesta obsidionis Damiatae* tells of the performance of the sacrament before battle at Damietta, for instance.

Analyses of Jacques de Vitry's portable altar have mostly been iconographic and have focused on the visual connections between items in the Namur collection, particularly the sun and moon imagery. Although also a conventional inclusion in medieval crucifixion iconography where they represented the Old and New Testaments, the sun and moon could also represent the masculine and the feminine principles of the universe, according to Cannuyer, who also suggests that these images concomitantly served something of a heraldic purpose for Jacques, identifying his seal, miter, and altar with the recognizable emblems of his episcopate.[40] As the portable altar was a functional object that did not particularly need to be so highly decorated, the pictorial scheme and iconography that *were* included on it suggest a highly personal resonance with the person who owned the object.[41]

One particularly significant element of the Namur portable altar in this regard is the inclusion of John the Evangelist. As we have seen on the parchment miter, the evangelists were not an uncommon element of episcopal iconography in general. But John the Evangelist seems to have been a saint to whom Marie of Oignies had been especially devoted: Jacques himself tells his readers that she "loved him with a special love." The *Vita Marie Oigniacensis* narrates that once, when Marie "had confessed a very little venial sin to a certain priest with many tears and groans and he asked why she was weeping, she said 'I cannot restrain my tears' for she saw an eagle on her breast which plunged its beak into it as if into a well and filled the air with great cries. Thus in the spirit did she understand that St John had borne to the Lord her tears and groans."[42] Thomas of Cantimpré also wrote that John the Evangelist had saved Marie from a "great rainfall," which fell from a "hideous storm cloud." Marie prayed for safety, and once the inundation ceased, she reported that "I saw John, the evangelist of Christ, in the air. By the command of almighty God he protected us from the great downpour of rain."[43] The presence of Mary and John the Evangelist was common in medieval crucifixion iconography until at least the fifteenth century. But given Marie of Oignies's particular interest in him, together with existing theological commentary on St. John, it is possible to also understand the image on the portable altar as a reminder of the closeness of the spiritual friendship between Jacques de Vitry and Marie.

Jeffrey Hamburger has shown that the relationship between St. John and Mary, signaled by their presence together in the visual culture of the Crucifixion, was explained by the theological concept of adoptive sonship derived from the Gospel of St. John (19:26–27).[44] During the Crucifixion, Christ said to Mary, "Behold thy son," and to John, he said, "Behold thy mother." For some commentators, these divine words effected a transformative moment wherein John's flesh and blood became the flesh and blood of Mary, and "from the hour that God said the word, John was as essentially Our Lady's son as if she had borne and given birth to him."[45] This quasi-Eucharistic episode emphasized John's likeness to Christ (as Mary's adoptive son through the grace of God) and "established the evangelist as the exemplary imitator of Christ's divinity."[46] This theology means that the iconography of John and Mary at the Crucifixion was not only an expression of witnessing or of mourning but also one of profound connection and kinship between these two individuals. Clerics like Robert of Arbrissel used John's adoptive relationship to Mary as a model for the relationship between men and women in double monasteries or shared communities like the priory at Oignies.[47]

The portable altar was first and foremost a practical item, and it was especially important for performing the Eucharistic ritual. This is why a number of portable altars include Crucifixion scenes—the Stavelot altar, for instance, has an elaborate program of images that emphasize the martyrdom of saints as elements in the story of Christ's death. Such scenes link participation in this liturgy with the redemption promised through the suffering Christ. Ecclesiasts like Jacques de Vitry who had the authority to perform the sacramental ritual were part of the process of communicating and administering access to Christianity's transcendent promise. Indeed, Jacques de Vitry was a key communicator of the Eucharist's power and effect through his preaching and hagiographical writing about Marie of Oignies. For Marie, according to Jacques, "life itself was for her the same as receiving Christ's body, and to be separated from this sacrament for a long time or to abstain from it was like death to her."[48] For Jacques, Marie was the model for a holy life, and her devotion to the Eucharist was a crucial part of that. Jacques's *Vita Marie Oigniacensis* must also be linked to the work of the Crusade. This was a work commissioned by Bishop Fulk of Toulouse in order to provide exempla of holy women to contrast the heretics in the south of France, and it includes a number of famous scenes in support of the Crusade and the protective power of the cross. Marie herself saw "crosses descending profusely from heaven on a multitude of men" in a vision; she saw "holy angels rejoicing and carrying the souls of those who had been killed [during the Albigensian Crusade] to the supernal joys without purgatory." She also saw a cross descend from heaven to protect the soul of a dying man.[49]

Likewise, Jacques's sermons and exempla stressed the importance of the Eucharist in the fight against heterodoxy. In one of his so-called *sermons vulgares* addressed to citizens and burghers, Jacques told the story of a man who would not receive the sacrament from an unworthy priest. He was sent a dream by God in which he saw a man who approached a well to drink but was refused by a leper, saying, "In what way will you accept water from the hand of a leper, you who scorn to accept the sacraments from an unworthy priest?" Jacques glossed this to explain that "most evil is the doctrine of heretics who say that the virtue of the sacraments depends on the [moral worthiness] of the minister."[50] Jacques's tract *De sacramentis*, which formed part of the *Historia occidentalis*, also grappled with the objections raised by heretics against the properties and claims of the Eucharist's strange and transformative materiality.[51]

The portable altar at Namur thus speaks of Jacques's itinerancy, his special role as an active participant in the dissemination of the holy, and his spiritual friendship with Marie of Oignies at Oignies. Although the altar's iconography seems conventional—even standard—it also holds layers of meaning that would have especially resonated with Jacques and the priory community that became its eventual custodian. Its very portability and materiality means that the altar transmits many memories—some liturgical, some biblical, some individual. It also brings together multiple temporalities: the long arc of Christian history, Jacques's decades-old connection with Oignies, and his time as an itinerant preacher and distributor of the sacrament in the Holy Land and beyond. At the center of all these allusions was the transformative and redemptive body of Christ.

CONTAINERS

It is perhaps easier to interpret objects when they display iconographic programs, such as the parchment miter and the portable altar, than it is to attach meaning to more utilitarian and undecorated objects. But items such as the containers that brought relics and other treasures to Oignies from the Holy Land and other places are also conduits of memory—the very portability of which, like Jacques de Vitry's altar, implies both distance and proximity, connection and alienation. There are several of these containers in the Namur collection, including ivory boxes and glass beakers. Whereas something like the portable altar memorializes multiple temporalities, the ivory and glass containers also signify multiple geographies by

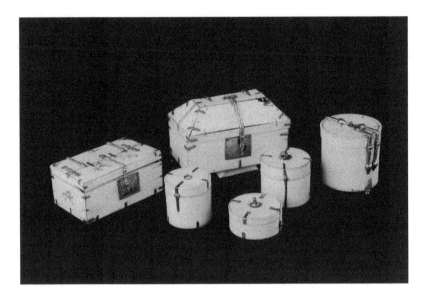

FIGURE 4 Ivory containers (closed). Société archéologique de Namur. Photo: Namur, SAN / Guy Focant, Vedrin.

embodying networks that stretch beyond their current location. As Julia Smith relates, these sorts of objects could be described as "portable Christianity" in that they "mediated the religious associations of specific places through material, highly moveable objects."[52]

There are ten ivory boxes now at Namur, six of which were made in Sicily and were sent back to Oignies by Jacques de Vitry. Sicily was a significant center of ivory craft during the twelfth century, although the manufacture of ivory art has had a much longer history and, as the evidence from China shows, a much more global reach. Trade in ivory renewed significantly during the thirteenth century as a result of trade routes that had managed to survive the volatility of the late Fatimid period. Some of these routes were indigenous African routes, while others were Mediterranean pathways, such as Genoese shipping routes that took the ivory to Western Europe. From North Africa and Egypt, ivory traveled through the Mediterranean to eventually end up in northern France in particular, where Gothic ivory sculpture flourished.[53] The Sicilian craft of ivory carving was thus facilitated by the island's proximity to both the main source of Western Europe's ivory and the sea routes that took ivory craft farther north.

The ivory carvings produced and exchanged in twelfth-century Sicily are most famously associated with the types of caskets and containers sent to

Oignies, although there are a number of more decorated examples in other collections. The latter category is mostly Islamic, such as the twelfth-century Sicilian casket now in the Art Institute of Chicago's collection and a similar twelfth-century example from Palermo in the Walters Art Museum.[54] These Islamic caskets are engraved or painted with images and inscriptions and were used as gifts, jewelry boxes, and storage. Boxes of a similar type were found throughout the Mediterranean world. Some had been taken as the spoils of war (such as the ivory caskets looted from Al-Mansuriyya in 1002 and displayed as trophies on the altar of San Pedro de Arlanza in Spain), while others were of more benign provenance, made in the royal courts of Sicily by artisans of diverse backgrounds.[55] Ivory caskets soon became used as relic containers in Western Christian culture both for transport and for storage. Unlike the more famous reliquaries of the high Middle Ages, the relics they housed were not necessarily visible, nor were the containers fashioned into the shape of the body part they contained. Nonetheless, as reliquaries, these ivory caskets assumed some of the same spiritual and mystical qualities and were certainly precious objects in themselves.

The Namur caskets are round or rectangular with clasps and mounts of gilded copper. They are mostly unpainted, although some have animal and bird drawings in ink, and they are similar in shape and composition to other Sicilian twelfth-century examples such as those now held at the Musée de Cluny, the Victoria and Albert Museum in London, the Palais des Beaux Arts at Lille, and the Fogg Museum at Harvard.[56] The relics they originally contained were sometimes wrapped in pieces of parchment and labeled. Other times, they traveled in textile pouches with an accompanying list of relics inside the casket with them. In the case of the Namur relics, some of these authentication labels are of a significantly later date or have been separated from the relics themselves, which makes it extremely difficult to verify connections between objects and the text.[57] But from the inventory lists, it is certainly clear that dozens of relics of varying sizes were sent by Jacques de Vitry to Oignies, including body fragments of numerous saints, a piece of the True Cross, drops of the Virgin's milk, crumbs from the Last Supper, and oil of Mary from the monastery of Saidnaya in Syria, which was a significant site of Marian devotion supported by the Templars.[58]

Glass vessels incorporated into reliquaries were also probably containers for relics that were transported from the Holy Land by Jacques de Vitry.

The Namur glasses are known as Hedwig beakers or Hedwig glasses, named because of their association with St. Hedwig of Silesia (1174–1243), who was said to have drunk from a glass that turned water into wine.[59] There are only thirteen surviving Hedwig glasses, two of which are part of the Namur treasury. The current thinking is that the Hedwig glasses were probably manufactured in Sicily, most likely during the reign of William of Hauteville (1166–89), using glass exported from Tyre, which was renowned for its glasshouses and the skill of its glassmakers.[60] Jacques de Vitry himself remarked on the "the purest glass . . . made with cunning workmanship out of the sands of the sea" that was produced in the glasshouses of Tyre.[61]

The style of the Hedwig beakers is quite distinctive. They are squat beakers of thick, colorless glass decorated with a variety of images, including lions, griffins, eagles, the Tree of Life, and occasionally a chalice, crescent moons, stars, and abstract designs. The triangular motifs on a number of these glasses have been linked by Rosemary Lierke to their Sicilian context of production.[62] The two glasses at Namur survive in the form of reliquaries, which were made by Hugh of Oignies. They are mounted on metal stands and have lids added to them. These are rather different from the more elaborate reliquaries dotted with gemstones and produced by Hugh to house, for instance, the rib of St. Peter or the True Cross. The Hedwig beaker reliquaries are simpler, and their key feature is the glass itself.

Nonetheless, the reliquary fashioned from one of the beakers transforms the vessel from a container to a reliquary monstrance specifically intended to display sacred relics.[63] At the same time, the central position of the beaker object meant that the glass was a key part of the visual experience of viewing the holy object, not just as a conveniently transparent medium but also as a meaningful material in itself. Rock crystal was understood by a number of medieval commentators to be a highly symbolic material. Many stressed the incorruptibility of crystal: Mary's virginity was likened to unbreakable crystal, some thought that the heavenly Jerusalem was made of crystal, and others understood that crystal was like the body of Christ in its uncompromising purity.[64] Crystal reliquary monstrances, mostly from Fatimid Egypt, date from the tenth and eleventh centuries, and there is ample evidence of the reuse of clear vessels for sacred display throughout the Middle Ages. The crusading period in particular brought a number of such containers to Europe, and some were repurposed either as a whole or in fragments to fashion reliquaries and reliquary monstrances. One example is the reliquary commissioned for some relics of the Fourth

Crusade brought to Halberstadt by Bishop Konrad von Krosigk. This reliquary was commissioned after his death in 1225 and features glass gems on it that were originally from an Islamic glass vessel that had probably come to Halberstadt as a container for relics, like the Namur glass. When it was broken, its fragments were stuck onto the reliquary for decoration.[65]

In the case of the Namur Hedwig glasses, the preciousness of the objects and their materials was also tied to their association with faraway places. These are items that traveled hundreds of miles with their sacred contents, transporting small pieces of the Christian past to their present destination. They were conduits of holiness in the same way as the ivory caskets, and like the caskets, they also evoked the networks and landscapes of elsewhere. Once these objects were relocated far from their place of production, they acquired new understandings of their context, meaning, and value. Such understandings also demonstrate that the significance of objects and their materials was relational and active. In other words, the object's meaning arises from its relationship with the people and places it encounters rather than deriving solely from the measurable properties and subjective qualities of its materials.[66] In this way, the reuse of the Hedwig beakers in the reliquaries of Namur brought together multiple geographies and their associations, making visible not just the sacred relics contained inside them but also the many distant places of their pasts.

CONCLUSION: MATERIALITY AND MEMORY

In this chapter, I have shown how memory was stimulated and anchored by the objects associated with Jacques de Vitry. The examples I have considered here—the parchment miter, the portable altar, and the ivory and glass relic containers—all demonstrate the importance of things in shaping the remembrance of people, places, and time. These objects mediated past and present, connected individual and collective experience, and contained and displayed spiritual truths. They did this through their materials and functions, both of which were already symbolically rich. That the materiality of things needs to be understood in order to comprehend their signification was expressed by St. Augustine in the following manner:

> Ignorance of things makes figurative expressions unclear. . . . Just as a knowledge of the habits of the snake clarifies the many analogies involving this animal regularly given in Scripture, so too an

ignorance of the numerous animals mentioned no less frequently in analogies is a great hindrance to understanding. The same is true of stones, herbs and anything that has roots. [We will not understand] that unbroken peace is signified by the olive branch brought by the dove when it returned to the ark unless we know that the smooth surface of oil is not easily broken by another liquid and also that the tree itself is in leaf all year round.[67]

Remembrance also connected the world of things and the world of signification, as we see in the objects at Namur. The objects I have discussed in this chapter reconstructed Jacques's own life experiences as preacher, Crusade participant, bishop, and friend by bringing things back to a location that had been critical for him. An object like the parchment miter, with its fleshly materiality, expressed the proximity of Jacques's own body to the priory and to the word of God. The miter and the portable altar also communicated Jacques's authority and legitimacy as a senior ecclesiast, connecting the priory and his friendships there to his status in the Church. In this way, the Namur objects were integrative by bringing together aspects of a personal life and locating them in a framework of collective belonging.

Time and space were also embodied in these objects not only in a biographical sense but also in a more transcendent way. The iconography and purpose of the altar and the parchment miter call to mind biblical history just as much as they signify Jacques's work as bishop. They link pre-Crusade time, Christian time, and the present, bringing Jacques and the priory into a set of differentiated but related temporalities. At the same time, the objects are spatial in their general connections to earthly locations and heavenly space. Ivory boxes and glass reliquaries denote multiple geographies, connecting Oignies with all sorts of spiritual, economic, and personal networks; they are reminders of distant landscapes. But ownership of these material objects also meant that Oignies itself, always a sacred space by virtue of its monastic consecration, was now specifically elevated as an especially important location where relics and other precious items were housed, cared for, and displayed. The objects thus both signified multiple terrains and times and deployed them in service of the present.

The modern team of forensic scientists at Namur is performing a different kind of commemorative work than that done by the priory of Oignies and its patron more than eight hundred years ago. But in the work of identification, dating, and preservation of Jacques de Vitry's remains, these scientists also participate in a remembrance project premised on the communicative nature of materiality. Just as the parchment miter, portable altar, and glass and ivory relic containers told of the connections between spaces, times, and people, so the body and bones of Jacques de Vitry carry traces of those stories to the present. As they do so, a new encounter unfolds, drawing together the many strands of memory that shaped Jacques's life and eventually brought him home to rest.

Conclusion

Remembering war serves many purposes—individual, collective, political, cultural, social, and ideological. National and nationalist narratives continue to be incorporated into stories of historical conflict as foundational and transformational moments in the formation of the modern state. Public rituals of remembrance are still played out to perpetuate and enshrine the place of war in cultural and collective memory. Memorials and monuments remain contested sites of war memory, crystallizing social and political anxieties about race, national belonging, recognition of past wrongs, and the representation of the past. Remembering is always about the present just as much as it is about the past. And remembering the past is always inclusive and exclusive in sometimes unequal measure—some stories are privileged, others are excluded; some narratives are dominant, others pushed aside. War memory is politicized in every regard: by those who seek to make prominent the experiences of veterans, those who wish to recognize and honor victims, those who wish to create a triumphant story of national progression, those who seek to mourn, those who seek to celebrate, those who wish to warn, and those who want to inspire. The interior cognitive act of remembering is swiftly eclipsed by the claims of cultural memory when it comes to war.

This book has used a particular historical moment, the Fifth Crusade, to unravel some of the many strands of war memory in the medieval past. I explored how war was remembered at a time when the nation-state did not provide an organizing framework or motivation and when understanding and giving meaning to conflict was clearly understood to be important.

The early thirteenth century was a significant moment in the history of war memory not because the Fifth Crusade itself was necessarily the most pivotal set of events for its refashioning but because the crusading movement itself was changing both shape and purpose while reflecting on its past during this time. As I indicated in the introduction to this book, the widening of the community of crusaders to encompass those who would never physically fight, the gradual integration of the new agenda of conversion, the writing of vernacular texts (especially crusading romance), and the diversification of crusading destinations were all important elements in the transforming history of the Crusade at this time. These were not sudden historical changes, but they did create a new landscape for crusading activity over the decades and provide new ways to talk about the nature of the holy war and its purpose. It has been the aim of this book to look at how and why remembering was such a significant part of crusading discourse at this particular time and to understand how war memory was created and understood in a premodern context.

Crusading always fostered fluid temporalities, given that it was part of an ongoing eschatological Christian story playing out in earthly and heavenly spheres. Crusaders understood that they were acting in service of the present, inspired by Christ's past sacrifice and the model of the Maccabees, in order to shape the terrestrial and eternal future. By the time of the Fifth Crusade, the efforts of previous crusaders were also being integrated into new mythologies about the trajectory of crusading history. Heroes of the First Crusade and ancestral and family figures had acquired motivational force, and their deeds were commemorated in text and visual culture. Crusaders knew that their own actions not only resonated now and in the future but also were framed by the past. Crusading itself was, in a number of ways, always a memorial exercise in its inherent spiritual character and justification. The religious quality of all these holy wars meant that remembering could always be expressed as part of the motivation and transcendent purpose of a Crusade. But crusading was also a military activity, and the war experience was part and parcel of what crusading involved. It was not just the spiritual value of crusading that was important to remember but war itself. This can be seen in the memorialization of particular battles or the commemoration of victory or defeat. Remembering war meant incorporating the individual experience into a collective or more generalized set of meanings. And it meant seeing the practice of war as worthy of being remembered. This book is not intended to be a military history of the Fifth Crusade, yet I have tried to show how the spiritual and military activities of the Crusade were brought together through what I have termed "remembrance projects" in order to explain and stimulate actions and events.

Crusaders tried to shape how they would be remembered in advance of battle by pragmatic means—taking care of their property and families—and by personal directives to care for their bodies should they not return. Those who wrote narratives about battle included motivational and consoling words in their representations of eve-of-battle speeches and prayers. In both these cases, crusaders and those who wrote about them worked to create a particular historical memory of themselves and other crusaders. Crusaders who wrote wills and testaments were preparing to be remembered; crusaders about to go into battle were represented as deserving of remembrance. These forms of what I have called "preparatory memory" also worked as a process of integration or socialization, whereby the individual crusader became identified as part of the more important collective. Remembrance was about not just ensuring an individual's legacy but establishing personal identification with the institution of the Crusade.

The authority to lay down these trails of future remembrance for the Fifth Crusade was, in part, invested in the eyewitness. The value of those who experienced the Crusade was understood in the context of Christian witnessing as well as individual experience. Men like Jacques de Vitry used the epistolary form to communicate their individual life experiences and make palpable the nature of the Crusade. Jacques also used emotions to bring his inner world to the external world of those hearing or reading about the Crusade. In so doing, he communicated to others what was important to remember about particular events. The narration of his own experience emerged from his immediate past to shape and direct the future memory of the Crusade. Simultaneously, deliberate decisions were made about who was worth remembering and who was not. Medieval war memory privileged the collective, although ties of kinship and association between individuals were certainly integrated into its communication. Men who were thought to offer models of exemplary conduct were named, while the personal and individual spiritual work of prayer meant that the behavior of each crusader was represented as critical to the Crusade's outcome. But mostly, remembrance was collective. Groups like the Frisians were singled out as especially worthy recipients of memory, as they provided a didactic and illustrative example of good conduct, right motivation, and pious gratitude. The texts that described such groups narrated their conduct in sometimes formulaic ways, using cultural scripts that were familiar to their audiences. They also imparted more general knowledge about the importance of commitment to God. Remembrance in this context was part of creating meaning for the Crusade and communicating the "right" sort of crusader to potential future recruiters and recruits.

Remembrance was thus an explanatory framework that brought together individual and collective experiences to give meaning to sometimes difficult events. In the case of the Fifth Crusade, which saw both Christian victory and ultimate failure, how to account for these events was not just about narrating a sequence of military actions. Explanation also meant locating the meaning of the Crusade in a wider context and communicating that meaning through text and space to current and future audiences. In this regard, Fifth Crusade texts sometimes sought to represent the Crusade as part of a prophesied story hinting at apocalyptic immanence. Sometimes suffering and sacrifice were emphasized to draw attention to the purposeful experience of combat. And material or spatial efforts to sacralize places like Damietta were attempts to create an enduring memorial to the evidence of God's will. That this latter attempt at memorialization gained immediate currency can be seen in the efforts of King Louis IX in the Seventh Crusade to regain ownership of the city.

There were renewed and careful efforts to connect the fundamental territorial claims of the Crusade with multiple locations in the early thirteenth century. A number of places, not just Damietta, were claimed, declared holy, and built to assert old claims of possession and display new claims of success. Communities like the monastery of São Vicente de Fora had their own agendas in maintaining memories of the Fifth Crusade, deciding which stories would be remembered. They created topographies of remembrance for local groups and for future crusaders not necessarily close to the main theater of combat. The mediation of past and present and their material embodiment may also be seen in the objects associated with Jacques de Vitry now held at Namur. These items represent and express the many connections between Jacques and the religious community at Oignies. Objects such as the parchment miter, the portable altar, and the glass and ivory containers can be seen to reconstruct the life experience of one individual as a preacher, friend, crusader, and senior ecclesiast. They also signify locations far from Oignies itself, bringing together biography and space in commemorative form and containing remembrance in their very materiality.

The chapters of this book deal mostly with what Jan and Aleida Assmann describe as communicative memory, or the creation and dissemination of memory during and immediately after an event. This is an especially useful time frame for the Fifth Crusade, given the rich narrative sources written by eyewitnesses throughout the Crusade that were meant to both report events and shape future memory of the events. Such sources also indicate that *what* is being remembered is only one part of the picture; *how* remembering is constituted and what it is supposed to achieve are even more significant. In text, image, object, place, and word, the Fifth Crusade shows that remembering was an active practice of representation, bringing past and present together in service of the imagined future. The sources for the Fifth Crusade are various, but the loudest voices within them are clerical and narrative, particularly the writings of Oliver of Paderborn and Jacques de Vitry. I have used Jacques as something of a link through most of these chapters, given his extraordinary presence in all forms of remembering the Crusade. He preached the Crusade, accompanied it to the Holy Land and Egypt, wrote letters about it, crafted histories about the East and West, and collected objects while on Crusade and in Acre. That his own body should be the most recently discovered link between Jacques and his precious items at Oignies adds to what we may come to know about this singular individual. As conduits of remembrance, the many texts—including writings and objects—associated with Jacques de Vitry tell us much about the modes of establishing and transmitting stories about the past and about the erasure of oppositional stories.

The spatiotemporal logic of crusading in the early thirteenth century invited reflection on the past in a myriad of ways. Remembering war at this time provided commentators and crusaders with opportunities to rehearse and disseminate the meaning of the Crusade through the interplay of individual experience and collective purpose. Remembering war allowed for claims of territorial possession to be extended to new frontiers. Remembering war created communities of belonging by articulating identification with the holy war and its aims. Remembering war drew together medieval Christians in a shared commitment to the endeavor of crusading wherever it was played out—on the plains and towns of the Holy Land; overlooking the ocean on the coast of Portugal; in monasteries, chapels, and priories in France or the Low Countries; or alongside long river Nile, which was thought to wend its way to the Mediterranean from Paradise itself. In all these ways, the many remembrance projects describing, explaining, and justifying the Crusade stitched together pieces of the past and the present to fashion a consoling, hopeful, and eternal future.

NOTES

Introduction

The first two epigraphs to this introduction are drawn from Jacques de Vitry, Letter 4, 109–10; the third is from Letter 6, 111. There are two modern accessible editions of Jacques's letters: Jacques de Vitry, *Lettres de Jacques de Vitry, 1160/1170–1240, évêque de Saint-Jean d'Acre,* ed. R. B. C. Huygens (Leiden: Brill, 1960); and de Vitry, *Lettres de la cinquième croisade,* ed. R. B. C. Huygens, trans. Gaston Duchet-Suchaux (Turnhout: Brepols, 1998), which is simply a reprint of Huygens's 1960 edition with a parallel French translation. There is an older edition by Reinhold Röhricht, "Briefe des Jacobus de Vitriaco (1216–21)," *Zeitschrift für Kirchengeschichte;* see volumes 14 (1894), 15 (1895), and 16 (1896). Citations here are to Huygens's edition. Some of the letters have also been translated into English in Malcolm Barber and Keith Bate, trans., *Letters from the East: Crusaders, Pilgrims and Settlers in the 12th–13th Centuries* (Farnham: Ashgate, 2010), and I follow these translations where appropriate. All other translations are mine. For the manuscripts of Jacques's work, see John Frederick Hinnebusch, "Extant Manuscripts of the Writings of Jacques de Vitry," *Scriptorium: Revue internationale des études relative aux manuscrits* 51 (1997): 156–64.

1. Jonathan Riley-Smith, "Crusading as an Act of Love," *History* 65 (1980): 177–92.

2. Jay Winter, "The Memory Boom in Contemporary Historical Studies," *Raritan* 21, no. 1 (2001): 52–66. For a collection of recent overviews on the history of memory, see Susannah Radstone and Bill Schwarz, eds., *Memory: Histories, Theories, Debates* (New York: Fordham University Press, 2010).

3. Kerwin Lee Klein, "On the Emergence of Memory in Historical Discourse," *Representations* 69 (2000): 143.

4. Pierre Nora, "Between Memory and History: Les lieux de mémoire," *Representations* 26 (Spring 1989): 7–24.

5. Siegfried Sassoon, "The Poet as Hero," in *Poetry of the First World War: An Anthology,* ed. Tim Kendall (Oxford: Oxford University Press, 2013), 94.

6. Stefan Goebel, *The Great War and Medieval Memory: War, Remembrance and Medievalism in Britain and Germany, 1914–1940* (Cambridge: Cambridge University Press, 2007). See also Allen J. Frantzen, *Bloody Good: Chivalry, Sacrifice, and the Great War* (Chicago: University of Chicago Press, 2004).

7. See David Matthews, *Medievalism: A Critical History* (Woodbridge: D. S. Brewer, 2015), for the cultural unfolding of medievalism from the sixteenth century.

8. Benedict R. Anderson, *Imagined Communities: Reflections on the Origin and Spread of Nationalism* (London: Verso, 1983); Eric Hobsbawm and Terence Ranger, eds., *The Invention of Tradition* (Cambridge: Cambridge University Press, 1983); Jasper van der Steen, *Memory Wars in the Low Countries, 1566–1700* (Leiden: Brill, 2015); Timothy G. Ashplant, Graham Dawson, and Michael Roper, eds., *The Politics of War Memory and Commemoration* (London: Routledge, 2000). For memory and modernity, see the essays in part 5, "Memory, Justice and the Contemporary Epoch," in Jeffery K. Olick, Vered Vinitzky-Seroussi, and Daniel Levy, eds., *The Collective Memory Reader* (Oxford: Oxford University Press, 2011).

9. Geoffrey Cubitt, *History and Memory* (Manchester: Manchester University Press, 2007).

10. Alon Confino, "History and Memory," in *Historical Writing Since 1945,* ed. Axel Schneider and Daniel Woolf, vol. 5, *The Oxford Handbook of Historical Writing* (Oxford: Oxford University Press, 2011), 36–51. See also Yosef H. Yerushalmi, *Zakhor: Jewish History and Jewish*

156 NOTES TO PAGES 5–9

Memory (Seattle: University of Washington Press, 1982); for the heated historical debates in the 1980s around the memory and legacy of the Holocaust in German history—the *Historikerstreit* debates—see, inter alia, Michael Burleigh, ed., *Confronting the Nazi Past: New Debates on Modern German History* (London: St. Martin's Press, 1996).

11. Confino, "History and Memory," 40.

12. Peter Carrier, "Holocaust Memoriography and the Impact of Memory on the Historiography of the Holocaust," in *Writing the History of Memory*, ed. Stefan Berger and Bill Niven (London: Bloomsbury, 2014).

13. Klein, "On the Emergence of *Memory*."

14. For recent studies along similar lines, see Erika Kuijpers et al., *Memory Before Modernity: Practices of Memory in Early Modern Europe* (Leiden: Brill, 2013). See also Kathleen Davis, "National Writing in the Ninth Century: A Reminder for Postcolonial Thinking About the Nation," *Journal of Medieval and Early Modern Studies* 28, no. 3 (1998): 611–37; Bruce W. Holsinger, "Medieval Studies, Postcolonial Studies, and the Genealogies of Critique," *Speculum* 77, no. 4 (2002): 1195–227.

15. Mary Carruthers, *The Craft of Thought: Meditation, Rhetoric, and the Making of Images, 400–1200* (New York: Cambridge University Press, 1998), 13.

16. Edmond Mikkers, "Un '*Speculum novitii*' inédit d'Etienne de Salley," *Collectanea cisterciensis ordinis reformatorum* 8 (1946): 17–68; Janet Coleman, *Ancient and Medieval Memories: Studies in the Reconstruction of the Past* (Cambridge: Cambridge University Press, 1992), 169–91.

17. See Megan Cassidy-Welch, "Confessing to Remembrance: Stephen of Sawley's *Speculum novitii* and Cistercian Uses of Memory," *Cistercian Studies Quarterly* 35, no. 1 (2000): 13–27.

18. See also Gabrielle M. Spiegel, "Memory and History: Liturgical Time and Historical Time," *History and Theory* 41, no. 2 (2002): 149–62, for the collapse of time in Jewish liturgical memory.

19. For Crusade exhortations and preaching, see Penny J. Cole, *The Preaching of the Crusades to the Holy Land, 1095–1270* (Cambridge: Medieval Academy of America, 1991); Christoph T.

Maier, *Preaching the Crusades: Mendicant Friars and the Cross in the Thirteenth Century* (New York: Cambridge University Press, 1998); Maier, *Crusade Propaganda and Ideology: Model Sermons for the Preaching of the Cross* (Cambridge: Cambridge University Press, 2000); Beverly Mayne Kienzle, *Cistercians, Heresy, and Crusade in Occitania, 1145–1229: Preaching in the Lord's Vineyard* (York: York Medieval Press, 2000).

20. Michael Lower, *The Barons' Crusade: A Call to Arms and Its Consequences* (Philadelphia: University of Pennsylvania Press, 2005). See also Anne E. Lester, "A Shared Imitation: Cistercian Convents and Crusader Families in Thirteenth-Century Champagne," *Journal of Medieval History* 35, no. 4 (2009): 353–70.

21. Elizabeth Lapina, *Warfare and the Miraculous in the Chronicles of the First Crusade* (University Park: Pennsylvania State University Press, 2015); Gabriela Signori, ed., *Dying for the Faith, Killing for the Faith: Old-Testament Faith-Warriors (1 and 2 Maccabees) in Historical Perspective* (Leiden: Brill, 2013); Sylvain Gouguenheim, "Les Maccabées: Modèles des guerriers chrétiens des origines au XIIe siècle," *Cahiers de civilisation médiévale* 54, no. 213 (2011): 3–20; Nicholas Morton, "The Defence of the Holy Land and the Memory of the Maccabees," *Journal of Medieval History* 36, no. 3 (2010): 275–93.

22. Guibert of Nogent, *Dei gesta per francos et cinq autres textes*, ed. R. B. C. Huygens, vol. 127A, *Corpus christianorum continuatio mediaevalis* (Turnhout: Brepols, 1996), 240; Eugenius III, *Quantum praedecessores*, translated in *The Second Crusade: Extending the Frontiers of Christendom*, ed. and trans. Jonathan Phillips (New Haven: Yale University Press, 2008), appendix I; Gregory VIII, *Audita tremendi*, in *Crusade and Christendom: Annotated Documents in Translation from Innocent III to the Fall of Acre, 1187–1291*, ed. Jessalynn Bird, Edward Peters, and James M. Powell (Philadelphia: University of Pennsylvania Press, 2013), 4–9.

23. Jay Rubenstein, *Armies of Heaven: The First Crusade and the Quest for Apocalypse* (New York: Basic Books, 2011); Damien Kempf and Marcus Bull, eds., *Writing the Early Crusades: Text, Transmission and Memory* (Woodbridge: Boydell Press, 2014).

24. Peter the Venerable, *The Letters of Peter the Venerable*, ed. Giles Constable, *Harvard Historical Studies* 78, no. 1 (Harvard: Harvard University Press, 1967): epistle 162, 395.

25. Gregory VIII, *Audita tremendi*, in *Crusade and Christendom*, ed. Bird, Peters, and Powell, 8.

26. M. Cecilia Gaposchkin, "From Pilgrimage to Crusade: The Liturgy of Departure, 1095–1300," *Speculum* 88, no. 1 (2013): 44–79; Gaposchkin, *Invisible Weapons: Liturgy and the Making of Crusade Ideology* (Ithaca: Cornell University Press, 2017).

27. Carl Erdmann, *Die Entstehung des Kreuzzugsgedankens* (Stuttgart: Verlag W. Kohlhammer, 1935). The English translation appeared as Erdmann, *The Origin of the Idea of Crusade*, trans. Marshall W. Baldwin and Walter Goffart (Princeton: Princeton University Press, 1977).

28. Lionel Rothkrug, "Popular Religion and Holy Shrines: Their Influence on the Origins of the German Reformation and Their Role in German Cultural Development," in *Religion and the People, 800–1700*, ed. James Obelkevich (Chapel Hill: University of North Carolina Press, 1979), 20–86.

29. For Outremer during this period, see Malcolm Barber, *The Crusader States* (New Haven: Yale University Press, 2012); for warfare and truces, see, inter alia, Christopher Marshall, *Warfare in the Latin East, 1192–1291* (Cambridge: Cambridge University Press, 1992).

30. Christopher Tyerman, "Were There Any Crusades in the Twelfth Century?," *English Historical Review* 110, no. 437 (1995): 553–77.

31. Nicholas L. Paul, "In Search of the Marshal's Lost Crusade: The Persistence of Memory, the Problems of History and the Painful Birth of Crusading Romance," *Journal of Medieval History* 40, no. 3 (2014): 292–310.

32. Nicholas L. Paul, *To Follow in Their Footsteps: The Crusades and Family Memory in the High Middle Ages* (Cornell: Cornell University Press, 2012); Megan Cassidy-Welch and Anne E. Lester, eds., "Crusades and Memory: Rethinking Past and Present," special issue, *Journal of Medieval History* 40, no. 3 (2014); Megan Cassidy-Welch, ed., *Remembering the Crusades and Crusading* (London: Routledge, 2016).

33. Paul, *To Follow in Their Footsteps*, 297–98.

34. The extent to which this was the preferred strategy of the Crusade has long been debated. See James M. Powell, *Anatomy of a Crusade, 1213–1221* (Philadelphia: University of Pennsylvania Press, 1986).

35. Jonathan Harris, "A Blow Sent By God: Changing Byzantine Memories of the Crusades," in *Remembering the Crusades and Crusading*, ed. Cassidy-Welch, 189–201; Thomas F. Madden, "The Venetian Version of the Fourth Crusade: Memory and the Conquest of Constantinople in Medieval Venice," *Speculum* 87, no. 2 (2012): 311–44; Thomas F. Madden, ed., *The Fourth Crusade: Event, Aftermath, and Perceptions* (Aldershot: Ashgate, 2008).

36. Guy Perry, *John of Brienne: King of Jerusalem, Emperor of Constantinople, c. 1175–1237* (Cambridge: Cambridge University Press, 2013). See also Thomas W. Smith, "Between Two Kings: Pope Honorius III and the Seizure of the Kingdom of Jerusalem by Frederick II in 1225," *Journal of Medieval History* 41, no. 1 (2015): 41–59.

37. Powell, *Anatomy of a Crusade*, 118.

38. Reinhold Röhricht, ed., *Deutsche Pilgerreisen nach dem Heiligen Lande* (Innsbruck: Wagner'schen Universitäts-Buchhandlung, 1900); Röhricht, ed., *Die Deutschen im Heiligen Lande* (Innsbruck: Wagner'schen Universitäts-Buchhandlung, 1894); Röhricht, ed., *Regesta regni Hierosolymitani: 1097–1291* (Innsbruck: Oeniponti, 1893); Röhricht, ed., *Addidamentum* (Innsbruck: Oeniponti, 1904); Röhricht, ed., *Testimonia minora de quinto bello sacro e chronicis occidentalibus* (Geneva, 1882); Röhricht, ed., *Quinti belli sacri scriptores minores* (Geneva: J.-G. Fick, 1879).

39. For an overview of this circle, see Christopher Tyerman, *The Debate on the Crusades, 1099–2010* (Manchester: Manchester University Press, 2011).

40. On the issue of motivation, see Jonathan Riley-Smith, *The First Crusade and the Idea of Crusading* (London: Athlone Press, 1986); Marcus Bull, *Knightly Piety and the Lay Response to the First Crusade: The Limousin and Gascony, c. 970–c. 1130* (Oxford: Clarendon Press, 1993). See also Giles Constable, "The Historiography of the Crusades," in *The Crusades from the*

158   NOTES TO PAGES 13–14

Perspective of Byzantium and the Muslim World, ed. Angeliki E. Laiou and Roy Parviz Mottahedeh (Washington: Dumbarton Oaks Research Library and Collection, 2001), 1–22.

41. Powell, *Anatomy of a Crusade*, 201. See also James M. Powell, "Honorius III and the Leadership of the Crusade," *Catholic Historical Review* 63, no. 4 (1977): 521–36; Powell's work may be contrasted with the more general overview provided by Thomas Curtis Van Cleve, "The Fifth Crusade," in *A History of the Crusades*, vol. 2, *The Later Crusades, 1189–1311*, ed. Kenneth M. Setton, Robert L. Wolff, and Harry W. Hazard (Philadelphia: University of Pennsylvania Press, 1962), 376–428; and the study by Joseph P. Donovan, *Pelagius and the Fifth Crusade* (Philadelphia: University of Pennsylvania Press, 1950).

42. For instance, Rebecca Rist, *The Papacy and Crusading in Europe, 1198–1245* (London: Continuum, 2009); Thomas W. Smith, *Curia and Crusade: Pope Honorius III and the Recovery of the Holy Land, 1216–1227* (Turnhout: Brepols, 2017); Pierre-Vincent Claverie, *Honorius III et l'orient (1216–1227): Étude et publication de sources inédites des archives vaticaines* (Leiden: Brill, 2013). For the papal registers, see Peter Pressutti, ed., *Regesta Honorii Papae III*, 2 vols. (Rome: Vatican, 1888–95).

43. Smith, "Between Two Kings," 42.

44. A new volume of essays seeks to expand the parameters of the conversation well beyond the European context. See E. J. Mylod et al., *The Fifth Crusade in Context: The Crusading Movement in the Early Thirteenth Century* (London: Routledge, 2017).

45. Jessalynn Bird, "The Victorines, Peter the Chanter's Circle, and the Crusade: Two Unpublished Crusading Appeals in Paris, Bibliothèque Nationale, MS Latin 14470," *Medieval Sermon Studies* 48 (2004): 5–28.

46. Jessalynn Bird, "Crusade and Conversion After the Fourth Lateran Council; Oliver of Paderborn's and James of Vitry's Missions to Muslims Reconsidered," *Essays in Medieval Studies* 21 (2004): 23–47; see also Benjamin Z. Kedar, *Crusade and Mission: European Approaches Toward the Muslims* (Princeton: Princeton University Press, 1984); Jean Richard, *La papauté et les missions d'Orient au Moyen*

Âge (XIIIe–XVe siècles) (Rome: École française de Rome, 1977).

47. The most recent study of this encounter is by John V. Tolan, *Saint Francis and the Sultan: The Curious History of a Christian-Muslim Encounter* (Oxford: Oxford University Press, 2009).

48. For Oliver of Paderborn, see Herman Hoogeweg, *Die Schriften des Kölner Domscholasters, Späteren Bischofs von Paderborn und Kardinal-Bischofs von S. Sabina Oliverus*, Bibliothek des Literarischen Vereins in Stuttgart, vol. 202 (Tübingen: Literarischen Vereins in Stuttgart, 1894), with a translation in Edward Peters, ed., *Christian Society and the Crusades, 1198–1229* (Philadelphia: University of Pennsylvania Press, 1971), 49–139. For Röhricht's collection, see *Quinti belli sacri*. For Jacques de Vitry's *Historia Hierosolymitana*, which was intended to be divided into three books, only two of which—the *Historia occidentalis* and the *Historia orientalis*—survive, see Jean Donnadieu, ed., *L'Historia orientalis de Jacques de Vitry* (Turnhout: Brepols, 2008); and Jacques de Vitry, *The Historia occidentalis of Jacques de Vitry: A Critical Edition*, ed. John Frederick Hinnebusch (Fribourg: University Press, 1972); and also Hinnebusch, "Extant Manuscripts."

49. See Powell, *Anatomy of a Crusade*, 260–63, for the longer list. Louis Weiland, ed., *Emonis Chronicon*, in Monumenta Germaniae Historica SS 23, ed. George H. Pertz (Hanover, 1874), 454–523; M. L. de Mas-Latrie, ed., *Chronique d'Ernoul et de Bernard le trésorier* (Paris: Mme Ve Jules Renouard, 1871), will be supplanted soon by a new edition by Peter Edbury. See Handyside's convenient résumé of the manuscripts and variants in Phillip D. Handyside, *The Old French William of Tyre* (Leiden: Brill, 2015). See Matthew Paris, *Chronica majora*, ed. Henry Richards Luard, 7 vols., Rolls Series, vol. 57 (London: Longmans, 1872–83); Ralph of Coggeshall, *Chronicon anglicanum*, ed. Joseph Stevenson, Rolls Series, vol. 66, no. 1 (London: Longmans, 1875); and Roger of Wendover, *Flores historiarum*, ed. H. G. Hewlett, 3 vols., Rolls Series, vol. 84 (London: Longmans, 1886–89). For the Hungarian participation, see L. von Heinemann, ed., *Ex Thomae historia pontificum Salonitanorum et Spalatinorum*, in Monumenta

Germaniae Historica SS 29, ed. Georg Waitz (Hanover, 1892), 568–98.

50. See, for instance, the idiosyncratic poem of Goswin, *De expugnatione Salaciae carmen*, which is included in the *Chronica regia coloniensis*, ed. Georg Waitz, in Monumenta Germaniae Historica SS 18 (Hanover, 1880), 349–54. Another often overlooked Cistercian source for the Crusade is Caesarius of Heisterbach's *Dialogus miraculorum*, ed. and trans. Nikolaus Nösges and Horst Schneider, 5 vols., *Fontes Christiani* 86 (Turnhout: Brepols, 2009). For a study of the Crusade in this text, see William J. Purkis, "Crusading and Crusade Memory in Caesarius of Heisterbach's *Dialogus miraculorum*." *Journal of Medieval History* 39, no. 1 (2013): 100–127.

51. For Crusade charters generally, see Giles Constable, "Medieval Charters as a Source for the History of the Crusades," in *Crusaders and Crusading in the Twelfth Century*, ed. Giles Constable (Aldershot: Ashgate, 2008); Riley-Smith, *The First Crusade and the Idea of Crusading*. For Fifth Crusade documents, see Powell, *Anatomy of a Crusade*, 259.

52. See Hoogeweg, *Die Schriften*.

53. Jaroslav Folda, *Crusader Art in the Holy Land, from the Third Crusade to the Fall of Acre, 1187–1291* (Cambridge: Cambridge University Press, 2005).

54. See Edmond Martène and Ursin Durand, eds., *Veterum scriptorum et monumentorum historicorum, dogmaticorum, moralium, amplissima collectio*, vol. 6 (Paris, 1730), 328–30, for the foundation history, which mentions Jacques. For a charter written by Prior Siger in the late thirteenth century, which connects the treasury with Jacques de Vitry, see vol. 1 (Paris, 1724), 1278–79; Ferdinand Courtoy, "Le trésor du prieuré d'Oignies aux soeurs de Notre-Dame à Namur et l'oeuvre de Frère Hugo," *Bulletin de la commission royale des monuments et des sites* 3 (1952): 119–256. For an account of the connections between East and West through a study of the gemstones, see Sharon Farmer, "Low Country Ascetics and Oriental Luxury: Jacques de Vitry, Marie of Oignies and the Treasures of Oignies," in *History in the Comic Mode: Medieval Communities and the Matter of Person*, ed. Rachel Fulton and Bruce W. Holsinger (New York: Columbia University Press, 2007), 205–22; Christian Cannuyer,

"Les emblèmes sigillaires de Jacques de Vitry reproduits sur trios pièces du trésor d'Oignies," *La vie wallonne* 387 (1984): 117–26.

55. Jay M. Winter, *Remembering War: The Great War Between Memory and History in the Twentieth Century* (New Haven: Yale University Press, 2006), 6; Emmanuel Sivan and Jay M. Winter, eds., *War and Remembrance in the Twentieth Century* (Cambridge: Cambridge University Press, 2000).

56. Jan Assmann, *Das kulturelle Gedächtnis: Schrift, Erinnerung und politische Identität in frühen Hochkulturen* (Munich: C. H. Beck, 1999); Jan Assmann, *Religion and Cultural Memory: Ten Studies*, trans. Rodney Livingstone (Stanford: Stanford University Press, 2005), 1–30; Aleida Assmann, *Der lange Schatten der Vergangenheit—Erinnerungskultur und Geschichtspolitik* (Munich: C. H. Beck, 2006).

Chapter 1

1. Andrew Carroll, ed., *War Letters: Extraordinary Correspondence from American Wars* (New York: Scribner, 2002), 194.

2. Siân Price, ed., *If You're Reading This: Last Letters from the Front Line* (London: Frontline Books, 2011), 3.

3. Paul, *To Follow in Their Footsteps*. See also Susan Boynton, *Shaping a Monastic Identity: Liturgy and History at the Imperial Abbey of Farfa, 1000–1125* (Ithaca: Cornell University Press, 2006).

4. Ashplant, Dawson, and Roper, eds., *Politics of War Memory*; Sivan and Winter, *War and Remembrance in the Twentieth Century*.

5. Dan Todman, *The Great War: Myth and Memory* (London: Bloomsbury Academic, 2005); Alistair Thomson, *ANZAC Memories: Living with the Legend*, 2nd ed. (Melbourne: Oxford University Press, 1994; Melbourne: Monash University, 2013).

6. James Fentress and Chris Wickham, *Social Memory: New Perspectives on the Past* (Oxford: Blackwell Press, 1992); Patrick J. Geary, *Phantoms of Remembrance: Memory and Oblivion at the End of the First Millennium* (Princeton: Princeton University Press, 1994).

7. Geary, *Phantoms of Remembrance*.

8. Nicholas Paul and Suzanne Yeager, eds., *Remembering the Crusades: Myth, Image, and*

160 NOTES TO PAGES 21–25

Identity (Baltimore: Johns Hopkins University Press, 2012).

9. Megan Cassidy-Welch and Anne E. Lester, "Memory and Interpretation: New Approaches to the Study of the Crusades," *Journal of Medieval History* 40, no. 3 (2014): 231. For women as keepers of memory, see Paul, *To Follow in Their Footsteps,* 64–65. For monks as custodians and creators of institutional memory, see Katherine Allen Smith, "Monastic Memories of the Early Crusading Movement," in *Remembering the Crusades and Crusading,* ed. Cassidy-Welch, 131–44.

10. Constance M. Rousseau, "Home Front and Battlefield: The Gendering of Papal Crusading Policy, 1095–1221," in *Gendering the Crusades,* ed. Susan B. Edgington and Sarah Lambert (New York: Columbia University Press, 2002); Powell, *Anatomy of a Crusade,* 93.

11. Riley-Smith, "Crusading as an Act of Love"; Bull, *Knightly Piety and the Lay Response*; Constable, "Medieval Charters," 93–116 (a revised version of the paper was originally published in Peter W. Edbury, ed., *Crusade and Settlement: Papers Read at the First Conference of the Study of Crusades and the Latin East and Presented to R. C. Smail* [Cardiff: University College Cardiff Press, 1985]).

12. Constable, "Medieval Charters," 82.

13. See also Bull, *Knightly Piety and the Lay Response*; and Bull, "The Diplomatic of the First Crusade," in *The First Crusade: Origins and Impact,* ed. Jonathan Phillips (Manchester: Manchester University Press, 1997).

14. Brigitte Bedos-Rezak, *When Ego Was Imago: Signs of Identity in the Middle Ages* (Leiden: Brill, 2011), 54.

15. Robert-Henri Bautier, "La collection des Chartes de Croisade dite 'collection Courtois,'" *Comptes rendus des séances de l'Académie des Inscriptions et Belles-Lettres* 100, no. 3 (1956): 382–86; David Abulafia, "Invented Italians in the Courtois Collection," in *Crusade and Settlement,* ed. Peter W. Edbury (Cardiff: University College Cardiff Press, 1985).

16. Steven Epstein, *Wills and Wealth in Medieval Genoa, 1150–1250* (Cambridge: Harvard University Press, 1984); Robert I. Burns, *Jews in the Notarial Culture: Latinate Wills in Mediterranean Spain, 1250–1350* (Berkeley: University of California Press, 1996).

17. Martha C. Howell, "Fixing Movables: Gifts by Testament in Late Medieval Douai," *Past and Present* 150 (1996): 3–45; Henri Auffroy, *Évolution du testament en France des origines au XIIIe siècle* (Paris: A. Rousseau, 1899); Philippe Godding, "La pratique testamentaire en Flandre au 13e siècle," *Tijdschrift voor Rechsgeschiedenis* 58 (1990): 281–300; Ellen E. Kittell, "Testaments of Two Cities: A Comparative Analysis of the Wills of Medieval Genoa and Douai," *European Review of History: Revue européenne d'histoire* 5, no. 1 (1998): 47–82.

18. Samuel P. Scott and Robert I. Burns, ed. and trans., "Law IV. How Knights Can Make Their Wills," *Las siete partidas,* vol. 5, *Underworlds: The Dead, the Criminal and the Marginalized (Partidas VI and VII)* (Philadelphia: University of Pennsylvania Press, 2001), 1178.

19. Barzella's will is to be found in *Annali bolognesi,* ed. Lodovico Vittorio Savioli (Bassano, 1784–95), 2:419–20; it is translated into English in W. S. Morris, "A Crusader's Last Testament," *Speculum* 27 (1952): 197–98; and with some commentary in Bird, Peters, and Powell, eds., *Crusade and Christendom.* A new edition edited by Hans Eberhard Mayer appears in "Bologna und der Fünfte Kreuzzug," *Crusades* 14 (2015): 153–66.

20. Women could take crusading vows but commuted them to money payments. Or, as Anne Lester has shown, women in religious houses performed supportive spiritual work for the Crusade. See Lester, "A Shared Imitation."

21. See Nicholas Paul and Jochen Schenk, "Family Memory and the Crusades," in *Remembering the Crusades and Crusading,* ed. Cassidy-Welch, 180.

22. For John of Harcourt's will, *Rotuli litterarum clausarum in Turri londinensi asservati,* vol. 1, *1204–1224,* ed. Thomas Duffus Hardy (London: Record Commission, 1833), 401. For the Harcourt family's connections with the Templars, see Beatrice A. Lees, ed., *Records of the Templars in England in the Twelfth Century: The Inquest of 1185 with Illustrative Charters*

and Documents (London: Oxford University Press, 1935), 208n2, 227n1, 232n6, 238–39n13.

23. When Hagan of Ervy, prior to departing on the Third Crusade in 1190, drew up his testament, he left half of his possessions and his body to Pontigny Abbey and asked for masses in his memory, to be paid for by a donation of one hundred solidi to the abbey's gatekeeper. He gave other gifts to the abbey too, including money to the infirmary and a vineyard. See Theodore Evergates, ed., *Feudal Society in Medieval France: Documents from the County of Champagne* (Philadelphia: University of Pennsylvania Press, 1993), 68–9.

24. Joseph Delaville Le Roulx, ed., *Cartulaire général de l'ordre des hospitaliers de Saint-Jean de Jérusalem (1100–1310)*, vol. 2, *1201–1260* (Paris: Ernest Leroux, 1897), 345, doc. 1830.

25. Ernest Strehlke, ed., *Tabulae ordinis teutonici* (Berlin, 1869), 143–45.

26. Delaville Le Roulx, ed., *Cartulaire général*, vol. 2, 298: "Anno domini M CC vicesimo primo, indictione VIII, XV kalendas novembris, manifestum sit cunctis quod ego, Henricus, De gratia comes ruthenensis, apud Accon gravi detentus infirmitate, compos tamen bone mentis et ordinator, dono et in perpetuum irrevocabiliter trado in hele-mosinam Deo et domui sancto Hospitalis Iherusalem, in manu fratris Garini de Mon-teacuto, ejusdem domus venerabilis magistri, pro redemptionem peccatorum meorum et antecessorum et successorum meorum, villam meam de Caneto, cum omnibus suis pertinenciis, sicut michi et meis pertinent et pertnuit. Dono et in presenti trado eidem Hospitali omnes mansos meos de Fontignano, et quicquid habeo vel habere debeo in Bastida de Sarnonenca et in omnibus suis pertinenciis, ita quod de cetero dicta domus Hospitalis dictam Bastidam cum omnibus suis perti-nenciis habeat libere et quiete. Et dono eidem Hospitali omnes homines, quos in eadem Bastida habeo, et mansos omnes, quos circa et juxta eadem Bastidam habeo, et mansos meos omes, qui sunt circa et juxta Canabeiros, et mansos omnes meos, qui sunt circa et juxta Bonum Locum. Et dono eidem Hospitali medietatem tocius terre quam comparavi ab Ugone de Caugnaco, et vineam meam totam quam ab eodem comparavi. Omnia predicta,

sicut mihi et meis antecessoribus pertinent et pertinere debent aliquo modo, dono, laudo et concedo, et perpetuo irrevocabiliter trado Deo et sancte domui Hospitalis Iherusalem, ita quod habeant, teneant, et possideant libere et quiete. Et est sciendum quod de predicta sancta domo multa et magna recepi servicia, quamdiu moram in partibus Sirie feci. Volens et desiderans bonorum omnium, que fient et facta sunt, esse participem et consor-tem, in die obitus mei volo suscipere habitum ejusdem domus et in suo cimiterio meam elegi sepulturam. Et rogo dominam A comitissam, uxorem meam karissimam, et Bernardum, filium meum karissimum, et de predicta helemosins, sine omni contradictione, dictum investiant Hospitale, ad omnes suas voluntates perpetuo faciendas. Actus est hoc Accon in domo Hospitalis."

27. Ibid., 308–9. Delaville Le Roulx suggests that there may have been a transcription error in the dating of the first will and that the two documents were composed at the same time. The slightly different witness list in the codicil, however, together with the evidence of strong spiritual connection to the Hospital as outlined above, may mitigate his suggestion.

28. Ibid., 270, document dated June 26, 1220.

29. Eugène de Buchère de Lépinois and Lucien Merlet, eds., *Cartulaire de Notre-Dame de Chartres*, vol. 2 (Chartres: Garnier, 1863), 94.

30. They were two of the many lords of Le Puiset who took up the cross from the time of the First Crusade. See John L. La Monte, "The Lords of Le Puiset on the Crusades," *Speculum* 17, no. 1 (1942): 100–118. For more on the relationship between the lords of Le Puiset and the cathedral, see Margot E. Fassler, *The Virgin of Chartres: Making History Through Liturgy and the Arts* (New Haven: Yale University Press, 2010).

31. Guillaume Doyen, *Histoire de la ville de Chartres*, vol. 1 (Chartres, 1786), 192. The scene for the window, if it was made, no longer survives.

32. J. W. Willis Bund, ed., *Episcopal Registers, Diocese of Worcester. Register of Bishop Godfrey Giffard, September 23rd 1268 to August 13th 1301*, vol. 2 (Oxford: James Parker, 1902), 7–9.

33. The wills are to be found in the register of the Genoese notary Lanfranc. See Hilmar C.

162 NOTES TO PAGES 28–32

Krueger and Robert L. Reynolds, eds., *Notai liguri del secoli XII e del XIII*, vol. 6, *Lanfranco* (Genoa, 1951–53). Steven Epstein noted that for the Third Crusade, only one Genoese will survives containing a bequest for the Crusade (of some 190 compiled between 1155 and 1204). See Epstein, *Wills and Wealth*.

34. Krueger and Reynolds, eds., *Notai ligur*, doc. 1319: "*Montanaria moglie di Martino de Mari drappiere fa testamento*, [21 dicembre 1216. 24]: Ego Montanaria uxor Martini de Mari draperii ultime voluntatis contemplatione corpus meum apud hospitale Sancti Johannis seppeliri volo. Sol. centum pro anima mea iudico, quorum decenum operi Sancti Laurentii relinquo. Residuum in obsequio sepulture mee volo dari per manum dicti viri mei. De aliis bonis meis sol. centum lego in servitio passagii ultramarini si non iero, si autem iero illos mecum portabo. Item dimitto sol. centum pro missis de toto anno celebrandis. Jacobe filie mee dimitto sol. centum. Simone filie mee lib .x. Florie nepti mee [*fo.* 73 y.] lib .v. [. . .] Petri de Porta sol. centum. Martineto nepoti meo sol. .x1. Palmere servienti mee sol .x1. Johanne consanguinee mee alios sol .x1. dimitto. Reliquorum bonorum meorum dictum virum meum et Ansaldum filium meum mihi equaliter heredes instituo. Hec est mea ultima voluntas que si non valet iure testamenti saltim vim codicillorum vel alicuius ultime voluntatis optineat. Testes Wilielmus caxarius, Baldoinus calegarius, Obertus calegarius, Conturius calegarius et Jacobus calegarius. Actum Janue, in domo Lanfranci notarii, .xxi°. die decembris, circa tertiam."

35. Powell, *Anatomy of a Crusade*, 105n38; de Vitry, *Lettres*. Regional variations in crusading bequests can be seen, for instance, in the number of Spanish wills that include money for ransoming captives. See James Brodman, *Ransoming Captives in Crusader Spain: The Order of Merced on the Christian-Islamic Frontier* (Philadelphia: University of Pennsylvania Press, 1986); Yvonne Friedman, *Encounter Between Enemies: Captivity and Ransom in the Latin Kingdom of Jerusalem* (Leiden: Brill, 2001).

36. Estella Weiss-Krejci, "Heart Burial in Medieval and Post-medieval Central Europe," in *Body Parts and Bodies Whole*, ed. Katharina

Rebay-Salisbury, Marie Louise Stig Sorensen, and Jessica Hughes, Studies in Funerary Archaeology 5 (Oxford: Oxbow Books, 2010), 119–34.

37. Paul, *To Follow in Their Footsteps*, 134–70.

38. Cited in Danielle Westerhof, "Celebrating Fragmentation: The Presence of Aristocratic Body Parts in Monastic Houses in Twelfth- and Thirteenth-Century England," in *Sepulturae cistercienses: Burial, Memorial and Patronage in Medieval Cistercian Monasteries*, ed. J. Hall and C. Kratzke. Comentarii cisterciensis 14 (Forges-Chimay: Cîteaux, 2005), 41. The source for this is the *Waverley Annals* in Henry Richards Luard, ed., *Annales monastici*, Rolls Series, vol. 36, no. 2 (London: Longmans, 1865), 292.

39. Delaville Le Roulx, ed., *Cartulaire général*, vol. 2, 394, dated before March 31, 1229.

40. Ibid., 532: "Item eligimus nobis sepulturam in domo Hospitalise Jerosolimitani de Aquis, ubi jacet pater noster bone memorie sepultus Idelfonsus, comes Provinciae quondam."

41. Johann von Frast, ed., *Das "Stiftungen-Buch" des Cistercienser-Klosters Zwetl* (Vienna: K. K. Hof und Staatsdruckerei, 1851), 96–100.

42. John R. E. Bliese, "Rhetoric and Morale: A Study of Battle Orations from the Central Middle Ages," *Journal of Medieval History* 15, no. 3 (1989): 203.

43. Fulcher of Chartres, *Historia Hierosolymitana (1095–1127)*, ed. Heinrich Hagenmeyer (Heidelberg: C. Winter, 1913); translated in Fulcher of Chartres, *A History of the Expedition to Jerusalem, 1095–1127*, ed. Harold S. Fink and trans. Frances R. Ryan (Knoxville: University of Tennessee Press, 1969), 157–58.

44. Gui, a household knight of the Viscount of Melun, late in 1249, "Letter to Master B. de Chartres," in Paris, *Chronica majora*, 6:155–62. Peter Jackson, trans., *The Seventh Crusade, 1244–1254: Sources and Documents* (Aldershot: Ashgate, 2009), 87.

45. For other contexts of "battlefield oration," see John R. E. Bliese, "The Courage of the Normans: A Comparative Study of Battle Rhetoric," *Nottingham Medieval Studies* 35 (1991): 1–26; John Bliese, "When Knightly Courage May Fail: Battle Orations

in Medieval Europe," *Historian* 53, no. 3 (1991): 489–504. See also David S. Bachrach, "Conforming with the Rhetorical Tradition of Plausibility: Clerical Representation of Battlefield Orations Against Muslims, 1080–1170," *International History Review* 26, no. 1 (March 2004): 1–19.

46. See *Gesta obsidionis Damiatae* in Röhricht, ed., *Quinti belli sacri*, 71–115, 81.

47. *Gesta obsidionis Damiatae*, 83.

48. Gaposchkin, *Invisible Weapons*, 125.

49. See Oliver of Paderborn, *Historia Damiatina*, in Hoogeweg, *Die Schriften*, 159–280, 183: "Clerici nudis pedibus per litus ambulabant supplicantes"; "Iacuit patriarcha ante lignum crucis prostratus in pulvere, stans nudis pedibus clerus indutus legitimis stolis clamavit in celum."

50. Oliver of Paderborn, *Historia Damiatina*, 197: "Pluvie et venti multum discriminis et difficultatis addiderunt nostris."

51. Jacques de Vitry, Letter 4, 106.

52. *Gesta obsidionis Damiatae*, 78.

53. Ibid., 79.

54. Ibid., 82–83: "Domine Iesu Christe, qui excitatus a Petro, cuius navicula demergebat, respondit: 'Modice fidei, quare dubitasti? Et statim imperasti ventis et mar et fact est tranquillitas magna. Intercede nunc, piissime Pater, super excitum tuum, impera mari et vento, ut revertantur ad locum suum, qui cum Patre vivis et regnas in secula seculorum. Amen.'"

55. Ibid., 98–99: "Domine Ihesu Christe, rex glorie, qui es potens in omnibus, adiuva servos tuos et libera nos ab illa flamma et a manibus iniquorum Sarracenorum."

56. Gaposchkin, *Invisible Weapons*, 195.

57. *Gesta obsidionis Damiatae*, 78.

58. Oliver of Paderborn, *Historia Damiatina*, 252: "Se ipsos diiudicarent, ne a iudice secretorum graviter iudicentur."

59. Caroline Smith, *Crusading in the Age of Joinville* (Aldershot: Ashgate, 2006).

60. Jessalynn Bird, "James of Vitry's Sermons to Pilgrims," *Essays in Medieval Studies* 25 (2008): 87. The sermon is edited in Bird's essay and also in Jean Longère, ed., *Sermones vulgares vel ad status*, in *Corpus christianorum continuatio mediaevalis* 255 (Turnhout: Brepols, 2013);

and translated in Bird, Peters, and Powell, eds., *Crusade and Christendom*, 143–54.

61. Bird, Peters, and Powell, eds., *Crusade and Christendom*, 149, 152.

62. Ibid., 143.

63. Ibid., 153.

64. For the text, see Röhricht, ed., *Quinti belli sacri*, 3–26. Also Powell, *Anatomy of a Crusade*, 52–63; Christopher Tyerman, *England and the Crusades, 1095–1588* (Chicago: University of Chicago Press, 1988), 164.

65. See also Morton, "The Defence of the Holy Land"; and the essays in Elizabeth Lapina and Nicholas Morton, eds., *The Uses of the Bible in Crusader Sources* (Leiden: Brill, 2017).

66. See *Quia maior*, in *Crusade and Christendom*, ed. Bird, Peters, and Powell, 108.

67. *Pium et Sanctum* (1213), in *Crusade and Christendom*, ed. Bird, Peters, and Powell, 113.

68. Innocent's letter to Duke Leopold IV of Austria, February 1208. See Innocent III, *Innocentii III romani pontifices opera omnia tomis quatuor distributa*, in *Patrologia latina* 215, ed. J. P. Migne (Paris, 1855), 1339–40.

69. Ibid.: "Vere pium est hoc propositum et tibi coelitus inspiratum. Intendi enim suscipiendo crucem reddere vicem Christo, quo tuos languores in ipsa pertulit, doloresque portavit'; 'ut in crucis victoriosae vexillo."

Chapter 2

1. De Vitry, Letter 6, 127: "Quod cum ingrederemus civitatem tot invenimus mortuorum cadaver super terram, eo, quod pauci vivi qui remanserant ex Sarracenis tot mortuos sepelire non poterant, quod fetorem et aeris corruptionem vix aliquis poterat sustinere."

2. Ibid., 133: "Ego autem iam debilis et confractus corde in pace et tranquillitate vitam meam finire desidero."

3. On Jacques de Vitry's career, see John W. Baldwin, *Masters, Princes, and Merchants: The Social Views of Peter Chanter and His Circle* (Princeton: Princeton University Press, 1970), 1:38–9; de Vitry, Historia occidentalis *of Jacques de Vitry*; the updated introductory notes provided by Jean Longère in Gaston Duchet-Suchaux, *Jacques de Vitry Histoire occidentale* (Paris: Editions du Cerf, 1997). Philipp Funk, *Jakob von Vitry: Leben und Werke*

(Berlin: Druck und Verlag von B. G. Teubner, 1909), is the only biography of Jacques. Jan Vandeburie's "Jacques de Vitry's *Historia orientalis*: Reform, Crusading, and the Holy Land After the Fourth Lateran Council" (PhD diss., University of Kent, 2015), examines the eighteen thirteenth-century manuscripts of Jacques's *Historia orientalis*. It provides a useful complement to Hinnebusch's older work on the *Historia occidentalis*; an edition of the *ad status* sermons was produced by Jean Baptiste Pitra, *Analecta novissima spicilegii Solesmensis: Altera continuatio*, vol. 2 (Paris, 1888). The errors in Pitra's edition are noted in Jessalynn Bird, "The Religious's Role in a Post-Fourth-Lateran World: Jacques de Vitry's *Sermones ad status* and *Historia occidentalis*," in *Medieval Monastic Preaching*, ed. Carolyn Muessig (Leiden: Brill, 1998), 210n2.

4. Seven of Jacques de Vitry's letters survive (one is of disputed authorship, hence most scholars generally accept that only six of the letters may confidently be attributed to Jacques), and four of those—the subject of this chapter—were written while he was on campaign in Egypt. These have been edited by de Vitry, *Lettres*. The Egypt letters are numbered 4, 5, 6, and 7 by Huygens. I follow this numbering here. There are eleven manuscripts containing the letters—for these, see de Vitry, *Lettres*, 6–51.

5. Alessandro Portelli, *The Death of Luigi Trastulli and Other Stories: Form and Meaning in Oral History* (Albany: State University of New York Press, 1991), 45–58.

6. Jeremy Cohen, *Living Letters of the Law: Ideas of the Jew in Medieval Christianity* (Berkeley: University of California Press, 1999), 33.

7. For a study of eyewitnessing in the context of the First Crusade, see Lapina, *Warfare and the Miraculous*.

8. Isidore of Seville, *The Etymologies of Isidore of Seville*, ed. and trans. Stephen A. Barney, W. J. Lewis, J. A. Beach, and Oliver Berghof (Cambridge: Cambridge University Press, 2006), bk. 1, 44.4, 67.

9. Peter Damian-Grint, *The New Historians of the Twelfth-Century Renaissance: Authorising History in the Vernacular Revolution* (Woodbridge: Boydell Press, 1999), 68–84.

10. Catherine Hanley, *War and Combat, 1150–1270: The Evidence from Old French Literature* (Woodbridge: D. S. Brewer, 2003), 54. See also Carol Sweetenham and Linda Paterson, eds., *The Canso d'Antioca: An Occitan Epic Chronicle of the First Crusade* (Aldershot: Ashgate, 2003), 123 and following.

11. Barbara Packard, "Remembering the First Crusade: Latin Narrative Histories, 1099–c. 1300" (PhD diss., Royal Holloway, University of London, 2011). Also see Yuval Noah Harari, "Eyewitnessing in Accounts of the First Crusade: The *Gesta francorum* and Other Contemporary Narratives," *Crusades* 3 (2004): 77–99.

12. Elizabeth Lapina, "*Nec signis nec testibus creditur*: The Problem of Eyewitnesses in the Chronicles of the First Crusade," *Viator* 38, no. 1 (2007): 117–39; and more recently Lapina, *Warfare and the Miraculous*. See also Marcus Bull, "The Eyewitness Accounts of the First Crusade as Political Scripts," *Reading Medieval Studies* 36 (2010): 23–37.

13. Carol Symes, "Popular Literacies and the First Historians of the First Crusade," *Past and Present* 235, no. 1 (May 2017): 67.

14. Symes, "Popular Literacies," 59.

15. Megan Cassidy-Welch, "Testimonies from a Fourteenth-Century Prison: Rumour, Evidence and Truth in the Midi," *French History* 16, no. 1 (2002): 3–27; Thelma Fenster and Daniel Lord Smail, eds., *Fama: The Politics of Talk and Reputation in Medieval Europe* (Ithaca: Cornell University Press, 2003).

16. Beate Schuster, "The Strange Pilgrimage of Odo of Deuil," in *Medieval Concepts of the Past: Ritual, Memory, Historiography*, ed. Gerd Althoff, Johannes Fried, and Patrick J. Geary (Washington, DC: Publications of the German Historical Institute, 2002), 253–78.

17. See Claude Gauvard, ed., *L'enquête au Moyen Âge* (Rome: École française de Rome, 2009); William Chester Jordan, *Louis IX and the Challenge of the Crusade: A Study in Rulership* (Princeton: Princeton University Press, 1979); Joseph Strayer, "La conscience du roi: Les enquêtes de 1258–1262 dans la Sénéchaussée de Carcassonne-Béziers," in *Mélanges Robert Aubanas* (Montpellier: La Société d'Histoire du droit et des institutions des anciens pays de droit écrit, 1984), 725–36.

18. De Vitry, Letter 2, 79–80: "Cupio autem quatinus, quamdiu vixeritis, recentem parvitatis mee memoriam habeatis, sicut vestri semper memoriam habeo, et per litteras, quando nuntium habere valeo, me ipsum memorie vestre libenter ingero et de statu meo vos certificare desidero."

19. Ibid., Letter 4, 101: "Unde, sicut in aliis litteris de his que in exercitu domini fuerunt et ab initio facta sunt vos certificavi, ita et presentibus litteris de his que postea factas unt vos certificare proposui." There are two versions of the letter, one addressed to Pope Honorius III (the A version) and the other addressed to "my most beloved friends in Christ," probably his fellow clerics in Acre (the B version). The *salutatio* differs in the two versions, although the body of the text, or *narratio*, is the same for both recipients. The letters conclude differently: the B version contains a list of those who had died, while the A version notes that "this letter was finished and the messenger was already hurrying to carry it to you when we received some further news" (which was that the Sultan had died and that more troops had arrived, including Pelagius, the papal legate).

20. See the brief but useful comments on letter-writing conventions in Martha Carlin and David Crouch, eds., *Lost Letters of Medieval Life: English Society, 1200–1250* (Philadelphia: University of Pennsylvania Press, 2013), 15–17; for fuller studies of medieval letters, see, inter alia, Giles Constable, *Letters and Letter-Collections*, vol. 17, *Typologie des sources du Moyen Âge occidental*, ed. B. van den Abeele and J. M. Yante (Turnhout: Brepols, 1976); Alain Boureau, "The Letter Writing Norm, a Mediaeval Invention," in *Correspondence: Models of Letter Writing from the Middle Ages to the Nineteenth Century*, ed. Roger Chartier, Alain Boureau, and Cécile Dauphin (Princeton: Princeton University Press, 1997), 24–58; Carol Poster and Linda C. Mitchell, eds., *Letter Writing Manuals and Instruction from Antiquity to the Present: Historical and Bibliographic Studies* (Columbia: USC Press, 2007).

21. De Vitry, Letter 5, 114: "Ego vero meum cum ducentis fere hominibus, quibusdam tamen ex illis interfectis et vulneratis, deduci feci, post hec vero barbotam meam cum viginti hominibus in flumine amisi, quorum sex captive ducti sunt, reliqui vero pugnando viriliter interfecti sunt."

22. Ibid., 115: "Submersi sunt cum plumbum in aquis vehementis."

23. Ibid., Letter 4, 103: "In eadem etiam terra est vinea balsami unde fit crisma, quod nusquam terrarum nisi in partibus illis reperitur."

24. Ibid., Letter 5, 112–13: "Qui relictis uxoribus et filiis et venditis terrenis hereditatibus, ut meliorem et eternam in celis consequerentur hereditatem exierunt . . . stimata in corpora suo portantes."

25. Ibid., 115: "Inmisit enim dominus nostris morbum nulla arte medicorum curabilem."

26. Ibid., 116: "Femoribus enim et tibiis primo ingrescentibus et deinde putrescentibus, carnibus etiam superfluis in ore subcrescentibus, diutius absque dolore magno languentes et paulatim corde deficientes."

27. See Powell, *Anatomy of a Crusade*, 150, for the real reason the Egyptians left (the discovery of a plot against their leader Al-Kamil).

28. De Vitry, Letter 5, 119: "Petrarias, trabucula, scalas et alia bellica preparantes instrumenta."

29. Ibid., 120: "Sciatis, quod per totam estate preteritam captioni civitatis per ingeniorum erectionem et frequenter per terram et aquam insultui vacavimus; et cum predictis operam daremus, Sarraceni, agminibus factis et bellis ordinatis, in manu potenti licias nostras expugnabant ita violenter, quod licias nostras semel intraverunt, quos nos potenter eiecimus et tam equorum quam personarum stragem fecimus copiosam."

30. Ibid., 120: "Consideraremus quod sine bello difficilitantum non opus perficeremus, habita prius magna deliberatio quis castra nostra custodiret et qui nobiscum egrederentur et quis galeas et vasa nostra dirigeret per flumen ad expugnanda vasa et capienda tentoria inimicorum nostrorum."

31. Ibid., 120.

32. Ibid., 121: "Armorum pondere cruciaretur."

33. Ibid.: "Revertentibus nobis quidam ex Sarracenis a latere, quidam ante, quidam retro, lanceis, sagittis, clavis et pilis et igne greco nos molestabant."

166 NOTES TO PAGES 52–57

34. Ibid.: "Magna pars calore et siti in sabulo fugiendo extincti sunt."

35. Ibid.: "Sarraceni vero in milites nostros postmodum ita vehementer irruerunt, quod nostris in personis et equitaturis intolerabilia damna intulerunt. Quod quidam ex militibus nostris non sustinentes, quidam inde indignati hostes impetebant; sed Sarraceni includentes dispersos quo eorum consuetudinem non noverant, eos in tantum clavis et ensibus, pilis et igne greco agitabant, quod ipsi succubuerunt."

36. Ibid., 122: "Sciatis quod quidam peregrine metu, quidam quia moram fecerant annuam in exercitu ad transfretandum se preparabant, quod remanentibus timorem pariter generat."

37. Ibid., 112: "Passa eclypsim tetendit ad occasum"; "tempore perfidi Machometi."

38. Ibid., 113: "Cuius afflictionem dominus respiciens in diebus nostris multis eiusdem ecclesie filiis inspiravit ut matris sue compaterentur doloribus."

39. Psalms 3, 76, 141, 36, 39, 146, and 125.

40. Christopher Allmand, "The Reporting of War in the Middle Ages," in *War and Society in Medieval and Early Modern Britain*, ed. Diana Dunn (Liverpool: Liverpool University Press, 2000), 17–33. Also Paul, *To Follow in Their Footsteps*, 88–89.

41. Paola Filippucci, "In a Ruined Country: Place and the Memory of War Destruction in Argonne (France)," in *Remembering Violence: Anthropological Perspectives on Intergenerational Transmission*, 2nd ed., ed. Nicholas Argenti and Katharina Schramm (New York: Berghahn Books, 2012), 182.

42. C. Stephen Jaeger and Ingrid Karsten, eds., *Codierungen von Emotionen im Mittelalter* (Berlin: Walter de Gruyter, 2003), viii.

43. Susanna A. Throop, *Crusading as an Act of Vengeance, 1095–1216* (Farnham: Ashgate, 2011).

44. See, most recently, Barbara H. Rosenwein and Riccardo Cristiani, *What Is the History of Emotions?* (Cambridge: Polity Press, 2018).

45. For a study of classical and medieval "emotion words," see Barbara Rosenwein, *Emotional Communities in the Early Middle Ages* (Ithaca: Cornell University Press, 2006). For important recent works in the history of emotions, see, inter alia, Nicole Eustace et al., "AHR Conversation: The Historical Study of the Emotions," *American Historical Review* 117, no. 5 (2012): 1487–531; Susan J. Matt and Peter N. Stearns, *Doing Emotions History* (Urbana: University of Illinois Press, 2014); Jan Plamper, *The History of Emotions: An Introduction* (Oxford: Oxford University Press, 2015).

46. William M. Reddy, *The Navigation of Feeling: A Framework for the History of Emotions* (Cambridge: Cambridge University Press, 2001).

47. See Jordan, *Louis IX*; Megan Cassidy-Welch, "Memories of Space in Thirteenth-Century France: Displaced People After the Albigensian Crusade," *Parergon* 27, no. 2 (2010): 111–31.

48. De Vitry, Letter 4, 108.

49. Ibid., 101: "Quam arta est via que ducit ad vitam, et pauci intrant per eam."

50. Maier, *Crusade Propaganda*, 125.

51. De Vitry, Letter 4, 106: "Peregrini, vero tam nobiles quam alii in sabulo sese procientes et pulverem super caput suum aspergentes cum lacrimis et gemitu clamabant ad dominum ut misereretur populi sui."

52. Ibid., 107: "Lacrimis et orationibus peregrinorum vegetati et in domino confortati."

53. Ibid., Letter 6, 126: "In stuporem et pusillanimitatem conversi et confusi."

54. Ibid., 129: "Illo die priusquam ad castra nostra perveniremus plusquam mille ex nostris amisimus, quibusdam gladio interfectis, aliis captis equis suis vulneratis et pre calore deficientibus, multis etiam ex peditibus propter estum solis siti extinctis; quidam etiam solo timore iusto licet occult dei iudicio in insaniam converse expiraverunt."

55. Ibid., 129: "Ego vero die illa absque armis cum cappa et suppellicio cum domno legato et patriarcha, qui sanctam crucem ferebat, exieram et non placuit domino cum suis martyribus indignum et miserum me vocare, sed adhuc voluit me ad laborem et dolorem reservare."

56. For Marie of Oignies and John of Nivelles and the hagiographical texts of Jacques de Vitry and Thomas of Cantimpré, see Anneke B. Mulder-Bakker, ed., *Mary of Oignies: Mother of Salvation* (Turnhout: Brepols, 2006).

57. Oliver of Paderborn, *Historia Damiatina*, 235: "Ingredientibus nobis occurrit fetor intolerabilis, aspectus miserabilis."

58. Gabrielle M. Spiegel, *Romancing the Past: The Rise of Vernacular Prose Historiography in Thirteenth-Century France* (Berkeley: University of California Press, 1993), 215.

59. Ibid., 219.

60. For the classic study in a monastic context, see Jean Leclercq, *The Love of Learning and the Desire for God: A Study of Monastic Culture*, trans. Catherine Misrahi (New York: Fordham University Press, 1982); for the scholastic context, see Brian Stock, *The Implications of Literacy: Written Language and Models of Interpretation in the Eleventh and Twelfth Centuries* (Princeton: Princeton University Press, 1983), 410–38.

61. Joan Scott, "The Evidence of Experience," *Critical Inquiry* 17, no. 4 (1991): 773–97.

62. Leonard V. Smith, *The Embattled Self: French Soldiers' Testimony of the Great War* (Ithaca: Cornell University Press, 2007), 13.

63. See Renaud Dulong, *Le témoin oculaire: Les conditions sociales de l'attestation personnelle* (Paris: Éditions de l'École des Hautes Études en Sciences Sociales, 1998), for a sociological analysis of the eyewitness.

64. Powell, *Anatomy of a Crusade*, 184.

Chapter 3

The first epigraph to this chapter is drawn from Aimeric de Pegulhan, *Ara parra qual seran enveyos*, in *Les troubadours et la cour des Malaspina*, ed. Gilda Caïti-Russo (Montpellier: Presses Universitaires de la Méditerranée, 2005), 100: "Avengutz es lo temps e la sazoz / on deu esser proat qual temon Dieu / qu'elh non somo mas los valens e.ls pros / car silh seran tostemps francames sieu / qui seran lai fi e bo sofredor/ ni afortit ni bon combatedor / e franc e larc e cortes e leyal / e remanran li menut e.l venal / que dels bos vol Dieus qu'ab bos fagz valens / se salvon lai, et es belhs salvamens." Occitan troubadour texts are on the Rialto website run by the University of Naples. See "Aimeric de Pegulhan," Rialto, accessed July 24, 2017, http://www.rialto .unina.it/AimPeg/10.11(Caïti-Russo).htm. The second epigraph derives from Jacques de Vitry,

Letter 3, 100: "Nunc ergo omnium nostrorum studium est et una voluntas." The attribution of this letter to de Vitry is disputed, although it is included in Huygens's edition. For some recent commentary on its authorship, see Jan Vandeburie, "The Preacher and the Pope: Jacques de Vitry and Honorius III at the Time of the Fifth Crusade, 1216–1227," in *Papacy, Crusade, and Christian-Muslim Relations*, ed. Jessalynn L. Bird (Amsterdam: Amsterdam University Press, 2018): 131–54.

1. Oliver of Paderborn, *Historia Damiatina; Gesta obsidionis Damiatae*, in Röhricht, ed., *Quinti belli sacri*, 73–115; for the attribution to Johannes Codagnellus, see Oswald Holder-Egger, "Über die historischen Werke des Johannes Codagnellus von Piacenza," *Neues Archiv* 16 (1890): 251–346, 473–509.

2. Ashplant, Dawson, and Roper, eds., *Politics of War Memory*, 22. See, for instance, Graham Dawson, *Soldier Heroes: British Adventure, Empire, and the Imagining of Masculinities* (London: Routledge, 1994). Some have maintained that individual remembering is not always culturally determined in this way and that subjective and emotional experience are not necessarily subsumed by dominant cultural forms—see Michael Roper, "Re-remembering the Soldier Hero: The Psychic and Social Construction of Memory in Personal Narratives of the Great War," *History Workshop Journal* 50 (2000): 181–204.

3. Assmann, *Das kulturelle Gedächtnis*. See the trenchant comments by Mary Carruthers in "Moving Back in Memory Studies," *History Workshop Journal* 77 (2014): 275–82. See also Assmann, *Der lange Schatten der Vergangenheit*.

4. Cited in Powell, *Anatomy of a Crusade*, 196.

5. For the relationship between the *Chronicle of Ernoul* and the Old French translation and continuation of William of Tyre, together with the former's representation of Frederick after 1225, see Peter Edbury, "Ernoul, Eracles and the Fifth Crusade," in *Fifth Crusade in Context*, ed. Mylod et al., 163–74. For a similarly disparaging view of Frederick II, see Janet Shirley, trans., *Crusader Syria in the Thirteenth Century: The Rothelin Continuation of the History of William*

of *Tyre with Part of the Eracles or Acre Text* (Aldershot: Ashgate, 1999), which narrates that Frederick was too close to the Saracens, had no plan for freeing the Holy Land, was full of guile trickery and deceit, and deferred his crusading vow, unlike the brave and good knights who went on Crusade when they said they would.

6. Jacques de Vitry, "Sermon to Pilgrims," in *Crusade and Christendom*, ed. Bird, Peters, and Powell, 147–48.

7. Paul, "In Search of the Marshal's Lost Crusade." Barbara Packard has shown quite clearly how the new literary turn to romance meant that the "lauding of heroes and their deeds appears to have been increasingly relegated to chansons and epic writings" ("Remembering the First Crusade," 119).

8. Packard, "Remembering the First Crusade," 124–25.

9. See also the recent discussion in Gaposchkin, *Invisible Weapons*, 110–21.

10. Riley-Smith, *The First Crusade*, 84.

11. J. P. Migne, ed., "Quia maior," in *Patrologia latina* 216 (Paris, 1855), 817–22; and translated in Bird, Peters, and Powell, eds., *Crusade and Christendom*, 111–12.

12. De Vitry, Letter 4, 107: "Peregrini vero tam nobiles quam alii."

13. Oliver of Paderborn, *Historia Damiatina*, 184.

14. Ibid.: "Christiani . . . rigatis vultibus dolorem, quem pro illis habuerunt, qui discrimen sustinuerunt in fluminis profundo, et totius Christianitatis dispendium protestando."

15. *Gesta obsidionis Damiatae*, 76.

16. Cited in Elina Gertsman, "'Going They Went and Wept': Tears in Medieval Discourse," in *Crying in the Middle Ages: Tears of History*, ed. Elina Gertsman (London: Routledge, 2011), xii.

17. *Gesta obsidionis Damiatae*, 76: "Ex oculis fluvium lachrymarum effundentes." See also Stephen Spencer, "The Emotional Rhetoric of Crusader Spirituality in the Narratives of the First Crusade," *Nottingham Medieval Studies* 58 (2014): 57–86, for a recent exploration of tears in crusading culture.

18. Piroska Nagy, "Religious Weeping as Ritual in the Medieval West," *Social Analysis* 48, no. 2 (2004): 119–37; Nagy, *Le don des larmes au Moyen Âge* (Paris: Albin Michel, 2000).

19. De Vitry, Letter 4, 106: "Sed in deo spem suam totam ponant."

20. *Gesta obsidionis Damiatae*, 99: "Ne permittas nos a minibus crudelium Paganorum perire."

21. *L'estoire de Eracles empereur et la conqueste de la terre d'outremer*, in *Recueil des historiens des croisades* I, Historiens occidentaux 2 (Paris, 1859), 337.

22. Oliver of Paderborn, *Historia Damiatina*, 184–85: "Miles quidam iuvenis Leodiensis diocesis primus turrim ascendit; Friso quidam iuvenculus tenens flagellum, quo granum excuti solet, sed ad pugnandum connexione catenarum preparatum, ad dextram et sinistram fortissime percussit et quendam tenentem signum croceum soldani stravit, vexillum et abstulit."

23. De Vitry, Letter 4, 106.

24. *Gesta obsidionis Damiatae*, 83. It is the Pisans who are described in the *Gesta* as possessing "magne fortitudinis et magnitudinis" (97). For miracles in Crusade narratives, see Lapina, *Warfare and the Miraculous*.

25. See J. J. van Moolenbroek, "Signs in the Heavens in Groningen and Friesland in 1214: Oliver of Cologne and Crusading Propaganda," *Journal of Medieval History* 13, no. 3 (1987): 251–72.

26. Dominic Francis, "Oliver of Paderborn and His Siege Engine at Damietta," *Nottingham Medieval Studies* 37 (1993): 28–32.

27. See Hinnebusch, "Extant Manuscripts," 157–58; and more recently, Thomas Smith, "Oliver of Cologne's *Historia Damiatina*: A New Manuscript Witness in Dublin, Trinity College Library MS 496," *Hermathena* 194 (2013): 37–68, which discusses a redaction of the *Historia Damiatina* composed for an English readership.

28. *Gesta obsidionis Damiatae*, 97, 93, 112.

29. Paul Magdalino, ed., *The Perception of the Past in Twelfth-Century Europe* (London: Hambledon Press, 1992), 184. For Codagnellus's other historical works, see Holder-Egger, "Über die historischen Werke"; and for a general overview, see G. Arnaldi, "Codagnello

Giovanni," in *Dizionario biografico degli italiani* (Rome: Instituto della Enciclopedia Italiana, 1982), xxvi.

30. Holder-Egger, "Über die historischen Werke." The other thirteenth-century manuscript is now Modena, Biblioteca Estense—Universitaria, Estense, Lat. 461 (its former shelfmark was MS VI.H.5), which also contains Sicard of Cremona's *De omnibus aetatibus*. The text of the *Gesta* was reproduced from this Modena manuscript in Ludovico Antonio Muratori, ed., "Memoriale potestatum Regensium," *Rerum Italicarum scriptores*, vol. 8 (Milan, 1726), 1073–74.

31. De Vitry, Letter 6, 130: "Dominus autem sibi soli victoriam reservabat . . . Confidimus autem in ipso qui portas nobis Egypti miraculose aperuit, quod christianorum imperio residuum subiciet Egypti tenebras illuminando et in fines orbis terre ecclesiam suam dilatando."

32. Ibid., Letter 4, 111: "Cum in nocte Pentecostes matutinas audisset, missa autem de die solempniter celebrata, flexo genu ante altare receipt viaticum. Expleto vero vespertino officio iussit sibi sterni lectum iuxta capellam nostrum in modico tentorio, nocte vero eum inunximus oleo sancto infirmorum. Ipse, continuo habens in ore eum quem fideliter in vita sua predicaverate, imminente diluculo cum laude dei et gratiarum actione migravit ad dominum."

33. Ibid., Letter 5, 116: "Vir litteratus et devotus, affabilis, liberalis et benignus, zelum dei habens et liberationem terre sancte ardenter desiderans."

34. Ibid., 126: "Quorum nomina scripta sunt in libro vite." Marcel Dickson and Christiane Dickson, "Le cardinal Robert de Courson: Sa vie," *Archives d'histoire doctrinale et littéraire du Moyen Âge* 9 (1934): 53–142.

35. Dickson and Dickson, "Le cardinal Robert de Courson," 122. See also de Vitry, Letter 6, where these men are named again.

36. Oliver of Paderborn, *Historia Damiatina*, 180.

37. Ibid., 188: "Multi pro Christo martires, plures in Christo confessores apud Damiatam rebus humanis exempti migraverunt ad Dominum."

38. De Vitry, Letter 4, 105.

39. *Gesta obsidionis Damiatae*, 101–2.

40. Oliver of Paderborn, *Historia Damiatina*, 205–7.

41. *Gesta obsidionis Damiatae*, 90: "Nulla quippe humana lingua sane potest explicare miserias, paupertates, tormenta, langores et infirmitates, quas Christiani in obsidione Damiate pro amore Iesu Christi passi fuerunt pro fide Christianitatis."

42. Ibid., 79, describes the suffering of the crusaders and the conditions in which they fought, saying how much blood and "putredine atque fetore pro interfectione eorum per plures dies Christiani steterunt, quod de fluminis aqua nullus bibere potuit nec coquina facere."

43. De Vitry, "Sermo ad crucesignatos vel signando," in Maier, *Crusade Propaganda*, 124–25: "Pusillanimes sunt et putridi quod crux illis non potest assui, qui tamquam panni vetustate consumpti et mulli usui apti suturum retinere non valent. Hii sunt formidolosi qui ad bellum non sunt ydonei, sed a Domino repobentur."

44. Oliver of Paderborn, *Historia Damiatina*, 218.

45. Samuel P. Scott and Robert I. Burns, ed. and trans., *Las siete partidas*, vol. 2, *Medieval Government: The World of Kings and Warriors* (Philadelphia: University of Pennsylvania Press, 2012), Title XXVII, Law 1; Part 2, Title XIX, 409.

46. Matthew Strickland, *War and Chivalry: The Conduct and Perception of War in England, and Normandy, 1066–1217* (Cambridge: Cambridge University Press, 1996), 120. For Richard I, see *Chronicon Richardi divinensis de tempore regis Ricardi primi*, ed. and trans. J. Appleby (London, 1963), 22: "Pedes pleno pede fugiens pedem perdat."

47. Calixtus II, *Epistolae et privilegia*, in *Patrologia latina* 163, ed. J. P. Migne (Paris, 1853), 45–46. See also Conor Kostick, "Courage and Cowardice on the First Crusade, 1096–1099," *War in History* 20, no. 1 (2013): 32–49.

48. Oliver of Paderborn, *Historia Damiatina*, 213–18.

49. Ibid., 213–18.

50. *Gesta obsidionis Damiatae*, 92–93.

51. Oliver of Paderborn, *Historia Damiatina*, 218.

52. De Vitry, Letter 6, 129.

53. E. Blochet, trans., *Extraits de l'histoire des patriarches d'Alexandrie relatifs au siège de Damiette sous le règne d'al-Malik al-Kāmil*, *Revue de l'orient latin* 11 (Paris, 1907), 245. Cited in Perry, *John of Brienne*, 100.

54. See William M. Aird, "'Many Others, Whose Names I Do Not Know, Fled with Them': Norman Courage and Cowardice on the First Crusade," in *Crusading and Pilgrimage in the Norman World*, ed. Kathryn Hurlock and Paul Oldfield (Woodbridge: Boydell Press, 2015), 13–29.

55. Oliver of Paderborn, *Historia Damiatina*, 248.

56. De Vitry, Letter 7, 135.

57. *Quia maior*, in *Crusade and Christendom*, ed. Bird, Peters, and Powell, 108.

58. Yves Gravelle, "Le problème des prisonniers de guerre pendant les croisades orientales (1095–1192)" (MA diss., Université de Sherbrooke, 1999), 120–22.

59. Suffering was literal in many cases. See Piers D. Mitchell, "The Torture of Military Captives in the Crusades to the Medieval Middle East," in *Noble Ideals and Bloody Realities: Warfare in the Middle Ages*, ed. Niall Christie and Maya Yazigi (Leiden: Brill, 2006), 97–118.

60. The most recent edition and translation of this song may be found at the University of Warwick's excellent *Troubadours, Trouvères and the Crusades* website, accessed August 8, 2017, http://www2.warwick.ac.uk/fac/arts/modernlanguages/research/french/crusades/texts/of/rs1576#page1.

61. William of Tyre, *Chronique*, ed. R. B. C. Huygens, *Corpus christianorum continuatio mediaevalis* 63 and 63A (Turnhout: Brepols, 1986), 18.14.

62. Ibid., 9.21.

63. Elizabeth Siberry, *Criticism of Crusading: 1095–1274* (Oxford: Clarendon Press, 1985).

64. A translation is available in Louise Riley-Smith and Jonathan Riley-Smith, *The Crusades: Idea and Reality, 1095–1274* (London: Edward Arnold, 1981), 57–59. For other examples of the trope, see, inter alia, Bernard of Clairvaux, "De consideratione ad Eugenium papam," in *Sancti Bernardi opera*, vol. 3, ed. Jean Leclercq and Henri Rochais (Rome, 1963), 379–493. A

convenient translation may be found in S. J. Allen and E. Amt, eds., *The Crusades: A Reader* (Peterborough: Broadview Press, 2003), 145–46.

65. De Vitry, Letter 6; Oliver of Paderborn, *Historia Damiatina*, 216–17.

66. Oliver of Paderborn, *Historia Damiatina*, 217: "Meror nostros occupavit, sed nulla desperatio. Pro certo enim habemus, quod pena peccati fuit hec castigatio."

67. *Epistola saluaris regi Babilnis ab auctore huius operis conscripta*, in Hoogeweg, *Die Schriften*, 296.

68. De Vitry, Letter 6, 127–28.

69. Ibid., 133, version B to John of Nivelles: "Misimus vobis duos parvulos de incendio Babylonis extractos."

70. Oliver of Paderborn, *Historia Damiatina*, 177.

71. Perry, *John of Brienne*; Powell, *Anatomy of a Crusade*. Guy Perry's discovery of a letter from John to Frederick II shows that they were in contact during the Crusade and that John represented himself as the leader of the Crusade.

72. Thomas Smith, "The Role of Pope Honorius III in the Fifth Crusade," in *Fifth Crusade in Context*, ed. Mylod et al., 15–26.

73. Oliver of Paderborn, *Historia Damiatina*, 207: "Plenus devotione, humilitate, obedientia, largitate."

74. Ibid., 213: "Et sic veraciter deprehensum est, sola virtute divina Damiatam in manus Christianorum fore tradendam."

75. De Mas-Latrie, ed., *Chronique d'Ernoul*, 417.

76. The Colbert Fontainebleu continuation is cited in Perry, *John of Brienne*, 101; de Vitry, Letter 6, 125: "Vir cautus et providus et in negotiis domini peragendis vigil et sollicitus."

77. See Perry, *John of Brienne*, 101–19.

78. Oliver of Paderborn, *Historia Damiatina*, 248: "Anteriorum oblitus ad posteriora se convertit"; de Vitry, Letter 7, 135–36.

79. Ashplant, Dawson, and Roper, eds., *Politics of War Memory*.

80. Wulf Kansteiner, "Finding Meaning in Memory: A Methodological Critique of Collective Memory Studies," *History and Theory* 41, no. 2 (May 2002): 197.

Chapter 4

The epigraph for this chapter is drawn from Oliver of Paderborn, *Historia Damiatina*, 281, 276, 282.

1. Hiram Kümper, "Oliver of Paderborn," in *The Encyclopedia of the Medieval Chronicle*, ed. Graeme Dunphy, 2 vols. (Leiden, 2010), 2:1166–67.

2. Peters, *Christian Society*, 142, 145.

3. George L. Mosse, *Fallen Soldiers: Reshaping the Memory of the World Wars* (New York: Oxford University Press, 1990), 7.

4. The most recent summary of the *Historia Damiatina* is Smith, "Oliver of Cologne's *Historia Damiatina*."

5. Ibid., citing Herman Hoogeweg, "Eine neue Schrift des Kölner Domscholasters Oliver," *Neues Archiv der Gesellschaft für Ältere Deutsche Geschichtskunde* 16 (1890): 191.

6. Herman Hoogeweg, "Die Kreuzpredigt des Jahres 1224 in Deutschland mit besonderer Rücksicht auf die Erzdiöcese Köln," *Deutsche Zeitschrift für Geschichtswissenschaft* 4, no. 2 (1890): 54–74.

7. Rubenstein, *Armies of Heaven*.

8. Matthew Gabriele, "From Prophecy to Apocalypse: The Verb Tenses of Jerusalem in Robert the Monk's *Historia* of the First Crusade," *Journal of Medieval History* 42, no. 3 (2016): 304–16. See also Jean Flori, *Chroniqueurs et propagandistes: Introduction critique aux sources de la première croisade* (Geneva: Droz, 2010).

9. Nicholas Morton, *Encountering Islam on the First Crusade* (Cambridge: Cambridge University Press, 2016), 217.

10. Guibert of Nogent, *Dei gesta per francos*, 113; Roger of Howden, *Gesta regis Henrici Secundi et Ricardi Primi*, ed. W. Stubbs, Rolls Series, vol. 49, no. 2. (London: Longmans, 1867), 151.

11. Lapina, *Warfare and the Miraculous*, 124 and 141.

12. For a discussion of the apocalyptic dimension of these letters, see Alfred J. Andrea, "Innocent III, the Fourth Crusade, and the Coming Apocalypse," in *The Medieval Crusade*, ed. Susan J. Ridyard (Woodbridge: Boydell Press, 2004), 97–106. For the papal letters, see Andrea's convenient translations in his *Contemporary Sources for the Fourth Crusade* (Leiden: Brill, 2000), 115–26 and 131–39.

13. Joachim of Fiore, *Expositio in apocalypsim* (Venice, 1527; repr., Frankfurt: Minerva, 1964).

14. *Quia maior*, in *Crusade and Christendom*, ed. Bird, Peters, and Powell, 108–9.

15. Hoogeweg, *Die Schriften*, 228–29: "Adultero quem diu tenuisti, proiecto ad priorem virum tuum reversa es"; "Acconensis episcopus ex te primitias aminarum Deo solvit parvulos tuos . . . etiam morti proximos baptismatis unda sacramentaliter mundando"; "et que prius parturiebas spurios amodo paries filios legitimos ad cultum filii Dei."

16. Ibid.: "Maius auxilium tulisti quam residuum totius regni Teutonici" (230); "Illustris imperator noster et rex Sicilie ardenter exspectatur a populo Dei ad negotii felicem comsummationem" (231).

17. The prophecy is printed in Röhricht, ed., *Quinti belli sacri*, 205–13. It survives in five manuscripts, none of which are Arabic.

18. See Bernard Hamilton, "The Lands of Prester John: Western Knowledge of Asia and Africa at the Time of the Crusades," *Haskins Society Journal* 15 (2006): 126–42; Bernard Hamilton, "The Impact of Prester John," in *Fifth Crusade in Context*, ed. Mylod et al., 53–68; Hamilton, "Continental Drift: Prester John's Progress Through the Indies," in *Prester John, the Mongols and the Ten Lost Tribes*, ed. Charles F. Beckingham and Bernard Hamilton (Aldershot: Variorum, 1996), 237–69.

19. De Vitry, Letter 7, 139: "Quasi claustrum monachorum."

20. Ibid., 150: "Christianorum autem exercitus predictis rumoribus exultabat et confortabatur in domino et maxime postquam litteras imperatoris Romanorum Frederici recepimus cum nuntiis eius affirmantibus, quod concedente domino cum magna virtute et magnifico apparatu venturus esset in proximo Augusto ad honorem dei et subsidium christianorum."

21. Ibid., 152: "Inde iudicium et finis."

22. Jan Vandeburie, "'Consenescentis mundi die vergente ad vesperam': James of Vitry's *Historia orientalis* and Eschatological Rhetoric

After the Fourth Lateran Council," in *Uses of the Bible in Crusader Sources*, ed. Lapina and Morton, 344.

23. Maier, *Crusade Propaganda*, 83–84.

24. Brett E. Whalen, *Dominion of God: Christendom and Apocalypse in the Middle Ages* (Cambridge: Harvard University Press, 2009); Geraldine Heng, *Empire of Magic: Medieval Romance and the Politics of Cultural Fantasy* (New York: Columbia University Press, 2003); Tolan, *Saint Francis and the Sultan*.

25. As Matthew Gabriele noted, prophecies could fail, but the apocalypse could not. See Gabriele, "From Prophecy to Apocalypse," 306.

26. See William Purkis, "Stigmata on the First Crusade," in *Signs, Wonders, Miracles: Representations of Divine Power in the Life of the Church*, ed. Kate Cooper and Jeremy Gregory, Studies in Church History 41 (Woodbridge: Boydell Press, 2005), 99–108.

27. Innocent III, *Innocentii III romani pontifices*, in *Patrologia latina* 214, ed. J. P. Migne (Paris, 1855), 1340.

28. Röhricht, ed., *Quinti belli sacri*, 13: "Dominus in cruce describit nobis totam vitam nostram, ut imitemur eum."

29. Oliver of Paderborn, *Historia Damiatina*, 193.

30. De Vitry, Letter 5, 116.

31. *Gesta obsidionis Damiatae*, 103; Apoc. 7:13.

32. Oliver of Paderborn, *Historia Damiatina*, 274.

33. David S. Bachrach, *Religion and the Conduct of War, c. 300–1215* (Woodbridge: Boydell Press, 2003), 128; Caroline Smith, "Martyrdom and Crusading in the Thirteenth Century: Remembering the Dead of Louis IX's Crusades," *Al-Masāq* 15, no. 2 (2003): 189–96; Packard, "Remembering the First Crusade," 117.

34. De Vitry, Letter 1, 78: "Vos autem instanter orate pro me et promeis, ut deus perducat nos ad portum Acconensis civitatis, et inde ad partum eterne beatitudinis."

35. Ibid., 71: "Inter varios dolores et labores continuos et frequentes mee peregrinationis molestias unicum est michi remedium et singulare solatium frequens amicorum meorum

memoria, quorum beneficio sustentatur spiritus meus ne corruat, quorum orationibus vegetatur anima mea ne penitus deficiat. Ex hac tamen medicinali memoria, cuius beneficio vulnera mea sanantur, aliquando novum vulnus cordi meo infigitur . . . circa notos et amicos meos mens mea adeo occupatur, ut fere omnia alia in tedium convertantur ita, quod appetitus orationis et desiderium lectionis ex hac frequendi afflictione frequenter in me evacuantur."

36. Ibid., Letter 2, 79: "Testis autem michi est dominus, pro cuius gratia continuis laboribus affligor, pro cuius nomine cotidianis expositus sum periculis, quod sine intermissione memoria memoriam vestri facio."

37. Ibid., 81: "Ego vero nullo modo adquievi propter malum exemplum, sed cum aliis volui suscipere commune periculum."

38. Ibid., Letter 5, 113: "Hiis vocibus vidua paupercula tempestate divulsa non cessat clamare et coram domino genua flectere et ad ostium misericordie eius indesinenter pulsare, cuius afflictionem dominus respiciens in diebus nostris multis eiusdem ecclesie filiis inspiravit ut matris sue compaterentur doloribus."

39. See Linda M. Paterson, *Singing the Crusades: French and Occitan Lyric Responses to the Crusading Movements, 1137–1336* (Cambridge: D. S. Brewer, 2018).

40. The University of Warwick project contains the Old French and Occitan together with the English translation that I have used here. See "Châtelain d'Arras," Warwick, accessed August 8, 2017, http://www2 .warwick.ac.uk/fac/arts/modernlanguages /research/french/crusades/texts/of/rs140/ #page1.

41. For the Crusade song, see generally Michael Routledge, "Songs," in *The Oxford Illustrated History of the Crusades*, ed. Jonathan Riley-Smith (Oxford: Oxford University Press, 1995), 91–111; Cathrynke T. J. Dijkstra, *La chanson de croisade: Étude thématique d'un genre hybride* (Amsterdam: Schiphouwer et Brinckman, 1995). For a recent study of the Châtelain d'Arras's Crusade song, see Marisa Galvez, "The Voice of the Unrepentant Crusader: 'Aler m'estuet' by the Châtelain d'Arras," in *Voice and Voicelessness in Medieval Europe*, ed. Irit Ruth

NOTES TO PAGES 97–103   173

Kleiman (Basingstoke: Palgrave Macmillan, 2015), 101–22; and most recently Paterson, *Singing the Crusades*.

42. For the translation, see "Aimeric de Pegulhan," Rialto, accessed August 8, 2017, http://www.rialto.unina.it/AimPeg/10.11 (Caïti-Russo).htm.

43. For the text and translation, see "Hugues de Berzé," Warwick, accessed August 8, 2017, http://www2.warwick.ac.uk/fac/arts /modernlanguages/research/french/crusades /texts/of/rs1126/#page1.

44. Routledge, "Songs," 101.

45. Lisa Perfetti, "Crusader as Lover: The Eroticized Poetics of Crusading in Medieval France," *Speculum* 88, no. 4 (2013): 957.

46. Much of the following appears in expanded form in Megan Cassidy-Welch, "The Stones of Damietta: Remembering the Fifth Crusade," in *Papacy, Crusade*, ed. Bird, 196–210. I thank Amsterdam University Press for permission to use part of that chapter here.

47. Hoogeweg, *Die Schriften*, 239. See also Denys Pringle, *The Churches of the Crusader Kingdom of Jerusalem: A Corpus*. vol. 1, *A–K* (*Excluding Acre and Jerusalem*) (Cambridge: Cambridge University Press, 1993), 203; Folda, *Crusader Art*.

48. De Vitry, Letter 6, 128.

49. Shirley, *Crusader Syria*, 89.

50. Ibid.

51. De Vitry, Letter 6, 127: "Cum lacrimis et magna populi devotione celebravit in qua etiam sedem archiepiscopalem instituit."

52. Amy Remensnyder, *La Conquistadora: The Virgin Mary at War and Peace in the Old and New Worlds* (New York: Oxford University Press, 2014), 29.

53. For a resume of thirteenth-century commentators on the consecration ritual, see Dawn Marie Hayes, *Body and Sacred Place in Medieval Europe, 1100–1389* (New York: Routledge, 2003).

54. Cited in Hayes, *Body and Sacred Place*, 13. For the critical edition of the Latin text, see William Durand, *Rationale divinorum officiorum*, ed. A. Davril and T. Thibodeau, vols. 140, 140A, 140B of *Corpus christianorum continuatio mediaevalis* (Turnhout: Brepols, 1995–2000). For an overview of the medieval

rite of consecration, see Dominique Iogna-Prat, "The Consecration of Church Space," in *Medieval Christianity in Practice*, ed. Miri Rubin (Princeton: Princeton University Press, 2009), 95–102.

55. Walter of Coventry, *Memoriale fratris Walteri de Coventria: The Historical Collections of Walter of Coventry*, ed. William Stubbs, Rolls Series, vol. 58 (London: Longmans, 1872–73), 2:242–43; and Paris, *Chronica majora*, 3:164. For Edmund as a crusading hero, see Frantzen, *Bloody Good*, 53–54.

56. Sarrasin's letter is translated in Bird, Peters, and Powell, eds., *Crusade and Christendom*, 354–60; see also Jeanette Beer, "The Letter of Jean Sarrasin, Crusader," in *Journeys Toward God: Pilgrimage and Crusade*, ed. Barbara N. Sargent-Bauer (Kalamazoo: Medieval Institute, 1992), 135–55.

57. Letter of Jean Beaumont, June 25, 1249, in Paul Riant, "Six lettres relatives aux croisades," *Archives de l'orient latin*, vol. 1 (Paris, 1881), 390.

58. See Pascal Buresi, "Les conversions d'églises et de mosquées en Espagne au XIe–XIIIe siècles," in *Religion et société urbaine au Moyen Âge: Études offertes à Jean-Louis Biget par ses anciens élèves* (Paris: Publications de la Sorbonne, 2000), 333–50.

59. Bird, Peters, and Powell, eds., *Crusade and Christendom*, 236.

60. Letter of Gui de Melun (1249), in Paris, *Chronica majora*, 6:160. See also a letter written by Blanche of Castile to Henry III in 1249, in which she reports that the Christian army entered the city barefoot, processing to the mosque "qui dudum in alia captione civitatis ejusdem ecclesia erat beatae Mariae Virginis" (*Chronica majora*, 6:166–67).

61. Ibid., 6:160: "Exercitus Christianus ad instar stagni, quod ex torrentibus inundantibus suscipit incrementum, cotidie dilatatur."

62. Ibid., 6:163: "Vovi et juravi hec venire, et terminum prout in me erat praefixi; sed non vovi me nec juravi hinc recedere, nec terminum mei recessus assignavi. Ideo colonorum instrumenta mecum apportavi."

63. For the Latin text of the charter, see Jean Richard, "La fondation d'une église latine en orient par saint Louis: Damiette," *Bibliothèque de l'école des chartes* 120 (1962): 39–54.

64. Ibid., 54: "Volumus etiam et precepimus quod, si premissa a nobis assignata non fuerint eidem ecclesie, in toto vel in parte, priusquam a partibus recesserimus cismarinis, quicumque dominum terre habuerit loco nostri ea integraliter teneatur eidem ecclesie, prout expressa sunt superius, assignare."

65. De Vitry, Letter 6, 130–31.

Chapter 5

The epigraph for this chapter is drawn from Doreen Massey, "Places and Their Pasts," *History Workshop Journal* 39, no. 1 (1995): 183.

1. *Gesta crucigerorum Rhenanorum*, in Röhricht, ed., *Quinti belli sacri*, 30: "Auriferus Thagus."

2. From *De expugnatione Ulixbonensi*, translated in James A. Brundage, *The Crusades: A Documentary Survey* (Milwaukee: Marquette University Press, 1962), 98.

3. For an account of these, see Stephen Lay, "Miracles, Martyrs, and Cult of Henry the Crusader in Lisbon," *Portuguese Studies* 24, no. 1 (2008): 7–31. For the sources, see Winand's letter, edited and transcribed in Susan B. Edington, "The Lisbon Letter of the Second Crusade," *Historical Research* 69, no. 170 (1996): 328–39; the letter by Duodecin is included in G. Waitz, ed., *Annales sancti disibodi*, in Monumenta Germaniae Historica SS 17, ed. George H. Pertz (Hanover, 1861), 27–29; Michel-Jean Joseph Brial, ed., *Epistola Arnulfi*, in *Recueil des historiens des Gaules et de la France*, vol. 14, ed. M. Bouquet (Paris: Imprimerie Impériale, 1806), 325–27; Charles Wendell David, trans. and ed., *De expugnatione Lyxbonensi: The Conquest of Lisbon* (New York: Columbia University Press, 1936).

4. *Indiculum fundationis monasterii sancti Vincentii*, in *Portugaliae monumenta historica scriptores*, vol. 1, fasc. 1 (Lisbon: Typis Academicis, 1856), 90–93; and Aires Nascimento, ed., *A conquista de Lisboa aos Mouros* (Lisbon: Vega, 2001), 177–201 (parallel Latin/Portuguese translation). The text was probably composed when preparations for the Third Crusade were under way, and internal evidence dates the account to 1188.

5. *Gesta crucigerorum Rhenanorum*, in Röhricht, ed., *Quinti belli sacri*, 30.

6. *De itinere Frisonum*, in Röhricht, ed., *Quinti belli sacri*, 62: "Ad orientem vero extra civitatem quoddam est venerabile cenobium, ubi palma de sepulchre martyris Christi [. . .] pulchre consurgens in aera demonstratur, [Heinricus], princeps miliciae Christiane, ante 70 annos ibidem cum suo armigero vitam finivit in Christo; qui nunc divina revelation canonizatus, Gloria temporali letatur et eterna."

7. De Vitry, "Sermon to Pilgrims," 145.

8. See, for instance, James E. Young, *The Texture of Memory: Holocaust Memorials and Meaning* (New Haven: Yale University Press, 1993); Jay Winter, *Sites of Memory, Sites of Mourning: The Great War in European Cultural History* (Cambridge: Cambridge University Press, 1995); Reinhart Koselleck, "War Memorials: Identity Formations of the Survivors," in *The Practice of Conceptual History: Timing History, Spacing Concepts*, ed. Reinhart Koselleck, trans. Todd Samuel Presner (Stanford: Stanford University Press, 2002), 285–326.

9. David, *De expugnatione Lyxbonensi*, 119.

10. Stephen Lay, "The Reconquest as Crusade in the Anonymous *De expugnatione Lyxbonensi*," *Al-Masāq* 14, no. 2 (2002).

11. In *De civitate dei* and *In Ioannis Evangelium*, cited in David Ganz, "The Ideology of Sharing: Apostolic Community and Ecclesiastical Property in the Early Middle Ages," in *Property and Power in the Early Middle Ages*, ed. Wendy Davies and Paul Fouracre (Cambridge: Cambridge University Press, 1995), 17–30. See D. J. MacQueen, "St. Augustine's Concept of Property Ownership," *Recherches augustiniennes* 8 (1972): 187–229.

12. Fulcher of Chartres, *Historia Hierosolymitana*, i, iii, 3–7, 324; translation in Fulcher of Chartres, *History of the Expedition to Jerusalem*, 66; *Audita tremendi* in Jonathan Phillips, *The Crusades, 1095–1204*, 2nd ed. (London: Routledge, 2014), doc. 20; *Post miserabile*, in *Crusade and Christendom*, ed. Bird, Peters, and Powell, 31.

13. Riley-Smith, "Crusading as an Act of Love," 191.

14. *Quia maior*, in *Crusade and Christendom*, ed. Bird, Peters, and Powell, 111–12.

15. Psalm 78:1: "Deus venerunt gentes in hereditatem tuam polluerunt templum sanctum tuum posuerunt Hierusalem in pomorum custodiam."

16. For the liturgies commemorating the fall of Jerusalem, see Gaposchkin, *Invisible Weapons*; and more generally, Amnon Linder, *Raising Arms: Liturgy in the Struggle to Liberate Jerusalem in the Late Middle Ages* (Turnhout: Brepols, 2003).

17. *Descriptio terre sancte*, the *Historia de ortu Jerusalem*, and the *Historia regum terre sancte* are all edited by Hoogeweg and appear in *Die Schriften*.

18. *Descriptio terre sancte*, 3–5.

19. Ibid., 6: "In Arabia est Mons regalis castrum habens munitissimum, quod Balduinus primus rex Francorum in Jherusalem ad tutelam regni firmavit et Christianis totam illam regionem subiugavit."

20. Ibid.: "Ante Tyrum est lapidis marmoreus super quem sedit Jhesus, illesus a tempore Christi usque ad expulsionem gentium de urbe, sed postea defraudatus est Francis necnon Veneticis."

21. Ibid., 17. See also Amy Remensnyder, *Remembering Kings Past: Monastic Foundation Legends in Medieval Southern France* (Ithaca: Cornell University Press, 1995), 155, for connections to the *Historia scholastica* of Peter Comestor, which told of this legend and its subsequent diffusion in a number of thirteenth-century manuscripts.

22. *Historia regum terre sancte*, 84.

23. Ibid., 156–57.

24. Oliver of Paderborn, *Historia Damiatina*, 262–63: "Magister huius horti christianus est habens sub se christianos et sarracenos ministros."

25. See Andrew Jotischky, *The Perfection of Solitude: Hermits and Monks in the Crusader States* (University Park: Pennsylvania State University Press, 1995); Denys Pringle, *The Churches of the Crusader Kingdom of Jerusalem: A Corpus*, vol. 2, *L–Z (Excluding Tyre)* (Cambridge: Cambridge University Press, 1997), 63–85.

26. See Veronica della Dora, "Gardens of Eden and Ladders to Heaven: Holy Mountain Geographies in Byzantium," in *Mapping Medieval Geographies: Geographical Encounters in the Latin West and Beyond, 300–1600*, ed. Keith D. Lilley (Cambridge: Cambridge University Press, 2013), 271–99.

27. Oliver of Paderborn, *Historia Damiatina*, 166.

28. *Descriptio terre sancte*, 11.

29. Nascimento, *A conquista de Lisboa*, 177–201. For commentary on the *Indiculum*, see Giles Constable, "A Further Note on the Conquest of Lisbon in 1147," in *The Experience of Crusading I: Western Approaches*, ed. Marcus Bull and Norman Housley (Cambridge: Cambridge University Press, 2003), 39–44; Sofia Seeger, "Gründungsbericht des Klosters S. Vicente in Lissabon: *Indiculum fundationis* (1188)," in *Mirakelberichte des frühen und hohen Mittelalters*, ed. Klaus Herbers, Lenka Jироušková, and Bernhard Vogel (Darmstadt: Wissenschaftliche Buchgesellschaft, 2005), 288–95. The following paragraphs first appeared in Megan Cassidy-Welch, "The Monastery of São Vicente de Fora in Lisbon as a Site of Crusading Memory," *Journal of Medieval Monastic Studies* 3 (2014): 1–20. I thank Brepols Publishers for permission to reproduce this section of the article here.

30. Nascimento, *A conquista de Lisboa*, 179: "Inimicorum crucis Christi mirificus extirpator"; "de diversorum partibus eptentrionis, zelo suo Dominus misit accensos."

31. Ibid., 184: "Quendam militem Coloniensem nomine Henricum, oriudum in villa que est ultra Coloniam per quatuor leugas nomine Bonna, virum utique stemate nobilem et moribus, in urbis corruisse conflictu." Armando de Sousa Pereira, "Guerra e santidade: O Cavaleiro-mártir Henrique de Bona e a conquista cristã de Lisboa," *Lusitania sacra* 17, 2nd series (2005): 15–38; Reinhard Jensen, "Heinrich von Bonn: Die Erinnerung an die Kreuzfahrer aus dem Romischen Reich in der portugeisischen Legendentradition," *Rheinische Vierteljahrsblätter* 30 (1965): 23–29.

32. Nascimento, *A conquista de Lisboa*, 184–86.

33. Ibid., 186.

34. Ibid., 192: "Omnes ergo male habentes ad sepulcrum illius, suplicandi gratia venientes, tollentes de palma illa suspendebant ad collum, vel redactam in pulverem bibebant statimque

176 NOTES TO PAGES 118–122

curabantur a quacumque detinebantur infirmitate."

35. David, *De expugnatione Lyxbonensi*, 135–36.

36. Nascimento, *A conquista de Lisboa*, 186: "Factus est autem ut populus ad certamen iturus, peractis missarum sollemnis, eulogiis, id est, pane benedicto cuperet premuniri. Ita enim cotidie consueverat. Cumque sacerdos vellet facere particulas quas singulis porigeret, et iam uni ex panibus secandis culter immiteretur, res miranda, ecce secati panis medietas cruentata reperitur [et] sanguis desudans. Tunc sacerdos omnesque qui aderant in stuporem converse sunt subitum, nam, visa re, vehementer fuerant perterriti. Cumque causam rei indagatione sedula quereretur, inventum est panem illum fuisse confectum cum usurpa farina, quam quidam moriens egenis preceperat erogari. Quod tandem cum annunciatum esset in castris ad spectaculum concurrunt universi, videntesque quod factum fuerat, revertebantur ammirantes, et divinum adiutorium secum esse non dubitantes, plena fide laudabant, et glorificabant Dominum, qui facit mirabilia solus."

37. Steven Justice, "Eucharistic Miracle and Eucharistic Doubt," *Journal of Medieval and Early Modern Studies* 42, no. 2 (2012): 307–32.

38. Miri Rubin, *Corpus Christi: The Eucharist in Late Medieval Culture* (Cambridge: Cambridge University Press, 1991).

39. Commentary of "Master Simon" from the Low Countries, writing in the mid-twelfth century. Cited in Rubin, *Corpus christi*, 38.

40. See Erwin Panofsky, *Abbot Suger on the Abbey Church of St. Denis and Its Art Treasures* (Princeton: Princeton University Press, 1979), 201–3.

41. Caroline Walker Bynum, *Holy Feast and Holy Fast: The Religious Significance of Food to Medieval Women* (Berkeley: University of California Press, 1987), 68.

42. Bynum, *Holy Feast and Holy Fast*, 63; and more recently, Caroline Walker Bynum, *Wonderful Blood: Theology and Practice in Late Medieval Northern Germany and Beyond* (Philadelphia: University of Pennsylvania Press, 2007).

43. Petri Vallium Sarnaii (Pierre des Vaux-de-Cernay), *Historia Albigensis*, ed. P. Guébin and E. D. Lyon, 3 vols. (Paris, 1926,

1930, 1939), bk. 1.25; Megan Cassidy-Welch, "Images of Blood in the *Historia Albigensis* of Pierre des Vaux-de-Cernay," *Journal of Religious History* 35, no. 4 (2011): 478–91.

44. Nascimento, *A conquista de Lisboa*, 190.

45. Ibid., 194: "Quare, inquit, principum ac regum est loca sancta ditare, benefactoribus concedere, possessionibus ampliare, iccirco ego rex Alfonsus vobis civibus Ulixbone atque omnibus aliis fidelibus, facio kartam possidendi mecum ecclesiam sancti Vicentii, quam in captione Ulixbone a Mauristuli, ut videlicet quicumque apud ipsam ecclesiam sepulturam suam habere suumue ibi beneficium vel elemosinas dare voluerint, ipsi et filii et progenies eorum sint mecum et filiis omnique progenie mea, heredes perpetuo in eadem ecclesia."

46. Röhricht, ed., *Quinti belli sacri*, 30: "Hanc civitatem construxit Ulixes, cum a troia post eius destruccionem discessisset, nunc autem ibi venerator beatu corpus Vincenii levite et martyris."

47. Ibid., 62: "Ibi miro scemate constructa in honore beateVirginis ostenditu ecclesias, in qua corpus beati Vincentii martyris in sarcophago requiescit argenteo. Ad orientem vero extra civitatem quoddam est venerabile cenobium, ubi palma de sepulchre martyris Christi domni Popteti Ulvinga pulchre consurgens in aera demonstratur, quo mutato nomine Heinricus, princeps miliciae Christiane, ante 70 annos ibidem cum suo armigero vitam finivit in Christo; qui nunc divina revelation canonizatus, Gloria temporali letatur et eterna."

48. Weiland, *Emonis Chronicon*, 454–572.

49. Ibid., 479: "Ibi miro scemate constructa in honore beateVirginis ostenditu ecclesias, in qua corpus beati Vincentii martyris in sarcophago requiescit argenteo. Ad orientem vero extra civitatem quoddam est venerabile cenobium, ubi palma de sepulchre martyris Christi domni Popteti Ulvinga pulchre consurgens in aera demonstratur, quo mutato nomine Heinricus, princeps miliciae Christiane, ante 70 annos ibidem cum suo armigero vitam finivit in Christo; qui nun divina revelation canonizatus, Gloria temporali letatur et eterna."

50. Goswin, *De expugnatione*, 349–54. Also *Indiculum fundationis monasterii sancti Vincentii*, 101–4.

51. Goswin, *De expugnatione*, 353: "Novit ulixboniam lux tercia post sacra luce / Festa iesu Christi subdere colla iugo / Post annos septem decies, binosque sub ipsa / Luce datur nobis alcaser, immo deo."

52. For the miracles associated with the preaching of the Fifth Crusade, see van Moolenbroek, "Signs in the Heavens." For the miracles assisting the troops at Alcácer do Sal, see Goswin, *De expugnatione*.

53. Katherine Allen Smith, *War and the Making of Medieval Monastic Culture* (Woodbridge: Boydell Press, 2011).

Chapter 6

The first epigraph to this chapter is drawn from Jacques de Vitry, Letter 2, 79: "Mentes quas spiritus sanctus coniunxit, locorum diversitas non disiungit; que autem caritatis sigillo mentibus amicorum imprimuntur, non facile temporis intervallo a memorialabuntur." The second epigraph derives from Marianne Hirsch, *The Generation of Postmemory: Writing and Visual Culture After the Holocaust* (New York: Columbia University Press, 2012), 178.

1. For the project and updates, see "Projet CROMIOSS: La tradition historique à la lumière de l'ADN," Société archéologique de Namur, accessed January 5, 2019, https://www.lasan.be/la-recherche/projet-cromioss.

2. Anne E. Lester, "What Remains: Women, Relics, and Remembrance in the Aftermath of the Fourth Crusade," *Journal of Medieval History* 40 (2014): 311–28; Lester, "Remembrance of Things Past: Memory and Material Objects in the Time of the Crusades, 1095–1291," in *Remembering the Crusades and Crusading*, ed. Cassidy-Welch, 73–94; Paul, *To Follow in Their Footsteps*.

3. Paul, *To Follow in Their Footsteps*.

4. For a recent analysis of the gemstones, see Farmer, "Low Country Ascetics."

5. Jean-François Foppens, ed., *Diplomatum belgicorum nova collection*, vol. 3 (Brussels, 1734), 407–8; and Edouard Poncelet, ed., *Chartes du Prieuré d'Oignies de l'Ordre de Saint-Augustin* (Namur: Wesmael-Charlier, 1913), 101–3n114.

6. Margot King, trans., "The Life of Mary of Oignies by James of Vitry," in Mulder-Bakker, *Mary of Oignies*, 70.

7. Thomas of Cantimpré, *Supplementum ad vitam beatae Mariae Oigniacensis, Acta sanctorum* 25 (Paris: Victor Palmé, 1867), 573–81; Mulder-Bakker, *Mary of Oignies*, 150.

8. See Jan Vandeburie, "'*Sancte fidei omnino deiciar*': Ugolino dei Conti di Segni's Doubts and Jacques de Vitry's Intervention," *Studies in Church History* 52 (2016): 87–101.

9. De Vitry, Letter 1, 72: "Unus ex cophinis meis plenus libris inter undas fluminis ferebatur, alius in quo matris mee Marie de Oegnis [*sic*] digitum reposeram, mulum meum sustentabat ne penitus mergeretur."

10. Joseph Greven, "Die Mitra des Jakob von Vitry und ihre Herkunft," *Zeitschrift für christliche Kunst* 20 (1907): 217–22.

11. Ruth Mellinkoff, *The Horned Moses in Medieval Art and Thought* (Berkeley: University of California Press, 1970), 94.

12. Durand, *Rationale divinorum officiorum*, bk. 3, chap. 13.

13. Charlotte Klack-Eitzen, Wiebke Haase, and Tanja Weißgraf, *Heilige Röcke: Kleider für Skulpturen im Kloster Wienhausen* (Regensburg: Schnell & Steiner, 2013).

14. University of Copenhagen, Arnamagnæanske Samling AM 666 b 4to.

15. Kunstgewerbemuseum, Staatliche Museenzu Berlin, inv. number K 6156.

16. Germanisches National Museum, inv. number K G709.

17. Cannuyer, "Les emblèmes sigillaires de Jacques de Vitry"; Folda, *Crusader Art*, 142–44.

18. Augustine, *Confessions*, trans. Francis J. Sheed, 2nd ed. (Indianapolis: Hackett, 2006), bk. 13.15.16, 299–300.

19. E. Jane Burns, *Medieval Fabrications: Dress, Textiles, Clothwork, and Other Cultural Imaginings* (New York: Palgrave Macmillan, 2016), 7: material clothing is "fashioned by the able hands of medieval commentators into metaphorical garments that resonate on a number of key cultural registers."

20. Sarah Kay, *Animal Skins and the Reading Self in Medieval Latin and French Bestiaries* (Chicago: University of Chicago Press, 2017).

NOTES TO PAGES 133–137

21. See the essays in Katie L. Walter, ed., *Reading Skin in Medieval Literature and Culture* (New York: Palgrave Macmillan, 2013).

22. Reinhold Röhricht, *Beitrage zur Geschichte der Kreuzzüge*, vol. 2 (Berlin, 1878), 127–28: "Sed quia presentium lator passiones nostras nobiscum sustinuit et in Christi nomine robur et sanguine suum offerens truncato et lacerate corpora impotens laborum et armorum opera inutile permansit, omnium ac singulorum rogamus pietatem, ut necessitates ipsius pie respiciatis, quatenus eleemosinarum vestrarum largitione iter posit peragere usque martirii et laboris sui nostrarum que orationum communionem."

23. In Mulder-Bakker, *Mary of Oignies*, 163.

24. Jaroslav Folda, "Before Louis IX: Aspects of Crusader Art at St Jean d'Acre, 1191–1244," in *France and the Holy Land: Frankish Culture at the End of the Crusades*, ed. Daniel H. Weiss and Lisa Mahoney (Baltimore: Johns Hopkins University Press, 2004), 138–57.

25. Ibid., 149–50.

26. Mulder-Bakker, *Mary of Oignies*, 141; Sarnaii, *Historia Albigensis*. See also Cole, *Preaching of the Crusades*. We also know that before he embarked on his journey to the Holy Land in 1216, Jacques had encountered some resistance against his Crusade preaching by French bishops who did not necessarily see the Fifth Crusade as a priority; see Brenda Bolton, "Faithful to Whom? Jacques De Vitry and the French Bishops," *Revue Mabillon*, n.s., 9 (1998): 53–72.

27. De Vitry, Letter 2, 86.

28. Ibid., 91.

29. De Vitry, *The Exempla or Illustrative Stories from the Sermones vulgares of Jacques de Vitry*, ed. Thomas Frederick Crane (London, 1890): exemplum 31, 12–13: "Similiter et Parisius accidit quod quidam discipulus post mortem magistro suo de die apparuit, qui indutus videbatur cappa ex pargameno minutis litteris conscripta. Cumque magister Sella, sic enim magister vocabatur, a discipulo quereret quid cappa illa et littere sibi vellent, respondit: 'Quelibet harum litterarum magis me gravat pondere suo quam si turrem hujus ecclesie super collum portarem,' ostensa sibi ecclesia Sancti Germani Parisiensis in cujus prato discipulus ejus apparuit illi. 'Hec,' inquit, 'littere sunt sophysmata et curiositates

in quibus dies meos consumpsi,' et addidit: 'Non possem tibi exprimere quanto ardore crucior sub hac cappa sed per unam guttam sudoris aliquot modo possem tibi ostendere.' Cumque magister extenderet palmam ut sudoris exciperet guttam, perforate est manus ejus a fervent gutta velud acutissima sagitta. Moxille magister scolas logice reliquit et ad ordinem Cystercientium se transferens ait: 'Linquo coax ranis, cracorvis, vanaque vanis, ad logicam pergo que mortis non timet ergo.' Quamdiu autem in ordine vixit manum perforatam habuit et usque ad tempora nostra, dum Parisius essemus, in scolis vixit manus sue foramen cunctis ostendens." See also Ian P. Wei, "From Twelfth-Century Schools to Thirteenth-Century Universities: The Disappearance of Biographical and Autobiographical Representations of Scholars," *Speculum* 86, no. 1 (2011): 42–78.

30. Another version of the tale has the cloak torturing the student with infernal heat. See J. A. Herbert, ed., *Catalogue of Romances in the Department of Manuscripts in the British Museum*, vol. 3 (London: British Museum, 1883–1910), 30. The tale is also told by Odo of Cheriton; this predates Jacques. For an analysis, see Barthélémy Hauréau, "Mémoire sur les récits d'apparitions dans les sermons du Moyen Âge," *Mémoires de l'Institut nationale de France* 28, no. 2 (1876): 239–63.

31. Courtoy, "Le trésor du prieuré d'Oignies."

32. Augustus Pugin's 1851 sketch of the altar (with other Namur items), now in the Victoria and Albert (V&A) Museum in London, delineates the proportions rather nicely (Prints, Drawings and Paintings Collection, museum number E.77:60–1970).

33. Thomas J. Welsh, *The Use of the Portable Altar: A Historical Synopsis and a Commentary* (Washington, DC: Catholic University of America Press, 1950), 4, 7–8, 12, and 15; and Éric Palazzo, *L'espace rituel et le sacré dans le christianisme: La liturgie de l'autel portatif dans l'Antiquité et au Moyen Âge* (Turnhout: Brepols, 2008), 74–78, 135–48; Palazzo, *L'espace et le sacre dans l'Antiquité et le haut Moyen Âge: Les autels portatifs*, Atti delle settimane di studio: Cristianità d'occidente e cristianità d'oriente

(secoli VI–XI) 51 (Spoleto: Centro italiano di studi sull'alto medioevo, 2004); Palazzo, "Performing the Liturgy," in *The Cambridge History of Christianity*, vol. 3, *Early Medieval Christianities, c. 600–c. 1100*, ed. Thomas F. X. Noble and Julia M. H. Smith (Cambridge: Cambridge University Press, 2008).

34. Lisa Bailey, "The Strange Case of the Portable Altar: Liturgy and the Limits of Episcopal Authority in Early Medieval Gaul," *Journal of the Australian Early Medieval Association* 8 (2012): 31–51.

35. Huneberc of Heidenheim, *Vita Willibaldi episcopi Eichstetensis*, ed. O. Holder-Egger, Monumenta Germaniae Historica SS 15.1, ed. Georg Waitz (Hanover: Hahnsche Buchhandlung, 1887), 98.

36. Palazzo, *L'espace rituel*.

37. Éric Palazzo and John H. Arnold, "*Missarum sollemnia*: Eucharistic Rituals in the Middle Ages," in *The Oxford Handbook of Medieval Christianity*, ed. John H. Arnold (Oxford: Oxford University Press, 2014), 238–55. For the symbolic representations of the altar, see the comments in Robert Favreau, "Les autels portatifs et leurs inscriptions," *Cahiers de civilisation médiévale* 46 (2003): 328.

38. Philippe George, *Reliques et arts précieux en pays mosan: Du haut Moyen Âge à l'époque contemporaine* (Liège: Éditions du Céfal, 2002).

39. Cited in Gaposchkin, *Invisible Weapons*, 98 (see Robert of Reims, *The Historia Iherosolimitana of Robert the Monk*, ed. D. Kempf and Marcus Bull [Woodbridge: Boydell, 2013], 98); William of Puylaurens is cited in Joseph F. O'Callaghan, *Reconquest and Crusade in Medieval Spain* (Philadelphia: University of Pennsylvania Press, 2013), 183.

40. Cannuyer, "Les emblèmes sigillaires."

41. Cynthia Hahn, "Portable Altars (and the *Rationale*): Liturgical Objects and Personal Devotion," in *Image and Altar, 800–1300, Papers from an International Conference in Copenhagen 24 October–27 October 2007*, ed. Paul Grinder Hansen (Copenhagen: University Press of Southern Denmark, 2014), 45–64.

42. Mulder-Bakker, *Mary of Oignies*, 113 of the translation.

43. Ibid., 146.

44. Jeffrey Hamburger, *St. John the Divine: The Deified Evangelist in Medieval Art and*

Theology (Berkeley: University of California Press, 2002), 2.

45. Ibid., 176.

46. Ibid., 166.

47. See Fiona J. Griffiths, "The Cross and the *Cura monialium*: Robert of Arbrissel, John the Evangelist, and the Pastoral Care of Women in the Age of Reform," *Speculum* 83 (2008): 303–30.

48. Mulder-Bakker, *Mary of Oignies*, 114.

49. Ibid., 107, 108. See also Lester, "A Shared Imitation," 369.

50. De Vitry, *Exempla or Illustrative Stories*, 68. For a discussion, see Lucy J. Sackville, *Heresy and Heretics in the Thirteenth Century: The Textual Representations* (Woodbridge: York Medieval Press, 2011), 73.

51. De Vitry, "*De sacramentis*," in *The Historia occidentalis*, 238–39.

52. Julia Smith, "Portable Christianity: Relics in the Medieval West (c. 700–1200)," *Proceedings of the British Academy* 181 (2012): 143–67.

53. For the thirteenth-century ivory trade, see Sarah M. Guérin, "Avorio d'ogni ragione: The Supply of Elephant Ivory to Northern Europe in the Gothic Era," *Journal of Medieval History* 36, no. 2 (2010): 156–74; Sarah M. Guérin, "Forgotten Routes? Italy, Ifrīqiya and the Trans-Saharan Ivory Trade," *Al-Masāq* 25, no. 1 (2013): 70–91.

54. Art Institute of Chicago, casket of Sicilian origin made from ivory, brass, tempera, and gold leaf, Samuel P. Avery Endowment, 1926.389; Walters Art Museum, Baltimore, cylindrical box of pyxis, ivory, and bone with paint and metal fittings, accession no. 71.308.

55. Avinoam Shalem, "From Royal Caskets to Relic Containers: Two Ivory Caskets from Burgos and Madrid," *Muqarnas* 12 (1995): 24–25.

56. For the Cluny examples, see Réunion des Musées Nationaux, "Coffret à couvercle à quatre pans," Agence photographique de la Réunion des Musées Nationaux-Grand Palais, accessed August 8, 2017, http://www.photo.rmn.fr/archive/09-508945 -2C6NU093RN4Z.html; and "Coffret en ivoirepeint: Cavaliers," Agence photographique de la Réunion des Musées Nationaux-Grand Palais, accessed August 8,

2017, http://www.photo.rmn.fr/archive/06 -522737-2C6NU0PA22SS.html; for the V&A, see "Saints and Other Figures Casket," V&A Collections, accessed August 8, 2017, http://collections.vam.ac.uk/item/O106774 /saints-and-other-figures-casket-unknown/; for Lille, see Réunion des Musées Nationaux, "Coffret à bijoux," Agence photographique de la Réunion des Musées Nationaux-Grand Palais, accessed August 8, 2017, http:// www.photo.rmn.fr/archive/10-509702 -2C6NU0Q44488I.html; and for the Harvard example, see Harvard Art Museum's "Tower Shaped Casket," accessed August 8, 2017, http://www.harvardartmuseums.org /collections/object/231637?position=8.

57. See Paul Bertrand, "Autour des authentiques de reliques du trésor dit d'Hugo d'Oignies," in *Actes de la journée d'étude Hugo d'Oignies: Contexte et perspective*, ed. Jacques Toussaint (Namur: Trema, 2013), 123–36.

58. See Jochen Schenk, "The Documentary Evidence for Templar Religion," in *The Templars and Their Sources*, ed. Karl Borchardt et al. (London: Routledge, 2017), 199–211.

59. Joseph Gottschalk, *St. Hedwig, Herzogin von Schlesien* (Köln: Böhlau, 1964).

60. See Fred Aldsworth et al., "Medieval Glassmaking at Tyre, Lebanon," *Journal of Glass Studies* 44 (2002): 49–66, for the Tyre glasshouses. William of Tyre remarked that the "glass is exported to distant provinces and it provides material suitable for vessels that are remarkable and of outstanding clarity" (Stefano Carboni, Giancarlo Lacerenza, and David Whitehouse, "Glassmaking in Medieval Tyre: The Written Evidence," *Journal of Glass Studies* 45 [2003]: 148). See also Rosemarie Lierke, *Die Hedwigsbecher: Das normannisch-sizilische Erbe der staufischen Kaiser* (Mainz: Verlag Franz Philipp Rutzen, 2005); and J. Kröger, "The Hedwig Beakers: Medieval European Glass Vessels Made in Sicily Around 1200," in *The Phenomenon of "Foreign" in Oriental Art*, ed. Annette Hagedorn (Wiesbaden: Reichert, 2006), 27–46.

61. Barbara Drake Boehm and Melanie Holcomb, eds., *Jerusalem, 1000–1400: Every People Under Heaven* (New York: Metropolitan Museum of Art, 2016), 44, citing the *Historia orientalis*.

62. Lierke, *Die Hedwigsbecher*; Rosemarie Lierke, "The Hedwig-Beaker Triangles: Signs of Origin," in *Annales du 17e Congrès de l'AIHV (Antwerp 2006)*, ed. K. Janssens et al. (Antwerp: University Press Antwerp, 2009), 289–94.

63. Cynthia Hahn, "*Visio Dei*: Changes in Medieval Visuality," in *Visuality Before and Beyond the Renaissance: Seeing as Others Saw*, ed. Robert S. Nelson (Cambridge: Cambridge University Press, 2000), 169–96; Jeffrey F. Hamburger and Anne-Marie Bouché, eds., *The Mind's Eye: Art and Theological Argument in the Middle Ages* (Princeton: Princeton University Press, 2006).

64. See, for instance, Heather Bruhn, "Late Gothic Architectural Monstrances in the Rhineland, c. 1380–1480: Objects in Context" (PhD diss., Pennsylvania State University, 2006); Farmer, "Low Country Ascetics"; Cynthia Hahn, *Strange Beauty: Issues in the Making and Meaning of Reliquaries, 400–circa 1204* (University Park: Penn State University Press, 2012).

65. They are green glass and so are likened to emeralds. Heraklius's *De coloribus et artibus romanorum* (book I) Cap. XIV, 8 in *Heraclius: Von den Farben und Künsten der Römer*, ed. Albert Ilg (Wien: W. Braumüller, 1873): 40–41, is one source on lapidic meaning. See Ingeborg Krueger, "Zu den 'Smaragden' auf dem Halberstädter Tafelreliquiar," *Journal of Glass Studies* 54 (2012): 247–53. See also Farmer, "Low Country Ascetics," for a discussion of the integration and meaning of gemstones in the reliquaries, including glass.

66. Tim Ingold, "Materials Against Materiality," *Archaeological Dialogues* 14, no. 1 (2007): 1–16.

67. Augustine, *De doctrina christiana: De vera religione*, ed. K. D. Daur and J. Martin, Corpus christianorum series latina 32 (Turnhout: Brepols, 1962), 2.16.24–25, 32, 49–50.

BIBLIOGRAPHY

Manuscripts

Brussels, Bibliothèque royale de Belgique, MS II-1146

Douai, Bibliothèque municipale, MS 503

Ghent, University Library, MS Gand 554

Leiden, University Library, MS VLQ 95

Leiden, University Library, MS VLQ 125

London, British Library, Add. MS 25440

London, British Library, Burney MS 351

London, Gray's Inn, MS 14

Paris, Bibliothèque Nationale de France, MS Lat. 5152A

Paris, Bibliothèque Nationale de France, MS Lat. 5695

Paris, Bibliothèque Saint-Geneviève, MS 3489

Vatican Library, MS Reg. Lat. 547

Primary Sources

Académie des Inscriptions et Belles-Lettres, ed. *Recueil des historiens des croisades: Historiens occidentaux.* Paris, 1844–95.

Aimeric de Pegulhan. "Ara parra qual seran enveyos." In *Les troubadours et la cour des Malaspina*, edited by Gilda Caïti-Russo, 100. Montpellier: Presses Universitaires de la Méditerranée, 2005.

Andrea, Alfred J. *Contemporary Sources for the Fourth Crusade.* Leiden: Brill, 2000.

Augustine. *Confessions.* 2nd ed. Translated by Francis Joseph Sheed. Indianapolis: Hackett, 2006.

———. *De doctrina christiana: De vera religione.* Edited by K. D. Daur and J. Martin. Corpus christianorum series latina 32. Turnhout: Brepols, 1962.

Barber, Malcolm, and Keith Bate, trans. *Letters from the East: Crusaders, Pilgrims and Settlers in the 12th–13th Centuries.* Farnham: Ashgate, 2010.

Benedict of Peterborough. *Gesta regis Henrici Secundi et Ricardi Primi.* Edited by W. Stubbs. Rolls Series, vol. 49, no. 2. London: Longmans, 1867.

Bernard of Clairvaux. "De consideratione ad Eugenium papam." In *Sancti Bernardi opera*, vol. 3, edited by Jean Leclercq and Henri Rochais, 379–493. Rome: Brepols, 1963.

Bird, Jessalynn, Edward Peters, and James M. Powell, eds. *Crusade and Christendom: Annotated Documents in Translation from Innocent III to the Fall of Acre, 1187–1291.* Philadelphia: University of Pennsylvania Press, 2013.

Blochet, E., trans. *Extraits de l'histoire des patriarches d'Alexandrie relatifs au siège de Damiette sous le règne d'al-Malik al-Kāmil.* Vol. 11 of *Revue de l'orient latin*, 240–60. Paris, 1907.

Brial, Michel-Jean Joseph, ed. *Epistola Arnulfi ad Milonem Tarvanensem episcopum.* Vol. 14 of *Recueil des historiens des Gaules et de la France*, edited by M. Bouquet, 325–27. Paris: Imprimerie Impériale, 1806.

Caesarius of Heisterbach. *Dialogus miraculorum: Dialog über die Wunder.* 5 vols. Edited and translated by Nikolaus Nösges and Horst Schneider. *Fontes Christiani* 86. Turnhout: Brepols, 2009.

Calixtus II. *Epistolae et privilegia.* Patrologia latina 163, edited by J. P. Migne, 1093–338. Paris, 1853.

Carroll, Andrew, ed. *War Letters: Extraordinary Correspondence from American Wars.* New York: Scribner, 2002.

David, Charles Wendell, ed. and trans. *De expugnatione lyxbonensi: The Conquest of Lisbon.* New York: Columbia University Press, 1936.

Delaville Le Roulx, Joseph, ed. *Cartulaire général de l'ordre des hospitaliers de Saint-Jean de Jérusalem (1100–1310).* Vol. 2, *1201–1260*. Paris: Ernest Leroux, 1897.

de Lépinois, Eugène de Buchère, and Lucien Merlet, eds. *Cartulaire de Notre-Dame de Chartres*. Vol. 2. Chartres: Garnier, 1863.

de Mas-Latrie, M. L., ed. *Chronique d'Ernoul et de Bernard le trésorier*. Paris: Mme Ve Jules Renouard, 1871.

de Vitry, Jacques. *The Exempla or Illustrative Stories from the Sermones vulgares of Jacques de Vitry*. Edited by Thomas Frederick Crane. London: Folklore Society, 1890.

———. *Histoire occidentale*. Edited by Gaston Duchet-Suchaux. Paris: Editions du Cerf, 1997.

———. *Histoire orientale: Historia orientalis*. Edited and translated by Jean Donnadieu. Turnhout: Brepols, 2008.

———. *The* Historia occidentalis *of Jacques de Vitry: A Critical Edition*. Edited by John Frederick Hinnebusch. Fribourg: University Press, 1972.

———. *Lettres de Jacques de Vitry, 1160/1170–1240, évêque de Saint-Jean d'Acre*. Edited by R. B. C. Huygens. Leiden: Brill, 1960.

———. "Sermo ad crucesignatos vel signando." In *Crusade Propaganda and Ideology: Model Sermons for the Preaching of the Cross*, edited by Christoph T. Maier, 124–25. Cambridge: Cambridge University Press, 2000.

———. "Sermon to Pilgrims." In *Crusade and Christendom: Annotated Documents in Translation from Innocent III to the Fall of Acre, 1187–1291*, edited by Jessalynn Bird, Edward Peters, and James M. Powell, 147–48. Philadelphia: University of Pennsylvania Press, 2013.

Edmond, Martène, and Ursin Durand, eds. *Veterum scriptorum et monumentorum historicorum, dogmatoricum, moralium, amplissima collectio*. Vols. 1 and 6. Paris, 1724, 1729.

Eugenius III. *Quantum praedecessores*. In *The Second Crusade: Extending the Frontiers of Christendom*, edited and translated

by Jonathan Phillips. New Haven: Yale University Press, 2008.

Foppens, Jean-François, ed. *Diplomatum belgicorum nova collectio*. Vol. 3. Brussels, 1734.

Fulcher of Chartres. *Historia Hierosolymitana (1095–1127)*. Edited by Heinrich Hagenmeyer. Heidelberg: C. Winter, 1913.

———. *A History of the Expedition to Jerusalem, 1095–1127*. Edited by Harold S. Fink. Translated by Frances R. Ryan. Knoxville: University of Tennessee Press, 1969.

Goswin. *De expugnatione Salaciae carmen*. In *Chronica regia coloniensis*, edited by Georg Waitz, 349–54. Monumenta Germaniae Historica SS: Rerum germanicarum, n.s., 18. Hanover, 1880.

Gregory VIII. *Audita tremendi*. In *Crusade and Christendom: Annotated Documents in Translation from Innocent III to the Fall of Acre, 1187–1291*, edited by Jessalynn Bird, Edward Peters, and James M. Powell, 4–9. Philadelphia: University of Pennsylvania Press, 2013.

———. *Audita tremendi*. In *The Crusades, 1095–1204*, 2nd ed., by Jonathan Phillips, doc. 20. London: Routledge, 2014.

Guibert of Nogent. *Dei gesta per francos et cinq autres textes*. Edited by R. B. C. Huygens. Vol. 127A of *Corpus christianorum continuatio mediaevalis*. Turnhout: Brepols, 1996.

Hardy, Thomas Duffus, ed. *Rotuli litterarum clausarum in Turri londinensi asservati*. Vol. 1, *1204–1224*. London: Record Commission, 1833.

Herbert, J. A., ed. *Catalogue of Romances in the Department of Manuscripts in the British Museum*. Vol. 3. London: British Museum, 1910.

Huneberc of Heidenheim. *Vita Willibaldi episcopi Eichstetensis*. Edited by O. Holder-Egger. Monumenta Germaniae Historica SS 15.1, edited by Georg Waitz, 86–106. Hanover, 1887.

Huygens, R. B. C., ed., and Gaston Duchet-Suchaux, trans. *Lettres de la cinquième croisade*. Turnhout: Brepols, 1998.

Indiculum fundationis monasterii sancti Vicentii. Vol. 1, fasc. 1 of *Portugaliae monumenta historica scriptores.* Lisbon: Typis Academicis, 1856.

Innocent III. *Innocentii III romani pontifices opera omnia tomis quatuor distributa.* Vols. 214–17 of *Patrologia latina,* edited by J. P. Migne. Paris, 1855.

Isidore of Seville. *The Etymologies of Isidore of Seville.* Edited and translated by Stephen A. Barney, W. J. Lewis, J. A. Beach, and Oliver Berghof. Cambridge: Cambridge University Press, 2006.

Jackson, Peter, trans. *The Seventh Crusade, 1244–1254: Sources and Documents.* Aldershot: Ashgate, 2007.

Joachim of Fiore. *Expositio in apocalypsim.* Frankfurt: Minerva Verlag, 1964. Facsimile of the first edition. Venice, 1527.

Krueger, Hilmar C., and Robert L. Reynolds, eds. *Notai liguri del secoli XII e del XIII.* Vol. 6. Genoa, 1951–53.

Lees, Beatrice A., ed. *Records of the Templars in England in the Twelfth Century: The Inquest of 1185 with Illustrative Charters and Documents.* London: Oxford University Press, 1935.

L'estoire de Eracles empereur et la conqueste de la terre d'outremer. In *Recueil des historiens des croisades* I. Historiens occidentaux 2. Paris, 1859.

Migne, J. P., ed. "Quia maior." Vol. 216 of *Patrologia latina,* 817–22. Paris, 1855.

Muratori, Ludovico Antonio, ed. "Memoriale potestatum regensium." Vol. 8 of *Rerum Italicarum scriptores,* 1073–174. Milan, 1726.

Oliver of Paderborn. *Die Schriften des Kölner Domscholasters, Späteren Bischofs von Paderborn und Kardinal-Bischofs von S. Sabina Oliverus.* Edited by H. Hoogeweg. Vol. 202 of *Bibliothek des Literarischen Vereins in Stuttgart.* Tübingen: Literarischen Vereins in Stuttgart, 1894.

Paris, Matthew. *Chronica majora.* 7 vols. Edited by Henry Richards Luard. Rolls Series, vol. 57. London: Longmans, 1872–83.

Peter the Venerable. *The Letters of Peter the Venerable.* Edited by Giles Constable. Harvard Historical Studies, vol. 78, no. 1. Cambridge: Harvard University Press, 1967.

Petri Vallium Sarnaii (Peter of Vaux-de-Cernay). *Historia Albigensis.* Edited by P. Guébin and E. D. Lyon. 3 vols. Paris, 1926, 1930, 1939.

Pitra, Jean Baptiste, ed. *Analecta novissima spicilegii solesmensis: Altera continuatio.* Vol. 2. Paris, 1888.

Poncelet, Edouard, ed. *Chartes du prieuré d'Oignies de l'ordre de Saint-Augustin.* Namur: Wesmael-Charlier, 1913.

Pressutti, Peter, ed. *Regesta Honorii Papae III.* 2 vols. Rome: Vatican, 1888–95.

Price, Siân, ed. *If You're Reading This: Last Letters from the Front Line.* London: Frontline Books, 2011.

Ralph of Coggeshall. *Chronicon anglicanum.* Edited by Joseph Stevenson. Rolls Series, vol. 66, no. 1. London: Longmans, 1875.

Riant, Paul. "Six lettres relatives aux croisades." Vol. 1 of *Archives de l'orient latin,* 383–92. Paris, 1881.

Richard of Devizes. *Chronicon Richardi divinensis de tempore regis Ricardi primi.* Edited and translated by J. Appleby. London: Nelson Medieval Texts, 1963.

Richards, Henry Luard, ed. *Annales monastici.* Rolls Series, vol. 36, no. 2. London: Longmans, 1865.

Roger of Howden. *Gesta regis Henrici Secundi et Ricardi Primi.* Edited by W. Stubbs. Rolls Series, vol. 49, no. 2. London: Longmans, 1867.

Roger of Wendover. *Flores historiarum.* Edited by H. G. Hewlett. 3 vols. Rolls Series, vol. 84. London: Longmans, 1886–89.

Röhricht, Reinhold, ed. *Addidamentum.* Innsbruck: Oeniponti, 1904.

———, ed. *Beitrage zur Geschichte der Kreuzzüge.* Vol. 2. Berlin: Weidmannsche Buchhandlung, 1878.

———. "Briefe des Jacobus de Vitriaco (1216–21)." *Zeitschrift für Kirchengeschichte* 14 (1894): 97–118; 15 (1895): 568–87; 16 (1896): 72–114.

184 BIBLIOGRAPHY

———, ed. *Deutsche Pilgerreisen nach dem Heiligen Lande*. Innsbruck: Wagner'schen Universitäts-Buchhandlung, 1900.

———, ed. *Die Deutschen im Heiligen Lande*. Innsbruck: Verlag der Wagnerschen, 1894.

———, ed. *Quinti belli sacri scriptores minores*. Geneva: J. G. Fick, 1879.

———, ed. *Regesta regni Hierosolymitani: 1097–1291*. Innsbruck: Oeniponti, 1893.

———, ed. *Testimonia minora de quinto bello sacro e chronicis occidentalibus*. Geneva, 1882.

Savioli, Lodovico Vittorio, ed. *Annali bolognesi*. 3 vols. Bassano, 1784–95.

Scott, Samuel P., and Robert I. Burns, ed. and trans. *Las siete partidas*. Vols. 2 and 5. Philadelphia: University of Pennsylvania Press, 2012.

Shirley, Janet, trans. *Crusader Syria in the Thirteenth Century: The Rothelin Continuation of the History of William of Tyre with Part of the Eracles or Acre Text*. Aldershot: Ashgate, 1999.

Strehlke, Ernest, ed. *Tabulae ordinis teutonici*. Berlin, 1869.

Suger. *Abbot Suger on the Abbey Church of St. Denis and Its Art Treasures*. Edited and translated by Erwin Panofsky. Princeton: Princeton University Press, 1979.

Sweetenham, Carol, and Linda Paterson, eds. *The Canso d'Antioca: An Occitan Epic Chronicle of the First Crusade*. Aldershot: Ashgate, 2003.

Thomas of Cantimpré. *Supplementum ad vitam beatae Mariae Oigniacensis*. Edited by Daniel Papebrochius. *Acta sanctorum*, 23 June, part 3, 666–76. Paris: Victor Palmé, 1867.

von Frast, Johann, ed. *Das "Stiftungen-Buch" des Cistercienser-Klosters Zwetl*. Vienna: K. K. Hof und Staatsdruckerei, 1851.

von Heinemann, L., ed. *Ex Thomae historia pontificum salonitanorum et spalatinorum*. Monumenta Germaniae Historica SS 29, edited by Georg Waitz, 568–98. Hanover, 1892.

Waitz, George, ed. *Annales sancti disibodi*. Monumenta Germaniae Historica SS 17, edited by George H. Pertz, 4–30. Hanover, 1861.

Walter of Coventry. *Memoriale fratris Walteri de Coventria: The Historical Collections of Walter of Coventry*. Edited by William Stubbs. 2 vols. Rolls Series, vol. 58. London: Longmans, 1872–73.

Weiland, Louis, ed. *Emonis chronicon*. Monumenta Germaniae Historica SS 23, edited by George H. Pertz, 454–523. Hanover, 1874.

William Durand. *Rationale divinorum officiorum*. Edited by A. Davril and Timothy M. Thibodeau. Vols. 140, 140A, 140B of *Corpus christianorum continuatio mediaevalis*. Turnhout: Brepols, 1995–2000.

William of Tyre. *Chronique*. Edited by R. B. C. Huygens. Vols. 63 and 63A of *Corpus christianorum continuatio mediaevalis*. Turnhout: Brepols, 1986.

Willis Bund, J. W., ed. *Episcopal Registers, Diocese of Worcester. Register of Bishop Godfrey Giffard, September 23rd, 1268 to August 15th, 1301*. Vol. 2. Oxford: James Parker, 1902.

Secondary Sources

Abulafia, David. "Invented Italians in the Courtois Collection." In *Crusade and Settlement*, edited by Peter W. Edbury, 135–43. Cardiff: University College Cardiff Press, 1985.

Aird, William M. "'Many Others, Whose Names I Do Not Know, Fled with Them': Norman Courage and Cowardice on the First Crusade." In *Crusading and Pilgrimage in the Norman World*, edited by Kathryn Hurlock and Paul Oldfield, 13–29. Woodbridge: Boydell Press, 2015.

Aldsworth, Fred, George Haggarty, Sarah Jennings, and David Whitehouse. "Medieval Glassmaking at Tyre, Lebanon." *Journal of Glass Studies* 44 (2002): 49–66.

Allen, S. J., and E. Amt, eds. *The Crusades: A Reader*. Peterborough: Broadview Press, 2003.

Allmand, Christopher. "The Reporting of War in the Middle Ages." In *War and Society in Medieval and Early Modern Britain*, edited by Diana Dunn, 17–33.

Liverpool: Liverpool University Press, 2000.

Anderson, Benedict R. *Imagined Communities: Reflections on the Origin and Spread of Nationalism.* London: Verso, 1983.

Andrea, Alfred J. "Innocent III, the Fourth Crusade, and the Coming Apocalypse." In *The Medieval Crusade,* edited by Susan J. Ridyard, 97–106. Woodbridge: Boydell Press, 2004.

Arnaldi, G. "Codagnello Giovanni." In *Dizionario biografico degli italiani,* vol. 26, 562–68. Rome: Instituto della Enciclopedia Italiana, 1982.

Ashplant, Timothy G., Graham Dawson, and Michael Roper, eds. *The Politics of War Memory and Commemoration.* London: Routledge, 2000.

Assmann, Aleida. *Der lange Schatten der Vergangenheit—Erinnerungskultur und Geschichtspolitik.* Munich: C. H. Beck, 2006.

Assmann, Jan. *Das kulturelle Gedächtnis: Schrift, Erinnerung und politische Identität in frühen Hochkulturen.* Munich: C. H. Beck, 1999.

———. *Religion and Cultural Memory: Ten Studies.* Translated by Rodney Livingstone. Stanford: Stanford University Press, 2005.

Auffroy, Henri. *Évolution du testament en France des origines au XIIIe siècle.* Paris: A. Rousseau, 1899.

Bachrach, David S. "Conforming with the Rhetorical Tradition of Plausibility: Clerical Representation of Battlefield Orations Against Muslims, 1080–170." *International History Review* 26, no. 1 (March 2004): 1–19.

———. *Religion and the Conduct of War, c. 300–1215.* Woodbridge: Boydell Press, 2003.

Bailey, Lisa. "The Strange Case of the Portable Altar: Liturgy and the Limits of Episcopal Authority in Early Medieval Gaul." *Journal of the Australian Early Medieval Association* 8 (2012): 31–51.

Baldwin, John W. *Masters, Princes, and Merchants: The Social Views of Peter Chanter and His Circle.* 2 vols. Princeton: Princeton University Press, 1970.

Barber, Malcolm. *The Crusader States.* New Haven: Yale University Press, 2012.

Bautier, Robert-Henri. "La collection des chartes de croisade, dite 'collection Courtois.'" *Comptes rendus des séances de l'Académie des Inscriptions et Belles-Lettres* 100, no. 3 (1956): 382–86.

Bedos-Rezak, Brigitte. *When Ego Was Imago: Signs of Identity in the Middle Ages.* Leiden: Brill, 2011.

Beer, Jeanette. "The Letter of Jean Sarrasin, Crusader." In *Journeys Toward God: Pilgrimage and Crusade,* edited by Barbara N. Sargent-Bauer, 135–55. Kalamazoo: Medieval Institute, 1992.

Bertrand, Paul. "Autour des authentiques de reliques du trésor dit d'Hugo d'Oignies." In *Actes de la journée d'étude Hugo d'Oignies: Contexte et perspective,* edited by Jacques Toussaint, 123–36. Namur: Trema, 2013.

Bird, Jessalynn. "Crusade and Conversion After the Fourth Lateran Council: Oliver of Paderborn's and James of Vitry's Missions to Muslims Reconsidered." *Essays in Medieval Studies* 21 (2004): 23–47.

———. "James of Vitry's Sermons to Pilgrims." *Essays in Medieval Studies* 25 (2008): 81–113.

———, ed. *Papacy, Crusade, and Christian-Muslim Relations.* Amsterdam: Amsterdam University Press, 2018.

———. "The Religious's Role in a Post-Fourth-Lateran World: Jacques de Vitry's *Sermones ad status* and *Historia occidentalis.*" In *Medieval Monastic Preaching,* edited by Carolyn Muessig, 209–30. Leiden: Brill, 1998.

———. "The Victorines, Peter the Chanter's Circle, and the Crusade: Two Unpublished Crusading Appeals in Paris, Bibliothèque Nationale, MS Latin 14470." *Medieval Sermon Studies* 48 (2004): 5–28.

Bliese, John R. E. "The Courage of the Normans: A Comparative Study of Battle Rhetoric." *Nottingham Medieval Studies* 35 (1991): 1–26.

———. "Rhetoric and Morale: A Study of Battle Orations from the Central

Middle Ages." *Journal of Medieval History* 15, no. 3 (1989): 201–26.

———. "When Knightly Courage May Fail: Battle Orations in Medieval Europe." *Historian* 53, no. 3 (1991): 489–504.

Boehm, Barbara Drake, and Melanie Holcomb, eds. *Jerusalem, 1000–1400: Every People Under Heaven.* New York: Metropolitan Museum of Art, 2016.

Bolton, Brenda. "Faithful to Whom? Jacques de Vitry and the French Bishops." *Revue Mabillon,* n.s., 9 (1998): 53–72.

Boureau, Alain. "The Letter Writing Norm, a Mediaeval Invention." In *Correspondence: Models of Letter Writing from the Middle Ages to the Nineteenth Century,* edited by Roger Chartier, Alain Boureau, and Cécile Dauphin, 24–58. Princeton: Princeton University Press, 1997.

Boynton, Susan. *Shaping a Monastic Identity: Liturgy and History at the Imperial Abbey of Farfa, 1000–1125.* Ithaca: Cornell University Press, 2006.

Brodman, James. *Ransoming Captives in Crusader Spain: The Order of Merced on the Christian-Islamic Frontier.* Philadelphia: University of Pennsylvania Press, 1986.

Bruhn, Heather. "Late Gothic Architectural Monstrances in the Rhineland, c. 1380–1480: Objects in Context." PhD diss., Pennsylvania State University, 2006.

Brundage, James A. *The Crusades: A Documentary Survey.* Milwaukee: Marquette University Press, 1962.

Bull, Marcus. "The Diplomatic of the First Crusade." In *The First Crusade: Origins and Impact,* edited by Jonathan Phillips, 35–56. Manchester: Manchester University Press, 1997.

———. "The Eyewitness Accounts of the First Crusade as Political Scripts." *Reading Medieval Studies* 36 (2010): 23–37.

———. *Knightly Piety and the Lay Response to the First Crusade: The Limousin and Gascony, c. 970–c. 1130.* Oxford: Clarendon Press, 1993.

Bull, Marcus, and Damien Kempf, eds. *Writing the Early Crusades: Text, Transmission and Memory.* Woodbridge: Boydell Press, 2014.

Buresi, Pascal. "Les conversions d'églises et de mosquées en Espagne au XIe–XIIIe siècles." In *Religion et société urbaine au Moyen Âge: Études offertes à Jean-Louis Biget par ses anciens élèves,* 333–50. Paris: Publications de la Sorbonne, 2000.

Burleigh, Michael, ed. *Confronting the Nazi Past: New Debates on Modern German History.* London: St. Martin's Press, 1996.

Burns, E. Jane. *Medieval Fabrications: Dress, Textiles, Clothwork, and Other Cultural Imaginings.* New York: Palgrave Macmillan, 2016.

Burns, Robert I. *Jews in the Notarial Culture: Latinate Wills in Mediterranean Spain, 1250–1350.* Berkeley: University of California Press, 1996.

Bynum, Caroline Walker. *Holy Feast and Holy Fast: The Religious Significance of Food to Medieval Women.* Berkeley: University of California Press, 1987.

———. *Wonderful Blood: Theology and Practice in Late Medieval Northern Germany and Beyond.* Philadelphia: University of Pennsylvania Press, 2007.

Cannuyer, Christian. "Les emblèmes sigillaires de Jacques de Vitry reproduits sur trois pièces du trésor d'Oignies." *La vie wallonne* 387 (1984): 117–26.

Carboni, Stefano, Giancarlo Lacerenza, and David Whitehouse. "Glassmaking in Medieval Tyre: The Written Evidence." *Journal of Glass Studies* 45 (2003): 139–49.

Carlin, Martha, and David Crouch, eds. *Lost Letters of Medieval Life: English Society, 1200–1250.* Philadelphia: University of Pennsylvania Press, 2013.

Carrier, Peter. "Holocaust Memoriography and the Impact of Memory on the Historiography of the Holocaust." In *Writing the History of Memory,* edited by Stefan Berger and Bill Niven, 199–218. London: Bloomsbury, 2014.

Carruthers, Mary J. *The Craft of Thought: Meditation, Rhetoric, and the Making of Images, 400–1200.* New York: Cambridge University Press, 1998.

———. "Moving Back in Memory Studies." *History Workshop Journal* 77, no. 1 (2014): 275–82.

Cassidy-Welch, Megan. "Confessing to Remembrance: Stephen of Sawley's *Speculum novitii* and Cistercian Uses of Memory." *Cistercian Studies Quarterly* 35, no. 1 (2000): 13–27.

———. "Images of Blood in the *Historia Albigensis* of Pierre des Vaux-de-Cernay." *Journal of Religious History* 35, no. 4 (2011): 478–91.

———. "Memories of Space in Thirteenth-Century France: Displaced People After the Albigensian Crusade." *Parergon* 27, no. 2 (2010): 111–31.

———. "The Monastery of São Vicente de Fora in Lisbon as a Site of Crusading Memory." *Journal of Medieval Monastic Studies* 3 (2014): 1–20.

———, ed. *Remembering the Crusades and Crusading*. London: Routledge, 2016.

———. "The Stones of Damietta: Remembering the Fifth Crusade." In *The Papacy, Crusade, and Christian-Muslim Relations*, edited by Jessalynn L. Bird, 195–210. Amsterdam: Amsterdam University Press, 2018.

———. "Testimonies from a Fourteenth-Century Prison: Rumour, Evidence and Truth in the Midi." *French History* 16, no. 1 (2002): 3–27.

Cassidy-Welch, Megan, and Anne E. Lester, eds. "Crusades and Memory: Rethinking Past and Present." Special issue, *Journal of Medieval History* 40, no. 3 (2014).

———. "Memory and Interpretation: New Approaches to the Study of the Crusades." *Journal of Medieval History* 40, no. 3 (2014): 225–36.

Claverie, Pierre-Vincent. *Honorius III et l'orient (1216–1227): Étude et publication de sources inédites des archives vaticanes*. Leiden: Brill, 2013.

Cohen, Jeremy. *Living Letters of the Law: Ideas of the Jew in Medieval Christianity*. Berkeley: University of California Press, 1999.

Cole, Penny J. *The Preaching of the Crusades to the Holy Land, 1095–1270*. Cambridge,

MA: Medieval Academy of America, 1991.

Coleman, Janet. *Ancient and Medieval Memories: Studies in the Reconstruction of the Past*. Cambridge: Cambridge University Press, 1992.

Confino, Alon. "History and Memory." In *Historical Writing Since 1945*, edited by Axel Schneider and Daniel Woolf. Vol. 5 of *The Oxford Handbook of Historical Writing*, 36–51. Oxford: Oxford University Press, 2011.

Constable, Giles. "A Further Note on the Conquest of Lisbon in 1147." In *The Experience of Crusading I: Western Approaches*, edited by Marcus Bull and Norman Housley, 39–44. Cambridge: Cambridge University Press, 2003.

———. "The Historiography of the Crusades." In *The Crusades from the Perspective of Byzantium and the Muslim World*, edited by Angeliki E. Laiou and Roy Parviz Mottahedeh, 1–22. Washington, DC: Dumbarton Oaks Research Library and Collection, 2001.

———. *Letters and Letter-Collections. Typologie des sources du Moyen Âge occidental*. Vol. 17, edited by B. van den Abeele and J. M. Yante. Turnhout: Brepols, 1976.

———. "Medieval Charters as a Source for the History of the Crusades." In *Crusaders and Crusading in the Twelfth Century*, edited by Giles Constable, 93–116. Aldershot: Ashgate, 2008.

Courtoy, Ferdinand. "Le trésor du prieuré d'Oignies aux soeurs de Notre-Dame à Namur et l'oeuvre de Frère Hugo." *Bulletin de la commission royale des monuments et des sites* 3 (1952): 119–256.

Cubitt, Geoffrey. *History and Memory*. Manchester: Manchester University Press, 2007.

Damian-Grint, Peter. *The New Historians of the Twelfth-Century Renaissance: Authorising History in the Vernacular Revolution*. Woodbridge: Boydell Press, 1999.

Davis, Kathleen. "National Writing in the Ninth Century: A Reminder for Postcolonial Thinking About the Nation."

Journal of Medieval and Early Modern Studies 28, no. 3 (1998): 611–37.

Dawson, Graham. *Soldier Heroes: British Adventure, Empire, and the Imagining of Masculinities.* London: Routledge, 1994.

della Dora, Veronica. "Gardens of Eden and Ladders to Heaven: Holy Mountain Geographies in Byzantium." In *Mapping Medieval Geographies: Geographical Encounters in the Latin West and Beyond, 300–1600,* edited by Keith D. Lilley, 271–99. Cambridge: Cambridge University Press, 2013.

Dickson, Marcel, and Christiane Dickson. "Le cardinal Robert de Courson: Sa vie." *Archives d'histoire doctrinale et littéraire du Moyen Âge* 9 (1934): 53–142.

Dijkstra, Cathrynke T. J. *La chanson de croisade: Étude thématique d'un genre hybride.* Amsterdam: Schiphouwer et Brinckman, 1995.

Donovan, Joseph P. *Pelagius and the Fifth Crusade.* Philadelphia: University of Pennsylvania Press, 1950.

Doyen, Guillaume, ed. *Histoire de la ville de Chartres.* Vol. 1. Chartres, 1786.

Dulong, Renaud. *Le témoin oculaire: Les conditions sociales de l'attestation personnelle.* Paris: Éditions de l'École des Hautes Études en Sciences Sociales, 1998.

Edbury, Peter W., ed. *Crusade and Settlement: Papers Read at the First Conference of the Study of Crusades and the Latin East and Presented to R. C. Smail.* Cardiff: University College Cardiff Press, 1985.

———. "Ernoul, Eracles and the Fifth Crusade." In *The Fifth Crusade in Context: The Crusading Movement in the Early Thirteenth Century,* edited by E. J. Mylod, Guy Perry, Thomas W. Smith, and Jan Vandeburie, 163–74. London: Routledge, 2017.

Edington, Susan B. "The Lisbon Letter of the Second Crusade." *Historical Research* 69, no. 170 (1996): 328–39.

Epstein, Steven. *Wills and Wealth in Medieval Genoa, 1150–1250.* Cambridge: Harvard University Press, 1984.

Erdmann, Carl. *Die Entstehung des Kreuzzugsgedankens.* Stuttgart: Verlag W.

Kohlhammer, 1935. In *The Origin of the Idea of Crusade,* translated by Marshall W. Baldwin and Walter Goffart. Princeton: Princeton University Press, 1977.

Eustace, Nicole, Eugenia Lean, Julie Livingston, Jan Plamper, William M. Reddy, and Barbara H. Rosenwein. "AHR Conversation: The Historical Study of the Emotions." *American Historical Review* 117, no. 5 (2012): 1487–531.

Evergates, Theodore, ed. *Feudal Society in Medieval France: Documents from the County of Champagne.* Philadelphia: University of Pennsylvania Press, 1993.

Farmer, Sharon. "Low Country Ascetics and Oriental Luxury: Jacques de Vitry, Marie of Oignies, and the Treasures of Oignies." In *History in the Comic Mode: Medieval Communities and the Matter of Person,* edited by Rachel Fulton and Bruce W. Holsinger, 205–22. New York: Columbia University Press, 2007.

Fassler, Margot E. *The Virgin of Chartres: Making History Through Liturgy and the Arts.* New Haven: Yale University Press, 2010.

Favreau, Robert. "Les autels portatifs et leurs inscriptions." *Cahiers de civilisation médiévale* 46 (2003): 327–52.

Fenster, Thelma, and Daniel Lord Smail, eds. *Fama: The Politics of Talk and Reputation in Medieval Europe.* Ithaca: Cornell University Press, 2003.

Fentress, James, and Chris Wickham. *Social Memory: New Perspectives on the Past.* Oxford: Blackwell Press, 1992.

Filippucci, Paola. "In a Ruined Country: Place and the Memory of War Destruction in Argonne (France)." In *Remembering Violence: Anthropological Perspectives on Intergenerational Transmission,* 2nd ed., edited by Nicholas Argenti and Katharina Schramm, 165–89. New York: Berghahn Books, 2012.

Flori, Jean. *Chroniqueurs et propagandistes: Introduction critique aux sources de la première croisade.* Geneva: Droz, 2010.

Folda, Jaroslav. "Before Louis IX: Aspects of Crusader Art at St. Jean d'Acre,

1191–1244." In *France and the Holy Land: Frankish Culture at the End of the Crusades*, edited by Daniel H. Weiss and Lisa Mahoney, 138–57. Baltimore: Johns Hopkins University Press, 2004.

———. *Crusader Art in the Holy Land, from the Third Crusade to the Fall of Acre, 1187–1291*. Cambridge: Cambridge University Press, 2005.

Francis, Dominic. "Oliver of Paderborn and His Siege Engine at Damietta." *Nottingham Medieval Studies* 37 (1993): 28–32.

Frantzen, Allen J. *Bloody Good: Chivalry, Sacrifice, and the Great War*. Chicago: University of Chicago Press, 2004.

Friedman, Yvonne. *Encounter Between Enemies: Captivity and Ransom in the Latin Kingdom of Jerusalem*. Leiden: Brill, 2001.

Funk, Philipp. *Jakob von Vitry: Leben und Werke*. Berlin: Druck und Verlag von B. G. Teubner, 1909.

Gabriele, Matthew. "From Prophecy to Apocalypse: The Verb Tenses of Jerusalem in Robert the Monk's *Historia* of the First Crusade." *Journal of Medieval History* 42, no. 3 (2016): 304–16.

Galvez, Marisa. "The Voice of the Unrepentant Crusader: 'Aler m'estuet' by the Châtelain d'Arras." In *Voice and Voicelessness in Medieval Europe*, edited by Irit Ruth Kleiman, 101–22. Basingstoke: Palgrave Macmillan, 2015.

Ganz, David. "The Ideology of Sharing: Apostolic Community and Ecclesiastical Property in the Early Middle Ages." In *Property and Power in the Early Middle Ages*, edited by Wendy Davies and Paul Fouracre, 17–30. Cambridge: Cambridge University Press, 1995.

Gaposchkin, M. Cecilia. "From Pilgrimage to Crusade: The Liturgy of Departure, 1095–1300." *Speculum* 88, no. 1 (2013): 44–79.

———. *Invisible Weapons: Liturgy and the Making of Crusade Ideology*. Ithaca: Cornell University Press, 2017.

Gauvard, Claude, ed. *L'enquête au Moyen Âge*. Rome: École française de Rome, 2009.

Geary, Patrick J. *Phantoms of Remembrance: Memory and Oblivion at the End of the First Millennium*. Princeton: Princeton University Press, 1994.

Gertsman, Elina. "'Going They Went and Wept': Tears in Medieval Discourse." In *Crying in the Middle Ages: Tears of History*, edited by Elina Gertsman, xi–xx. London: Routledge, 2011.

Godding, Philippe. "La pratique testamentaire en Flandre au 13e siècle." *Tijdschrift voor Rechsgeschiedenis* 58 (1990): 281–300.

Goebel, Stefan. *The Great War and Medieval Memory: War, Remembrance and Medievalism in Britain and Germany, 1914–1940*. Cambridge: Cambridge University Press, 2007.

Gottschalk, Joseph. *St. Hedwig, Herzogin von Schlesien*. Köln: Böhlau, 1964.

Gouguenheim, Sylvain. "Les Maccabées: Modèles des guerriers chrétiens des origines au XIIe siècle." *Cahiers de civilisation médiévale* 54, no. 213 (2011): 3–20.

Gravelle, Yves. "Le problème des prisonniers de guerre pendant les croisades orientales (1095–1192)." MA thesis, Université de Sherbrooke, 1999.

Greven, Joseph. "Die Mitra des Jakob von Vitry und ihre Herkunft." *Zeitschrift für christliche Kunst* 20 (1907): 217–22.

Griffiths, Fiona J. "The Cross and the *Cura monialium*: Robert of Arbrissel, John the Evangelist, and the Pastoral Care of Women in the Age of Reform." *Speculum* 83 (2008): 303–30.

Guérin, Sarah M. "Avorio d'ogni ragione: The Supply of Elephant Ivory to Northern Europe in the Gothic Era." *Journal of Medieval History* 36, no. 2 (2010): 156–74.

———. "Forgotten Routes? Italy, Ifrīqiya and the Trans-Saharan Ivory Trade." *Al-Masāq* 25, no. 1 (2013): 70–91.

Hahn, Cynthia. "Portable Altars (and the *Rationale*): Liturgical Objects and Personal Devotion." In *Image and Altar, 800–1300, Papers from an International Conference in Copenhagen 24 October–27 October 2007*, edited by Paul Grinder Hansen, 45–64.

Copenhagen: University Press of Southern Denmark, 2014.

———. *Strange Beauty: Issues in the Making and Meaning of Reliquaries, 400–circa 1204.* University Park: Pennsylvania State University Press, 2012.

———. *"Visio Dei:* Changes in Medieval Visuality." In *Visuality Before and Beyond the Renaissance: Seeing as Others Saw,* edited by Robert S. Nelson, 169–96. Cambridge: Cambridge University Press, 2000.

Hamburger, Jeffrey F. *St. John the Divine: The Deified Evangelist in Medieval Art and Theology.* Berkeley: University of California Press, 2002.

Hamburger, Jeffrey F., and Anne-Marie Bouché, eds. *The Mind's Eye: Art and Theological Argument in the Middle Ages.* Princeton: Princeton University Press, 2006.

Hamilton, Bernard. "Continental Drift: Prester John's Progress Through the Indies." In *Prester John, the Mongols and the Ten Lost Tribes,* edited by Charles F. Beckingham and Bernard Hamilton, 237–69. Aldershot: Variorum, 1996.

———. "The Impact of Prester John." In *The Fifth Crusade in Context: The Crusading Movement in the Early Thirteenth Century,* edited by E. J. Mylod, Guy Perry, Thomas W. Smith, and Jan Vandeburie, 53–68. London: Routledge, 2017.

———. "The Lands of Prester John: Western Knowledge of Asia and Africa at the Time of the Crusades." *Haskins Society Journal* 15 (2006): 126–42.

Handyside, Phillip D. *The Old French William of Tyre.* Leiden: Brill, 2015.

Hanley, Catherine. *War and Combat, 1150–1270: The Evidence from Old French Literature.* Woodbridge: D. S. Brewer, 2003.

Harari, Yuval Noah. "Eyewitnessing in Accounts of the First Crusade: The *Gesta francorum* and Other Contemporary Narratives." *Crusades* 3 (2004): 77–99.

Harris, Jonathan. "A Blow Sent By God: Changing Byzantine Memories of the Crusades." In *Remembering the Crusades and Crusading,* edited by Megan Cassidy-Welch, 189–201. London: Routledge, 2016.

Hauréau, Barthélémy. "Mémoire sur les récits d'apparitions dans les sermons du Moyen Âge." *Mémoires de l'Institut nationale de France* 28, no. 2 (1876): 239–63.

Hayes, Dawn Marie. *Body and Sacred Place in Medieval Europe, 1100–1389.* New York: Routledge, 2003.

Heng, Geraldine. *Empire of Magic: Medieval Romance and the Politics of Cultural Fantasy.* New York: Columbia University Press, 2003.

Hinnebusch, John F. "Extant Manuscripts of the Writings of Jacques de Vitry." *Scriptorium: Revue internationale des études relative aux manuscrits* 51 (1997): 156–64.

Hirsch, Marianne. *The Generation of Postmemory: Writing and Visual Culture After the Holocaust.* New York: Columbia University Press, 2012.

Hobsbawm, Eric, and Terence Ranger, eds. *The Invention of Tradition.* Cambridge: Cambridge University Press, 1983.

Holder-Egger, Oswald. "Über die historischen Werke des Johannes Codagnellus von Piacenza." *Neues Archiv der Gesellschaft für Ältere Deutsche Geschichtskunde* 16 (1890): 251–346, 473–509.

Holsinger, Bruce W. "Medieval Studies, Postcolonial Studies, and the Genealogies of Critique." *Speculum* 77, no. 4 (2002): 1195–227.

Hoogeweg, Herman. "Die Kreuzpredigt des Jahres 1224 in Deutschland mit besonderer Rücksicht auf die Erzdiöcese Köln." *Deutsche Zeitschrift für Geschichtswissenschaft* 4, no. 2 (1890): 54–74.

———. "Eine neue Schrift des Kölner Domscholasters Oliver." *Neues Archiv der Gesellschaft für Ältere Deutsche Geschichtskunde* 16 (1890): 186–92.

Howell, Martha C. "Fixing Movables: Gifts by Testament in Late Medieval Douai." *Past and Present* 150 (1996): 3–45.

Ing, Albert, ed. *Heraclius: Von den Farben und Künsten der Römer*. Wien: W. Braumüller, 1873.

Ingold, Tim. "Materials Against Materiality." *Archaeological Dialogues* 14, no. 1 (2007): 1–16.

Iogna-Prat, Dominique. "The Consecration of Church Space." In *Medieval Christianity in Practice*, edited by Miri Rubin, 95–102. Princeton: Princeton University Press, 2009.

Jaeger, C. Stephen, and Ingrid Karsten, eds. *Codierungen von Emotionen im Mittelalter*. Berlin: Walter de Gruyter, 2003.

Jensen, Reinhard. "Heinrich von Bonn: Die Erinnerung an die Kreuzfahrer aus dem römischen Reich in der portugiesischen Legendentradition." *Rheinische Vierteljahrsblätter* 30 (1965): 23–29.

Jordan, William Chester. *Louis IX and the Challenge of the Crusade: A Study in Rulership*. Princeton: Princeton University Press, 1979.

Jotischky, Andrew. *The Perfection of Solitude: Hermits and Monks in the Crusader States*. University Park: Pennsylvania State University Press, 1995.

Justice, Steven. "Eucharistic Miracle and Eucharistic Doubt." *Journal of Medieval and Early Modern Studies* 42, no. 2 (2012): 307–32.

Kansteiner, Wulf. "Finding Meaning in Memory: A Methodological Critique of Collective Memory Studies." *History and Theory* 41, no. 2 (May 2002): 179–97.

Kay, Sarah. *Animal Skins and the Reading Self in Medieval Latin and French Bestiaries*. Chicago: University of Chicago Press, 2017.

Kedar, Benjamin Z. *Crusade and Mission: European Approaches Toward the Muslims*. Princeton: Princeton University Press, 1984.

Kienzle, Beverly Mayne. *Cistercians, Heresy, and Crusade in Occitania, 1145–1229: Preaching in the Lord's Vineyard*. York: York Medieval Press, 2000.

King, Margot, trans. "The Life of Mary of Oignies by James of Vitry." In *Mary of Oignies: Mother of Salvation*, edited by Anneke B. Mulder-Bakker, 33–127. Turnhout: Brepols, 2006.

Kittell, Ellen E. "Testaments of Two Cities: A Comparative Analysis of the Wills of Medieval Genoa and Douai." *European Review of History: Revue européenne d'histoire* 5, no. 1 (1998): 47–82.

Klack-Eitzen, Charlotte, Wiebke Haase, and Tanja Weißgraf, eds. *Heilige Röcke: Kleider für Skulpturen im Kloster Wienhausen*. Regensburg: Schnell & Steiner, 2013.

Klein, Kerwin Lee. "On the Emergence of Memory in Historical Discourse." *Representations* 69 (2000): 127–50.

Koselleck, Reinhart. "War Memorials: Identity Formations of the Survivors." In *The Practice of Conceptual History: Timing History, Spacing Concepts*, edited by Reinhart Koselleck and translated by Todd Samuel Presner, 285–326. Stanford: Stanford University Press, 2002.

Kostick, Conor. "Courage and Cowardice on the First Crusade, 1096–1099." *War in History* 20, no. 1 (2013): 32–49.

Kröger, J. "The Hedwig Beakers: Medieval European Glass Vessels Made in Sicily Around 1200." In *The Phenomenon of "Foreign" in Oriental Art*, edited by Annette Hagedorn, 27–46. Wiesbaden: Reichert, 2006.

Krueger, Ingeborg. "Zu den 'Smaragden' auf dem Halberstädter Tafelreliquiar." *Journal of Glass Studies* 54 (2012): 247–53.

Kuijpers, Erika, Judith Pollmann, Johannes Müller, and Jasper van der Steen, eds. *Memory Before Modernity: Practices of Memory in Early Modern Europe*. Leiden: Brill, 2013.

Kümper, Hiram. "Oliver of Paderborn." In *The Encyclopedia of the Medieval Chronicle*, edited by Graeme Dunphy. 2 vols. Leiden, 2010.

La Monte, John L. "The Lords of Le Puiset on the Crusades." *Speculum* 17, no. 1 (1942): 100–118.

Lapina, Elizabeth. "*Nec signis nec testibus creditur*: The Problem of Eyewitnesses in the Chronicles of the First Crusade." *Viator* 38, no. 1 (2007): 117–39.

———. *Warfare and the Miraculous in the Chronicles of the First Crusade.*

University Park: Pennsylvania State University Press, 2015.

Lapina, Elizabeth, and Nicholas Morton, eds. *The Uses of the Bible in Crusader Sources*. Leiden: Brill, 2017.

Lay, Stephen. "Miracles, Martyrs, and the Cult of Henry the Crusader in Lisbon." *Portuguese Studies* 24, no. 1 (2008): 7–31.

———. "The Reconquest as Crusade in the Anonymous *De expugnatione Lyxbonensi*." *Al-Masāq* 14, no. 2 (2002): 123–30.

Leclercq, Jean. *The Love of Learning and the Desire for God: A Study of Monastic Culture*. Translated by Catherine Misrahi. New York: Fordham University Press, 1982.

Lester, Anne E. "Remembrance of Things Past: Memory and Material Objects in the Time of the Crusades, 1095–1291." In *Remembering the Crusades and Crusading*, edited by Megan Cassidy-Welch, 73–94. London: Routledge, 2016.

———. "A Shared Imitation: Cistercian Convents and Crusader Families in Thirteenth-Century Champagne." *Journal of Medieval History* 35, no. 4 (2009): 353–70.

———. "What Remains: Women, Relics, and Remembrance in the Aftermath of the Fourth Crusade." *Journal of Medieval History* 40, no. 3 (2014): 311–28.

Lierke, Rosemarie. *Die Hedwigsbecher: Das normannisch-sizilische Erbe der staufischen Kaiser*. Mainz: Verlag Franz Philipp Rutzen, 2005.

———. "The Hedwig-Beaker Triangles: Signs of Origin." In *Annales du 17e Congrès de l'AIHV (Antwerp 2006)*, edited by K. Janssens, P. Cosyns, J. Caen, and L. Van't dack, 289–94. Antwerp: University Press Antwerp, 2009.

Linder, Amnon. *Raising Arms: Liturgy in the Struggle to Liberate Jerusalem in the Late Middle Ages*. Turnhout: Brepols, 2003.

Lower, Michael. *The Barons' Crusade: A Call to Arms and Its Consequences*. Philadelphia: University of Pennsylvania Press, 2005.

MacQueen, D. J. "St. Augustine's Concept of Property Ownership." *Recherches augustiniennes* 8 (1972): 187–229.

Madden, Thomas F., ed. *The Fourth Crusade: Event, Aftermath, and Perceptions; Papers from the Sixth Conference of the Society for the Study of the Crusades and the Latin East. Istanbul, Turkey, 25–29 August 2004*. Aldershot: Ashgate, 2008.

———. "The Venetian Version of the Fourth Crusade: Memory and the Conquest of Constantinople in Medieval Venice." *Speculum* 87, no. 2 (2012): 311–44.

Magdalino, Paul, ed. *The Perception of the Past in Twelfth-Century Europe*. London: Hambledon Press, 1992.

Maier, Christoph T. *Crusade Propaganda and Ideology: Model Sermons for the Preaching of the Cross*. Cambridge: Cambridge University Press, 2000.

———. *Preaching the Crusades: Mendicant Friars and the Cross in the Thirteenth Century*. New York: Cambridge University Press, 1998.

Marshall, Christopher. *Warfare in the Latin East, 1192–1291*. Cambridge: Cambridge University Press, 1992.

Massey, Doreen. "Places and Their Pasts." *History Workshop Journal* 39, no. 1 (1995): 182–92.

Matt, Susan J., and Peter N. Stearns, eds. *Doing Emotions History*. Urbana: University of Illinois Press, 2014.

Matthews, David. *Medievalism: A Critical History*. Woodbridge: D. S. Brewer, 2015.

Mayer, Hans Eberhard. "Bologna und der Fünfte Kreuzzug." *Crusades* 14 (2015): 153–66.

Mellinkoff, Ruth. *The Horned Moses in Medieval Art and Thought*. Berkeley: University of California Press, 1970.

Mikkers, Edmond. "Un '*Speculum novitii*' inédit d'Etienne de Salley." *Collectanea cisterciensis ordinis reformatorum* 8 (1946): 17–68.

Mitchell, Piers D. "The Torture of Military Captives in the Crusades to the Medieval Middle East." In *Noble Ideals and Bloody Realities: Warfare in the Middle Ages*, edited by Niall Christie and Maya Yazigi, 97–118. Leiden: Brill, 2006.

Morris, W. S. "A Crusader's Last Testament." *Speculum* 27 (1952): 197–98.

Morton, Nicholas. "The Defence of the Holy Land and the Memory of the Maccabees." *Journal of Medieval History* 36, no. 3 (2010): 275–93.

———. *Encountering Islam on the First Crusade*. Cambridge: Cambridge University Press, 2016.

Mosse, George L. *Fallen Soldiers: Reshaping the Memory of the World Wars*. New York: Oxford University Press, 1990.

Mulder-Bakker, Anneke B., ed. *Mary of Oignies: Mother of Salvation*. Turnhout: Brepols, 2006.

Mylod, E. J., Guy Perry, Thomas W. Smith, and Jan Vandeburie, eds. *The Fifth Crusade in Context: The Crusading Movement in the Early Thirteenth Century*. London: Routledge, 2017.

Nagy, Piroska. *Le don des larmes au Moyen Âge*. Paris: Albin Michel, 2000.

———. "Religious Weeping as Ritual in the Medieval West." *Social Analysis* 48, no. 2 (2004): 119–37.

Nascimento, Aires Augusto, ed. *A conquista de Lisboa aos Mouros: Relato de um cruzado*. Lisbon: Vega, 2001.

Nora, Pierre. "Between Memory and History: Les lieux de mémoire." *Representations* 26 (Spring 1989): 7–24.

O'Callaghan, Joseph F. *Reconquest and Crusade in Medieval Spain*. Philadelphia: University of Pennsylvania Press, 2003.

Olick, Jeffrey K., Vered Vinitzky-Seroussi, and Daniel Levy, eds. *The Collective Memory Reader*. Oxford: Oxford University Press, 2011.

Packard, Barbara. "Remembering the First Crusade: Latin Narrative Histories 1099–c. 1300." PhD diss., Royal Holloway, University of London, 2011.

Palazzo, Éric. *L'espace et le sacre dans l'Antiquité et le haut Moyen Âge: Les autels portatifs*. Atti delle settimane di studio: Cristianità d'occidente e cristianità d'oriente (secoli VI–XI) 51. Spoleto: Centro italiano di studi sull'alto medioevo, 2004.

———. *L'espace rituel et le sacré dans le christianisme: La liturgie de l'autel portatif dans l'Antiquité et au Moyen Âge*. Turnhout: Brepols, 2008.

———. "*Missarum sollemnia*: Eucharistic Rituals in the Middle Ages." In *The Oxford Handbook of Medieval Christianity*, edited by John H. Arnold, 238–55. Oxford: Oxford University Press, 2014.

———. "Performing the Liturgy." In *The Cambridge History of Christianity*, vol. 3, *Early Medieval Christianities, c. 600–c. 1100*, edited by Thomas F. X. Noble and Julia M. H. Smith. Cambridge: Cambridge University Press, 2008.

Paterson, Linda M. *Singing the Crusades: French and Occitan Lyric Responses to the Crusading Movements, 1137–1336*. Cambridge: D. S. Brewer, 2018.

Paul, Nicholas L. *To Follow in Their Footsteps: The Crusades and Family Memory in the High Middle Ages*. Ithaca: Cornell University Press, 2012.

———. "In Search of the Marshal's Lost Crusade: The Persistence of Memory, the Problems of History and the Painful Birth of Crusading Romance." *Journal of Medieval History* 40, no. 3 (2014): 292–310.

Paul, Nicholas, and Suzanne Yeager, eds. *Remembering the Crusades: Myth, Image, and Identity*. Baltimore: Johns Hopkins University Press, 2012.

Pereira, Armando de Sousa. "Guerra e santidade: O cavaleiro-mártir Henrique de Bona e a conquista cristã de Lisboa." *Lusitania sacra* 17, 2nd series (2005): 15–38.

Perfetti, Lisa. "Crusader as Lover: The Eroticized Poetics of Crusading in Medieval France." *Speculum* 88, no. 4 (2013): 932–57.

Perry, Guy. *John of Brienne: King of Jerusalem, Emperor of Constantinople, c. 1175–1237*. Cambridge: Cambridge University Press, 2013.

Peters, Edward, ed. *Christian Society and the Crusades, 1198–1229*. Philadelphia: University of Pennsylvania Press, 1971.

Philippe, George. *Reliques et arts précieux en pays mosan: Du haut Moyen Âge à l'époque contemporaine*. Liège: Éditions du Céfal, 2002.

Phillips, Jonathan. *The Crusades, 1095–1204.* 2nd ed. London: Routledge, 2014.

Plamper, Jan. *The History of Emotions: An Introduction.* Translated by Keith Tribe. Oxford: Oxford University Press, 2015.

Portelli, Alessandro. *The Death of Luigi Trastulli and Other Stories: Form and Meaning in Oral History.* Albany: State University of New York Press, 1991.

Poster, Carol, and Linda C. Mitchell, eds. *Letter Writing Manuals and Instruction from Antiquity to the Present: Historical and Bibliographic Studies.* Columbia: University of South Carolina Press, 2007.

Powell, James M. *Anatomy of a Crusade, 1213–1221.* Philadelphia: University of Pennsylvania Press, 1986.

———. "Honorius III and the Leadership of the Crusade." *Catholic Historical Review* 63, no. 4 (1977): 521–36.

Pringle, Denys. *The Churches of the Crusader Kingdom of Jerusalem: A Corpus.* Vol. 1, *A–K (Excluding Acre and Jerusalem).* Cambridge: Cambridge University Press, 1993.

———. *The Churches of the Crusader Kingdom of Jerusalem: A Corpus.* Vol. 2, *L–Z (Excluding Tyre).* Cambridge: Cambridge University Press, 1997.

Purkis, William J. "Crusading and Crusade Memory in Caesarius of Heisterbach's *Dialogus miraculorum,*" *Journal of Medieval History* 39, no. 1 (2013): 100–127.

———. "Stigmata on the First Crusade." In *Signs, Wonders, Miracles: Representations of Divine Power in the Life of the Church,* edited by Kate Cooper and Jeremy Gregory. Studies in Church History 41, 99–108. Woodbridge: Boydell Press, 2005.

Radstone, Susannah, and Bill Schwarz, eds. *Memory: Histories, Theories, Debates.* New York: Fordham University Press, 2010.

Reddy, William M. *The Navigation of Feeling: A Framework for the History of Emotions.* Cambridge: Cambridge University Press, 2001.

Remensnyder, Amy G. *La Conquistadora: The Virgin Mary at War and Peace in the Old and New Worlds.* New York: Oxford University Press, 2014.

———. *Remembering Kings Past: Monastic Foundation Legends in Medieval Southern France.* Ithaca: Cornell University Press, 1995.

Richard, Jean. "La Fondation d'une église latine en orient par saint Louis: Damiette." *Bibliothèque de l'école des chartes* 120 (1962): 39–54.

———. *La papauté et les missions d'orient au Moyen Âge (XIIIe–XVe siècles).* Rome: École Française de Rome, 1977.

Riley-Smith, Jonathan. "Crusading as an Act of Love." *History* 65, no. 214 (1980): 177–92.

———. *The First Crusade and the Idea of Crusading.* London: Athlone Press, 1986.

Riley-Smith, Louise, and Jonathan Riley-Smith. *The Crusades: Idea and Reality, 1095–1274.* London: Edward Arnold, 1981.

Rist, Rebecca. *The Papacy and Crusading in Europe, 1198–1245.* London: Continuum, 2009.

Roper, Michael. "Re-remembering the Soldier Hero: The Psychic and Social Construction of Memory in Personal Narratives of the Great War." *History Workshop Journal* 50 (2000): 181–204.

Rosenwein, Barbara H. *Emotional Communities in the Early Middle Ages.* Ithaca: Cornell University Press, 2006.

Rosenwein, Barbara H., and Riccardo Cristiani. *What Is the History of Emotions?* Cambridge: Polity Press, 2018.

Rothkrug, Lionel. "Popular Religion and Holy Shrines: Their Influence on the Origins of the German Reformation and Their Role in German Cultural Development." In *Religion and the People, 800–1700: Studies in the History of Popular Religious Beliefs and Practices,* edited by James Obelkevich, 20–86. Chapel Hill: University of North Carolina Press, 1979.

Rousseau, Constance M. "Home Front and Battlefield: The Gendering of Papal Crusading Policy, 1095–1221." In *Gendering the Crusades,* edited by Susan B. Edgington and Sarah Lambert, 31–44.

New York: Columbia University Press, 2002.

Routledge, Michael. "Songs." In *The Oxford Illustrated History of the Crusades*, edited by Jonathan Riley-Smith, 91–111. Oxford: Oxford University Press, 1995.

Rubenstein, Jay. *Armies of Heaven: The First Crusade and the Quest for Apocalypse.* New York: Basic Books, 2011.

Rubin, Miri. *Corpus Christi: The Eucharist in Late Medieval Culture.* Cambridge: Cambridge University Press, 1991.

Sackville, Lucy J. *Heresy and Heretics in the Thirteenth Century: The Textual Representations.* Woodbridge: York Medieval Press, 2011.

Sassoon, Siegfried. "The Poet as Hero." In *Poetry of the First World War: An Anthology*, edited by Tim Kendall, 94. Oxford: Oxford University Press, 2013.

Schenk, Jochen. "The Documentary Evidence for Templar Religion." In *The Templars and Their Sources*, edited by Karl Borchardt, Karoline Döring, Philippe Josserand, and Helen J. Nicholson, 199–211. London: Routledge, 2017.

Schuster, Beate. "The Strange Pilgrimage of Odo of Deuil." In *Medieval Concepts of the Past: Ritual, Memory, Historiography*, edited by Gerd Althoff, Johannes Fried, and Patrick J. Geary, 253–78. Washington, DC: Publications of the German Historical Institute, 2002.

Scott, Joan W. "The Evidence of Experience." *Critical Inquiry* 17, no. 4 (1991): 773–97.

Seeger, Sofia. "Gründungsbericht des Klosters S. Vicente in Lissabon: *Indiculum fundationis* (1188)." In *Mirakelberichte des frühen und hohen Mittelalters*, edited by Klaus Herbers, Lenka Jiroušková, and Bernhard Vogel, 288–95. Darmstadt: Wissenschaftliche Buchgesellschaft, 2005.

Shalem, Avinoam. "From Royal Caskets to Relic Containers: Two Ivory Caskets from Burgos and Madrid." *Muqarnas* 12 (1995): 24–38.

Siberry, Elizabeth. *Criticism of Crusading: 1095–1274.* Oxford: Clarendon Press, 1985.

Signori, Gabriela, ed. *Dying for the Faith, Killing for the Faith: Old-Testament Faith-Warriors (1 and 2 Maccabees) in Historical Perspective.* Leiden: Brill, 2013.

Sivan, Emmanuel, and Jay Winter, eds. *War and Remembrance in the Twentieth Century.* Cambridge: Cambridge University Press, 2000.

Smith, Caroline. *Crusading in the Age of Joinville.* Aldershot: Ashgate, 2006.

———. "Martyrdom and Crusading in the Thirteenth Century: Remembering the Dead of Louis IX's Crusades." *Al-Masāq* 15, no. 2 (2003): 189–96.

Smith, Julia. "Portable Christianity: Relics in the Medieval West (c. 700–1200)." *Proceedings of the British Academy* 181 (2012): 143–67.

Smith, Katherine Allen. *War and the Making of Medieval Monastic Culture.* Woodbridge: Boydell Press, 2011.

Smith, Leonard V. *The Embattled Self: French Soldiers' Testimony of the Great War.* Ithaca: Cornell University Press, 2007.

Smith, Thomas W. "Between Two Kings: Pope Honorius III and the Seizure of the Kingdom of Jerusalem by Frederick II in 1225." *Journal of Medieval History* 41, no. 1 (2015): 41–59.

———. *Curia and Crusade: Pope Honorius III and the Recovery of the Holy Land, 1216–1227.* Turnhout: Brepols, 2017.

———. "Oliver of Cologne's *Historia Damiatina*: A New Manuscript Witness in Dublin, Trinity College Library MS 496." *Hermathena* 194 (2013): 37–68.

———. "The Role of Pope Honorius III in the Fifth Crusade." In *The Fifth Crusade in Context: The Crusading Movement in the Early Thirteenth Century*, edited by E. J. Mylod, Guy Perry, Thomas W. Smith, and J. Vandeburie, 15–26. London: Routledge, 2017.

Spencer, Stephen. "The Emotional Rhetoric of Crusader Spirituality in the Narratives of the First Crusade." *Nottingham Medieval Studies* 58 (2014): 57–86.

Spiegel, Gabrielle M. "Memory and History: Liturgical Time and Historical Time." *History and Theory* 41, no. 2 (2002): 149–62.

BIBLIOGRAPHY

———. *Romancing the Past: The Rise of Vernacular Prose Historiography in Thirteenth-Century France*. Berkeley: University of California Press, 1993.

Stock, Brian. *The Implications of Literacy: Written Language and Models of Interpretation in the Eleventh and Twelfth Centuries*. Princeton: Princeton University Press, 1983.

Strayer, Joseph R. "La conscience du roi: Les enquêtes de 1258–1262 dans la sénéchaussée de Carcassonne-Béziers." In *Mélanges Robert Aubenas*, 725–36. Montpellier: La Société d'Histoire du droit et des institutions des anciens pays de droit écrit, 1984.

Strickland, Matthew. *War and Chivalry: The Conduct and Perception of War in England, and Normandy, 1066–1217*. Cambridge: Cambridge University Press, 1996.

Symes, Carol. "Popular Literacies and the First Historians of the First Crusade." *Past and Present* 235, no. 1 (May 2017): 37–67.

Thomson, Alistair. *ANZAC Memories: Living with the Legend*. 2nd ed. Melbourne: Oxford University Press, 1994; Melbourne: Monash University, 2013.

Throop, Susanna A. *Crusading as an Act of Vengeance, 1095–1216*. Farnham: Ashgate, 2011.

Todman, Dan. *The Great War: Myth and Memory*. London: Bloomsbury Academic, 2005.

Tolan, John V. *Saint Francis and the Sultan: The Curious History of a Christian-Muslim Encounter*. Oxford: Oxford University Press, 2009.

Tyerman, Christopher. *The Debate on the Crusades, 1099–2010*. Manchester: Manchester University Press, 2011.

———. *England and the Crusades, 1095–1588*. Chicago: University of Chicago Press, 1988.

———. "Were There Any Crusades in the Twelfth Century?" *English Historical Review* 110, no. 437 (1995): 553–77.

Van Cleve, Thomas Curtis. "The Fifth Crusade." In *A History of the Crusades*, vol. 2, *The Later Crusades, 1189–1311*, edited by Kenneth M. Setton, Robert L. Wolff, and Harry W. Hazard, 376–428. Philadelphia: University of Pennsylvania Press, 1962.

Vandeburie, Jan. "'*Consenescentis mundi die vergente ad vesperam*': James of Vitry's *Historia orientalis* and Eschatological Rhetoric After the Fourth Lateran Council." In *The Uses of the Bible in Crusader Sources*, edited by Elizabeth Lapina and Nicholas Morton, 341–59. Leiden: Brill, 2017.

———. "Jacques de Vitry's *Historia orientalis*: Reform, Crusading, and the Holy Land After the Fourth Lateran Council." PhD diss., University of Kent, 2015.

———. "The Preacher and the Pope: Jacques de Vitry and Honorius III at the Time of the Fifth Crusade, 1216–1227." In *Papacy, Crusade, and Muslim-Christian Relations*, edited by Jessalynn L. Bird. Amsterdam: Amsterdam University Press, 2018.

———. "'*Sancte fidei omnino deiciar*': Ugolino dei Conti di Segni's Doubts and Jacques de Vitry's Intervention." *Studies in Church History* 52 (2016): 87–101.

van der Steen, Jasper. *Memory Wars in the Low Countries, 1566–1700*. Leiden: Brill, 2015.

van Moolenbroek, J. J. "Signs in the Heavens in Groningen and Friesland in 1214: Oliver of Cologne and Crusading Propaganda." *Journal of Medieval History* 13, no. 3 (1987): 251–72.

Walter, Katie L., ed. *Reading Skin in Medieval Literature and Culture*. New York: Palgrave Macmillan, 2013.

Wei, Ian P. "From Twelfth-Century Schools to Thirteenth-Century Universities: The Disappearance of Biographical and Autobiographical Representations of Scholars." *Speculum* 86, no. 1 (2011): 42–78.

Weiss-Krejci, Estella. "Heart Burial in Medieval and Post-medieval Central Europe." In *Body Parts and Bodies Whole*, edited by Katharina Rebay-Salisbury, Marie Louise Stig Sorensen, and Jessica Hughes. Studies in Funerary

Archaeology 5, 119–34. Oxford: Oxbow Books, 2010.

Welsh, Thomas J. *The Use of the Portable Altar: A Historical Synopsis and a Commentary*. Washington, DC: Catholic University of America Press, 1950.

Westerhof, Danielle. "Celebrating Fragmentation: The Presence of Aristocratic Body Parts in Monastic Houses in Twelfth- and Thirteenth-Century England." In *Sepulturae cistercienses: Burial, Memorial and Patronage in Medieval Cistercian Monasteries*, edited by J. Hall and C. Kratzke, Comentarii cisterciensis 14, no. 41. Forges-Chimay: Cîteaux, 2005.

Whalen, Brett E. *Dominion of God: Christendom and Apocalypse in the Middle Ages*. Cambridge: Harvard University Press, 2009.

Winter, Jay M. "The Memory Boom in Contemporary Historical Studies." *Raritan* 21, no. 1 (2001): 52–66.

———. *Remembering War: The Great War Between Memory and History*. New Haven: Yale University Press, 2006.

———. *Sites of Memory, Sites of Mourning: The Great War in European Cultural History*. Cambridge: Cambridge University Press, 1995.

Yerushalmi, Yosef H. *Zakhor: Jewish History and Jewish Memory*. Seattle: University of Washington Press, 1982.

Young, James E. *The Texture of Memory: Holocaust Memorials and Meaning*. New Haven: Yale University Press, 1993.

INDEX

Aachen, 112
Acre, 70–71, 76, 85
    hospital of Saint Jean in, 26, 29
    Jacques de Vitry and, 43, 61, 95–96, 131–32,
        134–35, 152
Adil, al- (sultan of Egypt), 115
Aelred of Rievaulx, 67
Afonso Henriques (king of Portugal), 106,
        116–18, 121
Aidela (wife of Oberti Nigrini), 28
al-Adil. *See* Adil, al-
Alcácer do Sal, 68, 122
Alexandria. *See* Babylon
al-Kamil. *See* Kamil, al-
al-Mansuriyya. *See* Mansuriyya, al-
Andreas de'Epoisse, 71, 78
Andreas de Nanteuil, 71
Andrew, Saint, 97, 137
Andrew II (king of Hungary), 12, 76
Antioch, 113, 121
    battle of, 65, 76
Armenia, 76
Arnold de Raisse, 128
Augustine, Saint, 45, 109–10, 132, 145
Austria, Duke of (Leopold IV), 87, 93
Aywières, 43, 48, 57, 87
Ayyubids, 11, 115

Babylon, 79, 114
Baldwin I (king of Jerusalem), 31
Baltic, 10, 14
Bartholomew, Saint, 66, 98–99, 132, 137
Barzella Merxadrus, 24–28, 30
Battle Abbey, 124
Beaumont, Viscount of (Jean d'Archies), 71
Beguines, 43, 87
Beirut, 134
Bernard, Saint, 137
Berta de Gala, 28
Bethlehem, 137
Betranno de Lavania, 28
Bohemond IV, Prince of Antioch, 12, 91

Bohemond of Tarento, 77
Bologna, 24–25
Brindisi, 26, 79
Brussels, 138
Byblos, 134
Byzantine Empire, 10

Cairo, 11, 81, 92–93, 101, 114
Canet, 26
Capetians, 58
    See also Louis IX
Carcassonne, 121
Catalonia, 23
Cathars, 10
Cecilia, Saint, 137
Charroux, 112
Chartres, Viscount of (Gaucher of Le Puiset), 27
Chastel-Blanc, 134
Chester, Earl of, 85
China, 142
Cistercians, 29, 43, 87, 131
Clermont, 88, 110, 113
Compostela, 107
Constantinople, 12, 89
Constant of Douai, 1, 70
Copenhagen, 131
Crac, 134
    See also Kerak
Cuthbert, Saint, 137
Cyprus, 10, 79

Damietta, 12, 29, 31, 33–35, 66, 76, 80–81, 93,
        114, 124, 138
    capture of, 27, 56–61, 73–75, 85–87, 89, 91, 111
    death and martyrdom in, 71, 73, 100
    mosque in, 98–99, 102–3
    prisoners in, 78–79
    siege of, 1, 11, 42–43, 49–52, 69, 73–75, 90,
        111, 113
    as site of memory, 15, 104, 151
    testaments made in, 24–25, 27

200 INDEX

Douai, 23
Durham, 137

Edessa, 78, 114
Edmund the Martyr, Saint, 101
Egypt, 15, 21, 26, 76, 82, 89–91, 101, 103–4, 107,
    112–15, 142, 144
    attack on, 11
    conversion of, 14, 35, 99
    failure of the Fifth Crusade in, 85, 92
    Jacques de Vitry and, 1, 43, 50, 65, 70, 152
    prisoners in, 78
    testaments made in, 23
    withdrawal from, 73–74, 81
Egyptians, 34, 52, 55–56, 72, 78, 81, 91, 94
Emo of Wittwerium, 14
England, 37, 124
Enguerrand of Boves, 37–38
Estonia, 114
Eudes of Châteauroux, 102
Eugenius III (pope), 8, 78
Eugesippus-Fretellus, 111

Flanders, 23
France, 23, 31–32, 58, 79, 103, 112
    northern France, 142
    southern France, 10, 26, 29, 48, 134, 140, 153
Franciscans, 14
Francis of Assisi, Saint, 14
Frederick II (Holy Roman emperor), 12, 60,
    64, 69, 79, 81, 90–91, 114
Frisians, 14, 82–83, 106–7, 117, 122, 150–51
    excellence in battle, 56, 65, 67–69
Frontignan, 26
Fulcher of Chartres, 31, 113
Fulk of Toulouse, 140

Garendon, 29
Gaucher of Le Puiset. See Chartres, Viscount of
Gaul, 137
Genghis Khan, 91
Genoa, 23, 28, 43
Genoese, 67, 80, 142
Germans, 12, 28, 106–7, 113–14, 122
    death and martyrdom, 72, 94, 117
    excellence in battle, 67–69
Germany, 90, 131, 134
Gibaut, Osbert, 27
Giles de Walcourt, 127

Gregory, Saint, 40, 111, 119
Gregory IX (pope), 129
Gregory VIII (pope), 9, 110
Groningen, 122
Guibert of Nogent, 8, 88
Guiletta Merxadrus, 25
Gui of Melun, 32, 102
Guy of Tremelay, 26

Hademar II of Kuenring, 28–30
Halberstadt, 145
Hattin, battle of, 38, 81, 112, 115
Hebron, 111
Hedwig of Silesia, Saint, 144
Henry I. See Rodez, Count of
Henry of Bonn, 107–8, 117–18, 122–23
Hervé of Vierzon, 71
Holy Land, the, 11, 21, 23, 28, 66, 68, 76, 79,
    87–88, 113, 115, 131, 152–53
    commemorating, 15, 126, 141
    loss and recovery of, 9–10, 71, 77, 89, 110–11,
        114
    pilgrimage to, 12, 27
Honorius III (pope), 11–13, 64, 79
    Jacques de Vitry's letters to, 43, 49, 55, 57,
        74, 87, 91
Hospitallers, 23, 26–27, 29, 67, 72, 133
Hugh I (king of Cyprus), 12
Hugh of Oignies, 127–28, 132, 144
Hugh of Saint Victor, 7
Hugo of Beauchamp, 37–38
Hugues de Berzé, 97
Huon of Saint-Quentin, 77

Iberian Peninsula, 10, 14, 77, 100, 109
Ibn Wasil, 102
Innocent III (pope), 10, 40, 76, 79, 113
    letters of, 89, 93
    Post miserabile issued by, 110
    Quia maior issued by, 11–12, 21, 39, 66, 76,
        89, 110–11, 115
Isidore of Seville, 45
Israelites, 8, 36
Italians, 23–24, 69, 75
Ithier of Toucy, 71

Jacobus de Voragine, 100
Jacques de Vitry, 12, 60–65, 68–69, 81, 86, 90,
    97, 100–101, 104–5, 114

condemnation of deserters, 75–77
friendship with Marie d'Oignies, 57, 127, 139–40
Historia occidentalis, 14
Historia orientalis, 14, 92
letters of, 1–2, 15, 33, 42–44, 47–59, 73, 82, 85, 87, 91, 94–96, 150
negotiator during the crusades, 78–79
preacher of the crusades, 11, 28, 36–38, 70, 74, 88, 107, 111, 134, 146
treasures of Oignies, 16, 125–29, 131–36, 138–47, 151–52
Jaffa, 10
James of Avesnes, 37–38
Jean d'Archies. *See* Beaumont, Viscount of
Jerusalem, 10–12, 15, 28–29, 81, 89–90, 112, 133, 144
   capture and loss of, 2, 9, 114
   pilgrimage to, 36
   recovery of, 92, 104–5, 113
Joachim of Fiore, 88–89
Johannes Codagnellus, 63, 68–69, 72, 75, 78, 80, 83, 94
John of Brienne (king of Jerusalem), 12–13, 76, 78–82, 116
John of Cambrai, 1, 70
John of Harcourt, 25
John of Nivelles, 43, 57, 79, 87
John of Tulbia, 14, 78, 81
John the Baptist, 52, 71, 94, 115, 121, 136
John the Evangelist, 139–40
Joseph of Arimathea, 137

Kamil, al- (sultan of Egypt), 11, 14, 60, 78, 81, 90
Kerak, 81
   See also Crac
Knights Templar. *See* Templars
Konrad von Krosigk, 145

La Bastide-Pradines, 26
Lanfranc of Bogossa, 26
Languedoc, 10
Las Navas de Tolosa, battle of, 138
Laurence, Saint, 137
Leonius (master), 70
Leopold IV. *See* Austria, Duke of
Levant, the, 23
Lille, 143
Lisbon, 15, 106–9, 116–17, 122–23

Livonia, 10, 114
London, 143
Louis IX (king of France), 31–32, 48, 101–4, 151

Maccabees, 8–9, 36, 38, 149
Mansuriyya, al-, 143
Manuel Comnenus (emperor of Byzantium), 91
Margat, 134
Maria of Jerusalem, 79
Marie of Oignies, 43, 57, 127–29, 134, 139–41
Mary (mother of Jesus), 99–101, 114, 120, 136, 139–40, 143–44
Matthew Paris, 14
Messina, 74, 79, 88
Meuse, region, 138
Milon de S. Florentin, lord of Puits, 27
Minden, 131
Montamaria (wife of Martini de Mara), 28
Montréal, 81, 112
Morocco, 14
Mount Sinai, 115
Mount Tabor, 15, 76, 97, 111, 115–16
Muhammad, 89
Muret, battle of, 138

Namur, 16, 57, 125–32, 135, 138–39, 141–46, 151
Nazareth, 116

Oberti Nigrini, 28
   See also Aidela
Odo of Chatillon, 78
Odysseus, 106, 122
Oignies, 87
   Jacques de Vitry and, 43, 57, 127–29, 132, 134, 136, 140–43, 151–52
   priory of St. Nicholas in, 57, 125–26, 136, 140, 146
   treasury of, 16, 127–28
   See also Hugh of Oignies; Jacques de Vitry: friendship with Marie d'Oignies
Oliver of Paderborn, 1, 12, 24, 33, 35, 57, 83, 92, 104
   condemnation of deserters by, 74–76
   preacher of the crusades, 11, 14, 68, 70, 73, 85–86, 88, 111–16, 123
   writings by, 14–15, 62–63, 66–76, 78, 80–81, 87, 89–90, 94–95, 98, 100–101, 111, 122, 152

202 INDEX

Otto of Freising, 69, 91
Outremer, 63

Palermo, 143
Paris, 43, 48, 57, 135
Paschal II (pope), 74
Pelagius of Albano, 12, 32–35, 68, 75, 79–82, 90, 92, 98
Peter, Saint, 98–99, 115, 137, 144
Peter Comestor, 112
Peter Lombard, 120
Peter Montacute, 86
Peter of Vaux-de-Cernay, 121
Peter the Chanter, 43, 71
Peter the Venerable, 9
Petrus Maurinus, 27
Philistines, 112
Piacenza, 69
Pippin, 113
Pisans, 67, 75, 80, 168 n. 24
Poland, 10
popes. See individual popes
Portugal, 10–11, 68, 107, 116, 122–23, 153
Prester John, 91
Provence, Count of (Raymond Berengar), 29
Prussia, 114

Ralph of Caen, 76
Ralph of Coggeshall, 14
Raymond Berengar. See Provence, Count of
Reinier, 1, 70
Reynald of Barbichon, 70–71
Rhineland, 138
Richard I (king of England), 74, 88
Robert of Arbrissel, 140
Robert of Courçon, 11, 26, 51, 71, 80, 85, 93
Robert of Reims, 138
Rodez, Count of (Henry I), 26
Roger of Howden, 88
Roger of Wendover, 14
Rome, 125
Rustico della Costa, 28

Saher IV of Quincy. See Winchester, Earl of
Saidnaya, monastery, 143
Saladin, 9, 11, 88–89, 112, 114–15
San Pedro de Arlanza, monastery, 143

São Vicente de Fora, monastery, 106–9, 116–17, 120–24, 151
Saracens, 33–34, 36–37, 50, 52, 56, 67, 75–76, 89, 110–11, 113–15, 117, 134
Saxony, 131, 138
Sicily, 90, 142–44
Sidon, 134
Simon de Montfort, count, 26
Simon of Saarbrücken, count, 79
Split, 76
Suger of St. Denis, 120
Syria, 10, 26, 97, 115, 143

Templars, 25–27, 50, 67, 72, 74, 76, 143
Teutonic Knights, 23, 26–28, 72
Thomas Aquinas, 59
Thomas Becket, 101
Thomas of Cantimpré, 57, 128, 133–34, 139
Three Indies, the, 91
Tommy Kennedy, lieutenant, 19
Tortosa, 134
Toulouse, 114
Tripoli, 134
Tyre, 10, 112, 134, 144

Urban II (pope), 88, 110, 113

Venetians, 80, 112
Vincent, Saint, 122, 137
Visigoths, 109
Vlaardingen, 68

Walter of Tournai, 1, 70
Waverley, 29
Wends, the, 10
Werner Kybourg, 29
Wienhausen, 131
William de Bello Campo (Beauchamp), 27
William Durand, 101, 129
William of Chartres, 71
William of Hauteville, 144
William of Puylaurens, 138
William of Tyre, 14, 67, 77, 80, 113
Winchester, Earl of (Saher IV of Quincy), 28–29

Zwettl, 28–30

Lightning Source UK Ltd.
Milton Keynes UK
UKHW011303290922
409648UK00012B/388